*Vampires, Mummies,*

*and Liberals*

# Vampires, Mummies, and Liberals

Bram Stoker

and the Politics

of Popular Fiction

## David Glover

Duke University Press

Durham and London

1996

Frontis illustration by W. V. Cockburn for Bram Stoker's
"The Invisible Giant," in *Under the Sunset* (1882). *Courtesy of
the National Library of Ireland.*

*For Cora*

# Contents

# Acknowledgments

 My first debt is to the large number of scholars and enthusiasts whose work has done so much to create a new interest in Stoker's writing; for though my dissent from many of their conclusions and positions will be evident enough, this book could not have been written without them.

I also want to thank the friends and colleagues whose generosity with suggestions and encouragement helped to sustain this project over several lean years, especially my American family: Paul, Beth, Emma, and the late Sidney Kaplan. Conversations with John Barrell, Denise Riley, and the late Bill Readings moved my work in unexpected directions—my special thanks to them. For their support and thoughtful criticism I would like to thank Rachel Bowlby, Ed Cohen, Nick Daly, Elin Diamond, Luke Gibbons, Paul Gilroy, Annie Janowitz, Ann Rosalind Jones, Alison Light, Tania Modleski, Alan Sinfield, Peter Stallybrass, Judith Walkowitz, and Carolyn Williams. For last minute research while I was otherwise engaged, my thanks to the elusive Ed Kaplan. At Duke University Press, Ken Wissoker has been an exemplary editor—imaginative, funny, and always ahead of the game. And I have been extraordinarily fortunate in my two readers for the press: their incisive and insightful comments were a model of constructive criticism, and this book has benefited immeasurably from their intelligence and commitment.

Two institutions provided an intellectual home while the bulk of this book was being completed. My warmest thanks to E. Ann Kaplan, Director of the Humanities Institute at SUNY-Stony Brook, for making my stay there as a Resident Fellow so productive; to Victoria de Grazia, Project Leader at the Rutgers Center for Historical Analysis, for an exceptionally stimulating year as a Research Associate; and lastly to Rudolph Bell for extending my time at Rutgers through the award of a Visiting Fellowship in the Department of History. I would also like to thank the staff of the following libraries for their assistance: the Fales Library, New York University; the New York Public Library; and the British Library, London. I owe a particular debt to Christopher Sheppard, Sub-Librarian of the Brotherton Collection, Leeds University Library; to Jean Rose, Deputy Group Librarian at the Octopus Publishing

Group Library, Rushden; and to Leslie Morris, Curator of History and Bibliography at the Rosenbach Museum and Library, Philadelphia.

Finally, my greatest debt is to Cora Kaplan: for her love and friendship which made it all possible and for her unwavering conviction that a good book is always worth shouting about, this one is for her.

Chapters 1 and 2, together with the Coda, reuse some material that was published in rather different versions elsewhere. Chapter 1 is a revised and expanded version of an essay entitled " 'Dark enough fur any man': Bram Stoker's Sexual Ethnology and the Question of Irish Nationalism," which is included in *Late Imperial Culture*, edited by Román de la Campa, E. Ann Kaplan, and Michael Sprinker and published by Verso (1995). Part of chapter 2 has appeared as "Bram Stoker and the Crisis of the Liberal Subject," *New Literary History* 23 (Autumn 1992), and is reprinted here by permission of the Johns Hopkins University Press. It was originally presented as a paper at the Commonwealth Center for Literary and Cultural Change at the University of Virginia; my thanks to its Director, Ralph Cohen, and to John Barrell and Jacqueline Rose for their invitation to speak at the Center. An earlier version of the Coda, "Travels in Romania: Myths of Origin, Myths of Blood," appeared in *Discourse* 16 (Fall 1993) and is reprinted here by permission of Indiana University Press.

# *Abbreviations*

Unless otherwise indicated, all references are to the editions listed below and are abbreviated as follows:

D      *Dracula* (1897; reprint, Harmondsworth: Penguin, 1979).

JSS      *The Jewel of Seven Stars* (London: William Heinemann, 1903).

LA      *Lady Athlyne* (New York: Paul R. Reynolds, 1908).

LS      *The Lady of the Shroud* (1909; reprint, London: William Rider & Co., 1925).

LWW      *The Lair of the White Worm* (London: William Rider & Son, 1911).

M      *The Man* (London: William Heinemann, 1905).

MS      *The Mystery of the Sea* (London: William Heinemann, 1902).

SP      *The Snake's Pass* (1890; reprint, Dingle, County Kerry: Brandon, 1990).

# Introduction

The liberal believes that a man, once stripped of his national and cultural identity, will become Everyman—citizen of the world. The conservative knows that, in fact, he will become bewildered, schizophrenic, unhappy and lonely. *Andrew Roberts* [1]

The "I" with which I shall occupy myself will not be the "I" that relates back strictly to myself, but something else, some residue, that remains after all the other words I have uttered have flowed back into me, something that neither relates back nor flows back. *Yukio Mishima* [2]

 Bram Stoker is a notoriously elusive subject. Despite three biographies and a growing interest in his work, we know very little about him beyond the bare outline of his public career and a few hints and whispers of skeletons in his closet.[3] Stoker's reputation as a "naturally secretive" man is now legendary and has become part of the machinery of speculation that has repeatedly sought to link the sensationalism of his fiction to a no less sensational private life.[4] The intricacies of Stoker's relationship to his sometime friend Oscar Wilde, the rumors of "a sexless marriage," his possible homosexuality, his alleged membership of a secret occult society like the Hermetic Order of the Golden Dawn, or the suggestion that his death was caused by syphilis have all been paraded as tantalizing mysteries or perhaps as clues to some other, unimaginably grotesque reality—the melodrama of secrecy writ large.[5] It is as if the many lives of *Dracula*, its multitude of readings and retellings, has produced an extended cultural narrative in which the author has become an indispensable character, to be addressed or dismissed at will. "I have read Stoker," sneers the vampire leader in Dan Simmons's Romanian thriller *Children of the Night* (1992). "I read his silly novel when it was published in 1897 and saw the first stage production in London."[6] And when Stoker appears in Brian W. Aldiss's time-travel vampire novel *Dracula Unbound* (1991), he fares little better: he is "the ginger man," a red-bearded Irish voluptuary obsessed with menstrual blood who is saved from syphilis by an American visitor from the year 1999.[7]

In Aldiss's science fiction, these twin fin-de-siècles—the Victorian and our own—are presented as parallel worlds and the same contrast is also implicit in Francis Ford Coppola's 1992 film *Bram Stoker's Dracula*. Parallel, but hierarchically arrayed—for, in our fascination with Stoker's life and times, there is always the presumption of our own present-day superiority, our ability to know better than our historical precursors. *Dracula's* continuing circulation in contemporary popular culture depends upon and sustains a powerful representation of the past as a domain of scandal and error, awaiting exposure by a franker, more enlightened gaze. One might even say that the bulk of our current post-*Dracula* narratives—those by Anne Rice, Fred Saberhagen, and T. M. Wright are among the most innovative—all adopt a variant of this stance, rescuing their de-repressed monsters from the dead weight of inherited ignorance and superstition, flaunting their guilty secrets and endowing them with a romanticized humanity. Interviews with vampires belong essentially to the genre of "true confessions," imaginative autobiographies whose fiction of patient documentation yields quickly to the pleasures of voyeurism and intimate gossip.

Yet this penchant for biography and autobiography, and the knowing self that is their reader, is something that we share with Stoker's own age; indeed, this commodified need to know is partly what connects the very different turning points of our two centuries to the same modernity. More specifically, the popular desire for a biographical or autobiographical mode of understanding derives much of its impetus from the increasingly powerful apparatuses of journalism and publicity, occupational and commercial cultures within which Stoker himself moved and worked at a time when these key institutions were beginning to assume their characteristically modern forms. To read Stoker's interviews in *The Daily Chronicle* with such literary, theatrical, and political luminaries as Sir Arthur Conan Doyle, Sir W. S. Gilbert, or Winston Churchill is to see the human interest story in embryo, with its detailed descriptions of the subject's home, revelations of his personal life, and itinerary of his working day. So too, with Stoker's *Personal Reminiscences of Henry Irving* (1906), an insider's memoir of his actor-manager employer, a biography that comes as close to autobiography as almost anything the author ever wrote.

Stoker's *Personal Reminiscences* encourages us to read his own life through that of Henry Irving and as a result the book conceals as much as it reveals. This blurring of biographer and subject returns us to one of the central paradoxes informing Stoker's career, for while he consistently evades the full glare of biographical exposure, his work seems equally consistently to incite it. The disturbing scenarios enacted in his Gothic

*Vampires, Mummies, and Liberals*

narratives have inspired a number of attempts to psychoanalyze the author through the text, reading *Dracula* as a case study in Oedipal rivalry or infantile trauma.[8] In a less clinical vein, it has become a critical commonplace to see in Count Dracula a fictional expression of Stoker's "ambiguous regard" for the dominant and domineering figure of Henry Irving, an interpretation necessarily requiring "an excursion into biography."[9] But, from the other side of the text, Stoker himself constantly invites a biographical reading by playfully scattering topical references and allusions throughout his work. It is possible to find elements of self-portraiture in several of his heroes and the places and people in his novels are not infrequently based on those he knew well. He confirmed, for example, that *Dracula*'s Professor van Helsing was "founded on a real character," though, typically, he gave no clue as to who this was.[10]

But whether these citations are so strategically placed that they permit a novel like *Dracula* to be read as an elaborate roman à clef is another matter. The fact that Stoker and Oscar Wilde were rivals for the hand of Florence Balcombe raises questions concerning Stoker's own sexuality and the precise nature of this rivalry, but these are topics for conjecture rather than conclusive analysis. It remains to be seen whether the crucifixes dreaded by the novel's vampires can be traced back, as in one recent account, to the little golden cross that Wilde gave to Florence just three years before she married Stoker. Certainly there is reasonable doubt as to whether *Dracula* is a text written in "a recognizable code that was, perhaps, designed to be broken," one whose correct deciphering reveals "Stoker's fear and anxiety as a closeted homosexual man during Oscar Wilde's trial."[11] Reasonable doubt, not because such a suggestion would be unthinkable, but because our knowledge of Stoker's own sexual inclinations is so slight and haphazard and riddled with inconsistencies. For example, the powerfully homoerotic candor of his 1872 fan letter to Walt Whitman needs to be placed in apposition to his contemporary reputation as a ladies' man; but how these two pieces of evidence are to be evaluated and whether they can be reconciled are surely open questions. The roguish "Uncle Bram" so playfully addressed by aspiring actresses and female illustrators remains as inscrutable as ever.[12]

Moreover, to fix identity too quickly is in effect to foreclose on the work of sexual representation performed by Stoker's texts, to simplify their convoluted movement around the determination of sexuality itself. In Stoker's writing there is a persistent yet deeply troubled attempt to reimagine the terms of heterosexual subjectivity, its desires and perversions, often mixing bold ideas with a measure of ambiguity, as if it were somehow perilous to press his conclusions too far. The presence of what Ken Gelder has shrewdly noted as the "undercoded moment[s]" in Stoker's writings make them susceptible to a variety of sexual readings—queer, heteronormative, and bisexual alike—which cannot easily be reduced to plain matters of biography, at least where Stoker's personal sexual orientation is at issue.[13] Nor are such problems at all new. We know, for example, that *Dracula* was read as a moral tract by some of the author's peers and acclaimed for its high moral tone in several newspaper editorials. But even here doubts could soon creep in. When Mrs. Boyd-Carpenter, the wife of the Bishop of Ripon, wrote to Stoker praising the novel as "an allegory of sin" directed against "those whose belle-lettres repel," she also worried that she might be "reading into it more than you meant."[14] Stoker's reply seems not to have survived, yet in response to a similar question from an interviewer a few days earlier "he would give no definite answer." "I suppose that every book of the kind must contain some lesson," he remarked; "but I prefer that readers should find it out for themselves."[15] Again, Stoker's reluctance to foreclose on matters of interpretation can be read in more than one way: either as a refusal to be drawn onto dangerous ground, or as a desire not to have the complex meanings of his novel pigeonholed too quickly by overzealous readers. Whatever reasons lay behind Stoker's reserve, its effect is both to arouse our curiosity *and* to deny the satisfaction of that curiosity by firmly placing the text within the domain of strictly public meanings.

Biography's pleasures and seductiveness are virtually irresistible and yet, in a sense, Stoker makes us aware of its limits, its restrictions. With Stoker there is always an unwillingness to vouchsafe a "definite answer" and we are invariably left with a feeling of incompleteness or omission, a series of lacunae which provide intimations of a self deliberately poised just beyond our reach. To be sure, secrecy is textualized in Stoker's writings in several ways, and his books are full of mystery, deception, and concealment, often bringing into play a kind of Masonic narrative in which—as in *Dracula*—a group of men and women privately pledge themselves to fight against some terrible and overwhelming force. But in *Vampires, Mummies, and Liberals* I try to put aside "the suspicions about [Stoker's] inner life that one formed simply from reading *Dracula*" and, in seeking to displace the methods of critical biography, I turn instead to those of cultural studies. Though it resists any easy, incontrovertible definition—cultural studies is, after all, a field of inquiry crossed by "multiple discourses," the product of "a number of different histories"— what has been immensely fruitful in this body of work is its focus upon the politics of culture, upon the interconnections between cultural practices and questions of power.[16]

Throughout this book I try to see Stoker's literary career as an episode, or series of episodes, in a wider cultural history in which the self-assuredness of what has been called the Victorian "age of equipoise," with its limited franchise, its gospel of self-help, and its nightwatchman state, began to unravel.[17] At the core of this long transformation, lasting from the 1880s to the 1920s, lies a crisis in the character of British liberalism which put into doubt many of the received ideas regarding the proper relationship between the state and civil society, between the public and the private. It is a crisis evident in the splits and divisions inside the Liberal Party itself, and ultimately in that party's eventual decline. But it is also manifest in the upheaval affecting the various knowledges and ideologies that fall within the gravitational pull of liberal thinking, that mixture of social theories and "common-sense ideas" which forms the "taken-for-granted points of moral reference" of liberalism's practical philosophy (the more diffuse "liberalism with a small *l*").[18] Put another way, these knowledges and ideologies—ranging from quasi-medical concepts like "moral hygiene" to changing notions of personal responsibility—provide the cultural resources that enable individual social and civic subjects to imagine and enact their own sense of agency, however imperfectly.

In the following chapters I consider Stoker's work as it engages with the moral, political, and scientific discourses of his day, finding in his "characteristic forms and devices, evidence of the deadlocks and unsolved problems of the society" in which he lived.[19] By shuttling between Stoker's fictional and nonfictional writing, my aim has been to produce a "sociology of narrative elements" in a double sense.[20] In the first place, I attempt to follow the regularities and substitutions that occur *within* Stoker's varied oeuvre, the repertoire of tropes, figures, and motifs whose meanings shift as they move in and out of different social and generic contexts and which together serve as the signature of his work. Secondly, I seek to show the local discursive continuities between Stoker's writing and the various "régimes of truth" upon which he draws, those systems, sciences, disciplines, theories, rhetorics, arguments, and statements whose routine task is to distinguish between true and false accounts of the phenomena of his world.[21] One of the most curious features of Stoker's texts is that they bear the mark of an occasional but nonetheless incorrigible theorist. This propensity for wild and even phantasmatic speculation raises some further methodological issues to which I will return in a moment.

My approach is not intended to dispense with biographical work completely; rather, I hope to redirect attention toward the often contradictory public allegiances that defined Stoker's literary career, to read him as a historical figure occupying a plurality of sometimes uncomfortable positions, rather than as a tormented clinical case history. At the very least, this has meant taking Stoker at his word, reading him as he most wanted to be read, as a popular writer. Stoker's crowded and colorful life in the theater and the *succès de scandale* enjoyed by *Dracula* have both tended to obscure the strength of his commitment to writing. As he explained in his application to the Royal Literary Fund, "I may say that I have already written fifteen books besides many articles for magazines and newspapers and a number of short stories as well as doing a fair share of ordinary journalism"—all in his "spare time."[22] This application was filed in February 1911, a year before he died, when illness had brought his work to a halt and his badly reduced circumstances had forced him to seek charitable assistance. But a month later he was hard at work on his final novel, *The Lair of the White Worm*, producing a few pages almost every day in his execrable longhand, until the book was completed early in June. Despite his poor health—and by this time he probably knew that he was about to die—the manuscript is fluently written, with very few revisions and only a handful of minor errors.[23] If it is hardly his best book, it is at least one of his best known—it was given a tongue-in-cheek film treatment by Ken Russell in 1988—and Stoker clearly tackled it with his usual professional aplomb, taking a keen interest in its illustrations and sending out copies to interested or influential friends.

Stoker's devotion to literature and the arts is apparent from the very beginning. Although he was a student of science and pure mathematics at Trinity College, Dublin, he gave talks on Shakespeare, Keats, and Shelley as an undergraduate and addressed the university Philosophical Society on the subject of "Sensationalism in Fiction and Society."[24] He also became a keen admirer of the poetry of Walt Whitman, joining Edward Dowden, Trinity's Professor of English Literature, in an impassioned defense of the *Leaves of Grass* at a time when the book was widely regarded as being "as offensive to morals as to taste."[25] Stoker had in fact left

Trinity and taken a job as a Civil Service clerk in 1870, the year before the university-based campaign on behalf of Whitman's poetry began, but he continued to play an active role in his old college societies. He was also busy writing and publishing during this period, carving out for himself a part-time career in journalism as the local Irish newspaper industry underwent a phase of rapid expansion.[26] In November 1871 he became the *Dublin Mail*'s drama critic and two years later he briefly served as editor for the ill-fated *Halfpenny Press*. According to bibliographer Richard Dalby, "Stoker wrote many pieces for Dublin newspapers and journals" in the 1870s, including stories for publications like *The Warder* and "editorials and news items for *The Irish Echo*," most of which were unsigned.[27] But his first published piece of fiction, a short story called "The Crystal Cup," appeared in an English monthly, *The London Society*, in September 1872. A Dublin periodical, *The Shamrock*, serialized his first horror story, "The Chain of Destiny," in May 1875.

Stoker's early experience as a jobbing newspaper columnist decisively shaped his identity as a writer, teaching him to meet deadlines quickly and punctually and to keep a sharp eye trained on the literary marketplace for new opportunities. He later boasted that he had "helped largely to effect a needed reform" by speeding up the writing of theater reviews so that they could appear in the press the morning following the evening performance.[28] He seems to have been tremendously self-disciplined, squeezing a steady stream of stories, novels, and essays out of the spaces in between his hectic round of professional commitments, whether as a civil servant or later as Irving's business and tour manager. His habit of dating each day's output shows just how concentrated his work could be: for example, the original draft of *Seven Golden Buttons*, the short historical novel that eventually appeared under the title *Miss Betty* in 1898, was completed in slightly less than three weeks.[29] And his literary pursuits were even more diverse than the published record suggests. His letters show that in the mid-1870s, encouraged by the American actress Geneviève Ward, he was enthusiastically researching and drafting a play set in revolutionary France based on the life and loves of the French Girondist Madame Roland.[30] But this seems to have come to nothing. In 1908, when he was desperately grubbing around for any work he could find following Irving's death, he again tried his hand at writing for the stage, but with little success. The actor-manager of St. James's Theatre in London thought his three-act play *Paul Ransome* to be "very clever and very dramatic" but ultimately unsuitable.[31]

Stoker was constantly writing. Yet, because of *Dracula's* success—Winston Churchill jokingly told Stoker that one of the reasons he agreed to be interviewed by him was "because you are the author of *Dracula*"—the bulk of Stoker's work has been eclipsed, shunted off to the sidelines of critical discussion. As a result, we have lost any sense of the range of his writings, as well as any real understanding of the issues with which they are preoccupied and how these changed over time. The problem has been exacerbated by the fact that after Stoker's death several of his books were reissued in severely edited form, in some cases having been partially rewritten by an unknown hand. *The Lady of the Shroud* (1909) has suffered particularly badly in this respect, for in its modern editions one-third of the text has been excised, entirely removing the novel's utopian finale. Similarly, since its first publication, *The Lair of the White Worm* has almost invariably been reprinted in a revised and significantly shortened version, so that it becomes impossible to judge the intensity of the novel's racial animus. In all fairness, it must be said that these abridgments continued a trend that Stoker himself helped to create. He was always willing to revise or adapt at a publisher's request. Indeed, his practice as a writer was to solicit suggestions and criticisms from friends and associates, not all of them literary figures, and to alter his manuscripts accordingly.[32] There are two different versions of his Egyptological tale *The Jewel of Seven Stars* (1903, 1912), each with a conclusion that is the opposite of the other, and he cut some 19,000 words from his novel *The Man* (1905) when it was published in the United States under the title of *The Gates of Life* (1908).

In this study I make no claims to be presenting the complete Stoker, however that unlikely construct may be construed. But I do try to offer a corrective to the current overconcentration on *Dracula* and to place that book in the context of some of Stoker's other writings, showing his consistent concern with questions of nationhood, character, and sexuality, and the close links between them. While his career had its vicissitudes, many of Stoker's novels sold well and received favorable notices when they originally appeared. *Harper's Weekly*, for example, called him "a born story-teller" and praised *The Jewel of Seven Stars* as "a very clever and masterly story . . . which is likely to command a popular audience."[33] And *The Lady of the Shroud*, sometimes seen as a successor to his famous vampire novel, went through twenty editions between 1909 and 1934. These lesser successes have always suffered from comparison with *Dracula's* immense popularity and they were overshadowed by Stoker's illness and relative poverty in the years immediately following Irving's death in 1905. If he never again attained the level of income that his employment in the theater had led him to expect, we should remember just how difficult it was to make one's living solely as a writer. As the reduction in his earnings began to bite, Stoker complained in a letter to one of his publisher's assistants in 1907 that, compared to bookselling, writing was a poor trade, and by January 1909 he was pressing Heinemann for money because he was "stony."[34] "I find the being debarred working is the worst part of the sickness," he wrote to Heinemann while recovering from a paralytic stroke in 1906. But he continued writing almost to the end.[35]

*Dracula* has been called "the first great *modern* novel in British literature."[36] Yet as one anonymous reviewer noted long ago, it is hard to "place the novels of Mr. Bram Stoker in the highest class of literary distinction." His books are "ingenious," "entertaining," and often "thoroughly readable," but he was no great stylist and in many cases his novels fail to cohere fully.[37] One might borrow Henry James's judgment of Henry Irving to describe Stoker as, at best, "a very superior amateur."[38] In another sense, however, Stoker's lapses and inconsistencies are what make his writing so compelling, for they show his novels and stories to be the work of a transitional figure, an author nervously glancing back at the past as he strides out into the future. As he moves swiftly through a world of cameras, phonographs, automobiles, and flying machines, all the marvelous paraphernalia of modernity, there is always a strong reminder that the old Liberal certainties are failing, that something solid is slipping away.

Stoker is a writer who stands at the center of a number of conflicted and conflicting currents. In part, this is an effect of his mobility within the commercial public sphere of late Victorian Britain, tacking between the arenas of publishing, journalism, and the theater. More strikingly, it is also related to the cultural and geographical mobility that defined his move from Dublin to London. Stoker's middle-class Irish Protestant origins provided him with models of respectability and penury that remained with him all his life. His father was a clerk at Dublin Castle—hence Stoker's own Civil Service appointment—and his mother, who came from an Irish military family, was a social reformer and workhouse visitor. There were seven children, and the five Stoker boys were all given a professional education, at considerable expense. When the time came for Stoker's father to retire, the family debts were so large that he and his wife moved to Naples with their two daughters in order to live more cheaply on his monthly pension and pay off the money they still owed.

Bram's younger brother Thomas was also sent to Trinity College, but the other three boys, William, Richard, and George, went to medical school. William, his elder brother, became a venerable member of the Irish metropolitan elite: he was a trustee and governor of Ireland's National Gallery, president of the country's Royal College of Surgeons and of the Royal Academy of Medicine, and the recipient of a knighthood in 1895 and a baronetcy in 1911. He was also the only Stoker brother to remain in Ireland. Thomas became an administrator in the Indian Civil Service and Richard joined the Indian Medical Service, while George became a doctor in London, working overseas as a surgeon during the wars in Turkey and the Balkans, and later in South Africa.[39] Stoker's exposure to these medical and legal-bureaucratic specialisms had an important influence on his work and, as any reader of *Dracula* will know, the communities of professional men who find themselves trying to make sense of a bizarre and initially inexplicable set of incidents frequently include doctors and lawyers. As I seek to show in chapter 2, Stoker's narratives often use established knowledge as a point of departure for wildly unconventional hypotheses, particularly regarding "the physio-psychists" and their new understanding of the mysteries of the human mind (*LA*, 126). It is not at all uncommon to find Stoker theorizing about how dreams work or about the physical and psychological bases of sexual attraction. And even where medical men are absent, scientific thought is introduced to fill the breach. Contrasting dreams with material reality at one point, Stoker analogically invokes the physicist Sir Oliver Lodge's remarks on "the modern scientific view" of aether and matter: "Matter is turning out to be a filmy thing in comparison with aether" (*LA*, 249).

On the one hand, Stoker's excursions into medicine and law belong to the mechanics of his plots. As his working notes for *Dracula* show, Stoker carefully checked the details of the lunatic Renfield's fatal injuries with his brother William, and probably many of the medical and scientific references in the novel derive from the same source.[40] Similarly, when working on *Lady Athlyne* (1908), a romance whose climax turns on the idiosyncracies of the Scottish matrimonial laws, Stoker—who passed his bar examinations in 1890—patiently researched the legal background he needed to give his tale its plausibility. But on a larger scale, the forays into cultural criticism or the conjectures on history or religion in Stoker's

*Vampires, Mummies, and Liberals*

novels frequently draw upon medicine or science. Different discourses predominate in different texts: thus criminal anthropology plays an important role in *Dracula*, while sexology is crucial to *Lady Athlyne*. And Stoker's search for new epistemological points of departure also extended to the pseudosciences or parasciences: *The Jewel of Seven Stars* and *The Lady of the Shroud* partly situate themselves in relation to "psychical research," for example, and throughout the author's journalism and fiction one finds a continuing interest in physiognomy and phrenology, a predilection that he shared with Whitman. Describing the novelist William De Morgan in an interview, Stoker highlighted his "most interesting physical personality," emphasizing the "bold forehead, wide between those ridges which phrenologists call the 'bumps of imagination.' "[41] Or, in *The Jewel of Seven Stars*, we learn that the barrister Malcolm Ross regularly uses physiognomy in the courtroom as a way of "weighing up" the personality of clients and witnesses (*JSS*, 30). However far-fetched such ideas might sound today, in Stoker's texts a pseudoscience of character like physiognomy serves as a species of professional knowledge informing the trained eyes of his various narrators.

At the same time, these claims to scientific knowledge also connect with the author's political allegiances, since they reflect the "admiration for science" that has been one of the hallmarks of liberalism.[42] As I argue more fully in chapter 1, Stoker always regarded himself as a Liberal, though the meaning of this affiliation was never constant. Stoker's political sympathies took many forms, depending upon whether these were appropriate to the public duties of the citizen or the private conversations of the gentleman. When the death of the popular Liberal MP John Bright led to a by-election in Birmingham in 1889, Stoker was certainly interested enough in local politics to jot down the results and make notes on their likely implications.[43] And his correspondence reveals that his circle of friends and acquaintances in London contained a significant number of Liberal journalists and politicians, contacts who were probably instrumental in helping Stoker to find work on newspapers and periodicals after Irving's death.[44] Insofar as Stoker's writing can be taken as a case study of the stresses and strains by which liberalism was convulsed during the late Victorian and Edwardian periods, however, it is invariably directed to the difficult but pressing questions of moral and political renewal.

At the most general level, one finds traces of a classically liberal individualist philosophy throughout Stoker's writings—even in his least liberal moments. Thus in his 1908 essay "The Censorship of Fiction," Stoker's argument is a remarkable display of a liberalism divided against itself, torn between the old liberal suspicion of too much government and the newer liberal emphasis upon the ethical responsibilities of the State. His demand for censorship by the State is motivated by seeing how "a simple course of *laissez faire*" has brought into being "a continuous market" for "a class of literature so vile that it is actually corrupting the nation." Worse still, the problem had been exacerbated by the failure of the press, that key safeguard in liberal political theory, to provide the necessary criticism and moral leadership. In Stoker's eyes, the dangers of corruption were primarily located in the uncontrolled reaches of the individual imagination, not in some deracinated mass psychology, however destructive the onslaught of market forces might be. Here Stoker's atomistic view of society made it impossible for him to imagine the problem except in individualistic terms, for he argued that even in a "crowded" public forum like the theater such works could only "appeal to a nation . . . through its units, and so must be taken as dealing with individuals."[45] If Stoker's individualism shows the mid-Victorian roots of his Liberal convictions, his calls for government control came at a moment when support for State intervention within the party was growing, partly as a result of its advocacy by "New Liberals" like L. T. Hobhouse or C. F. G. Masterman.

Stoker's liberalism was further complicated by his Irish background. Ireland was of course one of the most intractable issues troubling English Liberals, and in 1885 Gladstone's conversion to the cause of Irish Home Rule split the party.[46] In his *Personal Reminiscences,* Stoker refers to his own Irish nationalist sentiments—a source of disagreement with Irving—but he also makes it clear that he had enormous respect for Gladstone and was sympathetic to the Liberal plans for devolution as laid out in the first Home Rule Bill.[47] Stoker's brand of Irish nationalism seems to have been a far cry from the politics of Charles Parnell, and there was no love lost between Parnell and Irish Liberals. Nevertheless, as I show in chapter 1, Stoker was in touch with a broad swathe of people who were active in the nationalist cause, ranging from Lord and Lady Wilde to Michael Davitt and William O'Brien.[48] But Stoker's relationship to his home country was a complex one and his Irish and English loyalties pulled him in different directions. His managerial post in Irving's company allowed him permanently to leave behind him what he felt to be the provincialism of Irish life and to ensconce himself in the heart of London society,

*Vampires, Mummies, and Liberals*

where he and his wife were known for their generous hospitality. Yet he is always remembered as an Irishman, someone who spoke with a recognizably Irish burr that became more pronounced in the heat of an argument, and his Irish origins are well to the fore in the early autobiographical sections of his tribute to Irving.[49]

One sign of the ambiguities inherent in Stoker's Irishness is how little he used his native land as a setting for his fiction. His only substantially Irish work is his first novel, *The Snake's Pass* (1890), and in a number of his stories the Scottish countryside or Scottish people appear to stand in for their counterparts across the Irish Sea. In the wake of the disillusionment following the collapse of Gladstonian Home Rule, Scotland functioned as a sublimated Ireland, a place of folk legends, resourceful subjects, and immense natural beauty.[50] In some stories, Scottishness and Irishness combine, as in the Sent Leger family in *The Lady of the Shroud* or in the character of the "natural" aristocrat Lord Athlyne, "2nd Viscount Roscommon (in the Peerage of Ireland)" and "30th Baron Ceann-da-Shail (in the Peerage of Scotland)" (*LA*, 18). And when Stoker tries to imagine a liberal utopia that will bring a small underdeveloped but fiercely independent statelet into the twentieth century, what he invents in *The Lady of the Shroud* is a Scottish-Balkan hybrid, a robust mixture of rugged folk traditions and modern science.

Like many advanced Liberals, Stoker looked to scientific growth as the key to modernization, and in an article he published in *The World's Work* in May 1907 one finds an account of Ireland's developmental potential that closely mirrors his Scottish-Balkan utopia. Writing about Dublin's International Exhibition on the site of the old Donnybrook Fair, Stoker argues that "the days of the stage Irishman and the stagey Irish play, of Fenianism and landlordism are rapidly passing away" to be replaced by "a strenuous, industrious spirit," "a new career of industrial progress" which "will introduce Patrick to his new self." Science will help to produce a new national identity, bringing to an end this insular country's "ignorance of itself and of the outside world," and he therefore believes that the Exhibition will have "a concentrating effect," acting as "a national centripetal force" that will overcome the old "historical bitterness."[51] These hopes for Irish renewal prefigure the futuristic vision at the close of *The Lady of the Shroud*, a dream of social improvement that owed much to the Edwardian cult of "national efficiency" in which the application of scientific expertise to Britain's economy and society was expected to restore the country's health.[52]

But as often as not, late-Victorian science seemed to reveal the obstacles to progress, impediments that weighed heavily upon the advanced Liberal conscience. Proponents of eugenics like Karl Pearson attacked Liberal meliorists for their "ignorance" of the "great biological truths," truths that made "so much of Liberal social effort vain. You cannot, sir, reform man, until you understand the factors which control his growth."[53] In *The Snake's Pass* and elsewhere, we see Stoker struggling with the new sciences of race as these bear upon the determination of Irishness, using the specter of the black woman to defend the attractiveness of the Irish colleen against a racializing English discourse which turns all colonial subjects into physically typed outsiders. These biopolitical questions of race and reproduction occur in a different mode in Stoker's later novels like *The Man* and *Lady Athlyne*, which attempt to formulate the "truths" of sexuality in order to ward off the threat of feminism and women's social and political rights. Here science takes the form of sexology or sexual psychology and in Stoker's hands it underwrites a normative heterosexuality that holds the key to national regeneration. Progress is nothing less than the restoration of an erotic social bond that has been purged of the ill-informed presumption and emotional excesses of misguided women who seek to negate their own natures. Sexology allows us to recognize those exemplary men and women in whose physical and mental superiority the future of the race resides. As a personal friend of Gladstone and a man with impeccable Liberal credentials, Bram Stoker is nevertheless a writer who has much to teach us about the underside of progressivism, the places and things it fears or that it wishes not to see.

In one of Stoker's later stories, "In the Valley of the Shadow" (1907), a sick man narrates his own delirium from a Scottish hospital bed. He imagines himself "borne in a winged machine, up into the cool air," but then realizes that H. G. Wells is "partially responsible for this little excursion." He asks the male night-nurse for a cigarette and upon being refused curses him for an hour and a half, though he subsequently thinks that "Mr Kipling is responsible for at least the meticulosity of my comminations." At one point he imagines "a cinematographic entertainment on a stupendous scale" before his eyes, but soon comes to feel that "they were not pictures at all, but real events in the process of happening," events he could bring to a halt if only he could answer "a question put to me by a mysterious voice." Yet he cannot. As his fever subsides and he becomes "sane again" he asks for a copy of Bunyan's *Pilgrim's Progress*, but when he turns to Christian's passage through the Valley of the Shadow he feels that, compared to what he has heard and seen, the book's demons are "merely *simulacra*."[54]

In his commentary on this story, Peter Haining reads Stoker literally: he is describing his own suffering, the effects of the illnesses of his final years. But, however accurate this may be, "In the Valley of the Shadow" partakes of the nightmarish quality so common to Stoker's fiction: the mingling of modernity and the archaic, John Bunyan and the silver screen, in a narrative that blurs the point of demarcation between them. Somewhere amid the hypnotic flicker of illusions and the chatter of received phrases, there is a fugitive glimpse of the real, a question whose answer eludes us. And always there are demons close at hand. Despite its touches of sardonic humor, the story is a thoroughly Gothic dream in which the recovery of one's reason in no way annuls the vivid presence of one's madness, a dream from which there may be no real awakening.

Paradoxically, for all their obsession with scientific knowledge and factual accuracy, Stoker's narratives are best understood as fantasy, as their frequent evocation of states of reverie, unconsciousness, dream, and daydream ought perhaps to suggest. I would argue that the genres that Stoker prefers and in which he excels—Gothic horror, romance, utopias—are those that, in their departure from the idioms of classical realism, most readily lend themselves to the ruses of fantasy. "For," as the narrator of *The Jewel of Seven Stars* remarks, "it is in the arcana of dreams that existences merge and renew themselves, change and yet keep the same—like the soul of a musician in a fugue" ( *JSS*, 2). If this image romantically links the enigmatic impulses of the mind to the process of artistic creation, the emphasis upon the imaginative renewal of what the speaker calls "existences," those altered states that somehow reassuringly retain their familiarity, might serve as an epigraph for much of Stoker's work.

To speak of fantasy might seem to return us to biography, to the realm of the private inner voice, to the inaccessible stirrings of the unconscious. But that is not my intention here. In this study I read Stoker's fiction as public and primarily conscious fantasies, narratives that are formally structured and designed for popular consumption, despite the occasional intrusion of recherché elements or references belonging to the author's individual myth. Indeed, it is essential to see that the anxieties that animate these novels are inextricably bound up with the most deeply rooted dilemmas facing late Victorian culture. Though we tend to think of fantasy in purely personal terms, psychoanalysis stresses its "mixed nature," "in which both the structural and the imaginary can be found" to varying degrees. As Laplanche and Pontalis note, "Freud always held the model fantasy to be the reverie, that form of novelette, both stereotyped and infinitely variable, which the subject composes and relates to himself in a waking state."[55] And in his 1908 essay on "Creative Writers and Daydreaming," Freud suggests a series of links between fantasy and play, dreams and daydreams, and artistic creativity and audience response, proposing a continuum that stretches from "personal day-dreams" to "the wishful phantasies of whole nations."[56] While psychoanalysis denies any absolute distinction between conscious and unconscious fantasies, the more conscious forms like daydreams "are characterised much more by narrative coherence and by the *stability* of the position of the subject within the scenario."[57] In technical terms, conscious fantasies are regulated or "stabilized by the secondary process"; that is, they are organized so as to satisfy the criteria of intelligibility and verisimilitude demanded by the outside world.[58]

Put differently, conscious fantasies can be said to be governed by "the reality principle," that aspect of mental functioning whose role is to temper what the mind finds "agreeable" with what is "real, even if it happened to be disagreeable."[59] But it is precisely around the workings of the reality principle in public fantasies that complications arise. As Freud observes in his essay on creative writers, a vital part of the artist's skill lies in drawing us into the fantasy life of another, bribing us "by the purely formal—that is, aesthetic—yield of pleasure which he offers" and freeing us from the "tensions in our minds," the "self-reproach or shame" that daydreams evoke.[60] Thus, the aesthetic accreditation of fantasy implies a subtle and resourceful negotiation of the real. In Freud's view, the great writer is someone who resists the instinctual sacrifices demanded by the reality principle, yet whose turn to fantasy provides the occasion for the discovery of new truths which bring us back to reality. However, it is far from clear that the coils of fantasy are always so conveniently transcended. Taking a more agonistic view, one might argue instead that, in Fredric Jameson's words, "the truth value of fantasy, the epistemological *bon usage* or proper use of daydreaming as an instrument of philosophical speculation," lies less in outflanking the reality principle than in "triumphantly wresting from it what can . . . in our or its own time be dreamt or fantasied as such"—an observation that might better help to explain the kind of wild theorizing habitually displayed in Stoker's fiction.[61] Here

*Vampires, Mummies, and Liberals*

fantasy comes to hold sway over the real, giving the two terms a finely balanced interdependence, so that each is defined by what the other excludes.

The various phases of this implicit *fort-da* game with the real—pushing it aside, holding it close—can be used to describe some of the main forms taken by fantasy. For example, Gilles Deleuze has argued that masochism is a disciplined "art of fantasy" in which the real is not so much discarded as "suspended," producing idealized scenarios that combine "an indefinite awaiting of pleasure" with "an intense expectation of pain."[62] Deleuze's suggestion that such conscious fantasies may shore themselves up by incorporating a version of the reality principle into their very structure is an important insight. In Sacher-Masoch's novels the protagonists resort to an explicit contract with the objects of their desires in order to ensure the strict and punitive application of the law, which is the precondition for their subsequent pleasures. But Deleuze's point can be generalized beyond psychoanalytic definitions of specific perversions. For, as Slavoj Žižek has noted, the process of reality testing is inevitably "precarious," since there is no secure position from which the individual subject can enjoy a full release from the lure of fantasy. From Žižek's Lacanian standpoint, our sense of reality can never be wholly separated from the fantasmatic domain against which it is counterposed. Rather, what counts as real depends upon, or is framed by, the contrasting residue of "hallucinatory fantasy." In short, "there is no reality without its fantasmatic support."[63]

In Stoker's work the nature of the real world is usually a matter for conjecture, and his stories are "full of strange surmises" (*JSS*, 252). His writing is incurably speculative, toying with hypotheses and explanations, and projecting his characters into situations that allow for experimental reasoning and counterfactual contingencies. But however exotic his narratives become, their payoff always involves the transfiguration of a readily identifiable terrain. At various moments in his novels Stoker imagines a new Ireland, a new womanhood purged of the disturbance of feminism, and a new cosmology that reconciles science and religion in a daringly supernatural mode—as well as populating his texts with specters, illusions, and monsters. In each case, Stoker starts from some contemporary branch of learning, a set of observations or a stray theory, and uses it to elaborate a blatantly phantasmagoric order of possibilities in which men and women can be reborn or remade. At the root of this work of reconstruction is the desire to provide a revised structure of heterosexuality, what might be described as a renegotiation of the "dominant fiction" of sexual difference.[64]

According to Kaja Silverman, our ordinary everyday sense of reality requires "the male subject to see himself, and the female subject to recognize and desire him, only through the medium of images of an unimpaired masculinity."[65] That is to say, by tacitly denying the Oedipal crisis, such images, and the narratives in which they are embedded, provide a society with its ideological conditions of existence. Thus the dominant fiction grounds sexual identity in an asymmetrical opposition between "male" and "female" upon which rests our "most fundamental image of unity, the family," and these representations in turn form the bedrock for our images of community, town, or nation.[66] In Silverman's account, then, the task of the dominant fiction is to naturalize social relations by connecting the basic laws of human culture like the incest taboo to historically specific ideologies of class, gender, and ethnicity. This formulation has, I think, a particular resonance for the liberal tradition whose political history can be written as the attempt "to construct a law that is absolute sovereign over nature, but that must and can find its motives only in nature."[67] In liberal political philosophy the question of how much government or regulation is necessary to safeguard the free and natural development of humankind has always been a source of intense difficulty. But it was enormously complicated both by the scale of the problems that late Victorian industrialism posed and by the growing influence of biological and medical knowledge upon nineteenth-century social and political theory.

From this perspective, Stoker's work might be said to be engaged in interrogating the dominant fiction of his time on behalf of liberalism, trying to conjure new ideals of masculinity and femininity in the face of political movements he distrusted and scientific findings whose significance were much disputed. To be sure, the results are fragmentary and incomplete, as he turns restlessly from one set of ideas to another or grapples with different issues, pitting the resources of fantasy against the unconscionable real. Thus the interdependence between fantasy and the real is omnipresent in these fictions, and their close imbrication provides the preconditions for a series of thought experiments or possible worlds built around the hopes and fears associated with an unprecedented moment for British Liberalism, a moment when the cherished tenets of the Gladstonian settlement had finally lost their hold. There is no better image for this confrontation between the old and the new than that of

*Vampires, Mummies, and Liberals*

Gladstone in his declining years, comfortably ensconced in Hawarden Castle, but imaginarily transported to that other, Transylvanian castle as he leafs through the presentation copy of the novel Stoker had sent to him.[68]

*Vampires, Mummies, and Liberals* opens with a chapter that examines the troubled question of Ireland and Irishness in Stoker's work. *The Snake's Pass*, Stoker's first and his only Irish novel, initially appeared as a serial in the London *People* and several provincial newspapers in 1889, during the turbulent interlude between the first and second Home Rule bills. Its publication in book form in November 1890 coincided, as Stoker noted in his *Personal Reminiscences*, with Parnell's attack on Gladstone in the manifesto "To the People of Ireland." For all his nationalist sympathies, Stoker, like the majority of the Irish Party, took Gladstone's side.[69] In *The Snake's Pass* we see Stoker wrestling with a dual allegiance: to the Ireland of his birth with whose national aspirations he identified, and to the "scientific" racial theories of his day, many of which accorded the Irish only a degraded and inferior status. There is, of course, no comfortable rapprochement between these two sets of commitments, but attempts to resolve the tensions they engender can be seen in the strategic marriages between different national subjects that are a common form of closure in Stoker's novels, beginning with *The Snake's Pass*. Echoes of these Irish dilemmas can also be found in *Dracula*, a book that is heavily preoccupied with the politics of racial decline and healthy breeding. In this chapter, *Dracula* emerges as a staging post in a sociobiological trajectory whose most fully developed statement can be found in Stoker's penultimate novel, *The Lady of the Shroud*. Sometimes dismissed as "warmed-over *Dracula*," this book fantasizes the bringing of a modernizing constitutional monarchy to an underdeveloped land of peasants and fighting priests in a remote part of the Balkans.[70]

Chapter 2 returns to *Dracula*'s Gothic terrain, which it reads together with Stoker's Egyptological romance *The Jewel of Seven Stars*, as an extended meditation on the various sciences of character in the modern era: physiognomy, degeneration theory, mental physiology, and criminal anthropology. Both of these texts question whether a manly self strong enough to withstand the rigors of a rapidly changing foreign and domestic order was still possible in an age when "the spirit of adventure" had been "curbed."[71] The tests of character that Stoker's heroes and heroines undergo probe the limits of the normal and the pathological, and these novels are haunted by anxious thoughts of nervous breakdown, racial debasement, male and female hysteria, unconscious and uncontrollable mental processes, and sexual perversion, phenomena which are confronted and theorized in a number of ways. While Stoker's focus upon questions of character invokes an imperial topography wherein races and nations struggle for dominance, the psychological ramifications of these conflicts forced him to draw upon the newly emerging conceptions of mental space and function, notions of psychic health and inner weakness that pointed beyond even "ordinary unconsciousness" (*JSS*, 59). These ideas frequently diverge and conflict, straining the interpretive coherence of Stoker's narratives. In *The Jewel of Seven Stars*, for example, the uncertain status of the conjectural theories explored in the novel produces rival visions of history whose implications are worked out in the contrasting and mutually contradictory endings found in the 1903 and 1912 editions of the book.

Race and reproduction occupy such a central place in Stoker's writings that the issues of gender and sexuality which they raise are never far away. Chapter 3 concentrates on Stoker's treatment of "the Woman Question" in his later fiction from the Edwardian era. In part, Stoker's novels like *The Man* and *Lady Athlyne* were conceived as angry ripostes to the growing movement for women's suffrage. But they also reflected broader social and cultural currents too. By this period, new collectivist forms of liberal thought were coming into prominence and these were often aligned with attempts to investigate and control the private sphere, the realm of sexual relations and family life. Stoker's essays on censorship reveal his outrage at the increasingly outspoken discussion of sexual matters in the so-called "sex novel," and it is clear that, as with early feminism, he regarded this as further proof of the breakdown of the old liberal order. Yet, like many other disillusioned liberals, he could scarcely avoid taking account of the influential thinking on sexual life embodied in eugenics, social hygiene, or the new science of sexology. In open competition with the "sex novel," Stoker's Edwardian romances attempt to install and celebrate a wholesome, but frankly erotic, depiction of our "natural instincts," that touchstone of sexological inquiry. Both *The Man* and *Lady Athlyne* take the national trauma of the Boer War as their point of departure, organizing their narratives of degeneration and regeneration around an exalted heterosexuality. These books are saturated with reflections on the causes of sexual difference and sexual deviance and the sexological provenance of Stoker's fantasies of natural desire places them

*Vampires, Mummies, and Liberals*

in a genealogy of "serious sexual fiction" that includes writers as different as D. H. Lawrence and Radclyffe Hall.

Finally, as a coda to this study, the last chapter considers the legacy of Stoker's work by examining some recent attempts to retell the story of *Dracula* for a contemporary audience. If the nosferatu have always been valued for their unconventional sexual prowess, latterly there has been a turn away from imagining the vampire purely as a site of the polymorphously perverse, seeing it instead as a tormented racialized Other, a meaning that returns us, however unintentionally, to the biopolitical concerns of Stoker's own writings. Though they are frequently heavily romanticized, vampires have come to figure among the most common symbols of political reaction and resurgent tribalism, a usage that can be found in such diverse cultural forms as graffiti and in-depth journalism. Two texts which appeared in 1992, Francis Ford Coppola's film *Bram Stoker's Dracula* and Dan Simmons's Romanian horror novel *Children of the Night*, provide key examples of this current trend in modern Stokeriana and their analysis is used to throw fresh light on the relationship between myth and popular culture.

This book is an attempt to track the movements of fantasy across a career in writing, to follow its forced march and unexpected detours into the strange territories that abutted on Stoker's crumbling Liberal domain. The result is a series of linked essays, roughly chronological in organization but with anticipations, flashbacks, and sideways glances where these help to fill out the wider cultural narrative to which Stoker's novels belong. It is a journey that ends in an even less orderly present, but one which Stoker might well have recognized.

# 1 *"Dark enough fur any man"*

## Sexual Ethnology and Irish Nationalism

I ask for a history that deliberately makes visible, within the very structure of its narrative forms, its own repressive strategies and practices, the part it plays in collusion with the narratives of citizenships in assimilating to the projects of the modern state all other possibilities of human solidarity.
*Dipesh Chakrabarty* [1]

Looking back in 1896 at "the growth of a doctrine of nationalities as the basis of a new right of nations"—one of "the most conspicuous features of nineteenth-century history"—the Irish writer and Liberal Unionist MP William E. H. Lecky noted that the nationalism of his day was rarely "a movement . . . drawing together men who had long been politically separated," but tended instead to act as "a disintegrating force," winnowing out what he called "the different race elements."[2] Today, however one assesses his judgment of the past, Lecky's observations seem remarkably prescient of a present in which our cultural identities increasingly bear the stamp of a dual process of deterritorialization. On the one hand, the breakup of old political empires and, on the other, the experience of mass migrations have brought about a loss of continuity in the popular consciousness of place and the rise of new ethnolinguistic communities and nationalisms. As a result, it has become more and more difficult for people—whatever their origins—to imagine themselves and the communities to which they feel they belong in the ways that they once did.

The scale of these changes can partly be gauged from the shifting etymology of the word *ethnic* itself, a term which has now become so indispensable as to defy our ability to think of it as having an etymology at all. Yet in premodern times it had a broad religious connotation which has since been narrowed into what is ultimately a far more restrictive definition. Originally, an "ethnic" community was one that stood beyond the Judeo-Christian pale, signifying its heathen or pagan Otherness. When a seventeenth-century writer like Thomas Hobbes spoke of "Ethnique Princes," for example, he was not only drawing a rough and ready line between civilized peoples and unbelievers but also pointing to the common interests shared by Christendom's frequently antagonistic dynasties and principalities. This usage persisted as late as the 1850s, but by then the term was already becoming freighted with new racial connotations stemming from the growing tendency in scientific discourse to think of humankind as irremediably fractured by moral, mental, and biological differences.[3] Superseding the stark division of the world into two broad ethico-religious camps, the impact of biological and anthropological theorizing effectively transformed "ethnicity" into a concept which deterministically treated the human species as a set of irreconcilable racial types—hence the term *ethnology* to designate the putative "science" of race. The new meaning of *ethnicity* was further complicated by its intersection with the growth of nationalism in the nineteenth century (an "-ism" which only came into common English currency in the 1830s), and consequently, when it was used synonymously for *nation*, the term *ethnic* and its derivations helped to thematize nationality in essentially racial terms.

Although Bram Stoker is not an author whose writings are commonly associated with questions of national identity, careful observation of his fiction and journalism reveals that such concerns occupy a central, if frequently uneasy, place in both his early and his later work. Stoker lived through some of the formative years of Irish nationalism and, though he died nearly a decade before independent statehood was achieved, he was a cautious but convinced advocate of Irish Home Rule from at least his early twenties. At the same time, however, his writings reveal the competing attractions of different national identities, suggesting a tension between his sense of his own local Protestant Irish origins and his desire for a more formal imperial-metropolitan ideal of citizenship. The question of boundaries, and of the political and scientific criteria by which one's membership within a national collectivity is to be decided, are issues which seem constantly to be rising to the surface of his fiction.

Despite innumerable difficulties during the nineteenth century, Ireland eventually produced "a national movement powerful enough to lead one of the first successful independence struggles within the British Empire, a struggle which in turn became a model for other colonized nations."[4] But then, as now, that movement was a highly controversial one, and Stoker's own troubled relationship to it underscores the divided loyalties that categories of ethnic identity and national belonging have often bequeathed to nationalism's potential supporters and subjects. In Stoker's time, European defenders of nationalist movements were often deeply at odds with each other over Irish claims to full self-rule. More specifically, though Ireland's radical intelligentsia and political organizations could boast a nationalist pedigree second to none, the rationales emerging in justification of such newly unified nation-states as Germany and Italy seemed to point toward different and sharply opposed conclusions.

For some, the German and Italian examples epitomized a progressive and typically liberal spirit of nation-building in which a scattering of peoples and territories were being brought together ostensibly to the benefit of the whole citizenry. If a nation was truly to flourish, such liberals reasoned, it required an optimum size, though few agreed on how this should be determined.[5] In practice, because of the uncertainty inherent in this so-called "threshold principle," appeals were also made to the cultural distinctiveness of race, language, or customs, positive sources of identity that could be taken as indicators that national viability had been achieved. However, these auxiliary arguments were equally inconclusive and, in fact, midcentury discussion of Ireland shows just how fuzzy both sorts of criteria could actually be. Whereas the English liberal philosopher John Stuart Mill argued that its population size alone was enough to validate Ireland's claims to independence, Mazzini—as the nationalist theoretician of the Young Italy movement—not only thought that the Irish were too few in number but also felt that they were not sufficiently different from the English to be granted self-determination on cultural grounds.

There is a double irony here, for after the Great Famine (1845–49) Ireland's population fell dramatically and cultural nationalism became an increasingly important strand in the independence movement, as attempts in the 1880s to "de-anglicize" Ireland by reviving the Gaelic language clearly show. In this respect, Ireland provided a prototype for challenges to the expansionary and assimilationist premises inherent in the liberal theory of nations as, toward the century's close, calls for national sovereignty solely on the basis of ethnic, linguistic, or cultural difference were heard with growing frequency.[6] Unfortunately, appeals to ethnic distinctiveness cut both ways, and one of the trickiest problems for cultural nationalists lay in knowing what sense to make of the new "advanced" sciences of race whose pejorative judgments were typically used against them and other subject peoples, structuring the relationship between dominant and subordinate groups and underwriting racist and imperialist sentiments. Lecky, whose response to nationalism was pragmatic at best, and who was certainly no supporter of Irish Home Rule, argued that in view of the extremely hybrid populations "in most European countries" race was "usually a most obscure and deceptive guide" to national identity, but added the crucial qualification: "except when it is marked by colour."[7]

## Fictions of Exile

The trajectory of Stoker's own complex response to the paradoxes of nationalism can best be seen through three very different novels: *The Snake's Pass* (1890), *Dracula* (1897), and *The Lady of the Shroud* (1909). Written over a twenty-year period that saw a slump in the prospects for Irish Home Rule and the concomitant rise of Ulster Unionism in the North, these books move between the extremes of euphoria and despair, recounting tales of romantic love in which the fate of a people is ultimately at stake. If Stoker's manner and matter are intensely melodramatic, then this is melodrama that always carries a political charge, drawing up blueprints for change or intimating imminent disaster and decline. But it is a sign of the refractoriness of the Irish question that, time and again, Ireland's condition proved so difficult to name. *The Snake's Pass*, Stoker's first novel set in Ireland, was also his last.

Paradoxically it is *Dracula*, at first glance among the least Irish of all Stoker's texts, that goes furthest in establishing his pedigree as a distinctively Irish writer. For *Dracula* properly belongs within the Anglo-Irish Gothic tradition, a predominantly nineteenth-century mode of writing which struggled obsessively with the cultural meaning of Ireland and Irishness. In this local subgenre the social and psychic fears that had been mobilized in the uncanny scenarios of English writers like Ann Radcliffe and Matthew "Monk" Lewis were subtly inflected into a monstrous vision of Ireland as imagined through the eyes of some of the poorer members of the Protestant Ascendancy, the country's socially and culturally dominant elite. Economically dependent upon mainland Britain for their readers, and awkwardly placed in relation to Ireland's turbulent politics, these authors produced out of their cultural marginality a motley fiction, marked by eerie displacements and curious evasions, in which commonplace Gothic tropes like the evocation of a decaying, haunted mansion or a Catholic European setting could acquire disturbing new resonances in Irish Protestant hands. Dissimulation and indirection were thus definitive of "a remarkable line among certain writers of the ascendancy, running from Charles Robert Maturin at the beginning of the century to Bram Stoker at its close: compounders of fantasies and tales of the grotesque, set everywhere save in Ireland."[8] Figuratively, and even sometimes literally, this was "a fiction of exile."[9]

In Stoker's case this exile was more than symbolic. Much of his life was spent not only in England, but also on the road in his role as theater manager for the celebrated Victorian actor Henry Irving. In fact, it was the fruits of his travels overseas that first brought Stoker fame as a writer on contemporary affairs. After touring the United States with Irving's company, Stoker wrote up his impressions from these two visits into a lecture which he delivered at the London Institution on December 28, 1885. Summing up his experiences in the United States just eleven days after Gladstone had announced his conversion to Irish Home Rule, Stoker told a cheering audience that "the workings of the institutions of America" satisfied him that "in future developments of country or of race, or of politics, which are to sway the world, we need never fear the developments of popular government."[10] Subsequently published as *A Glimpse of America* (1886), this strikingly eulogistic pamphlet drew praise from another traveler, the Anglo-American Henry Morton Stanley. Stoker still warmly remembered this tribute two decades later, and his admiration for Stanley and for other figures like the explorer Sir Richard Burton indicates the wider imperial context in which his writings also need to be placed. In Stoker's romances the foot-loose adventurer, home from Australia, the Balkans, or South Africa, is a favorite device, and one of the most fascinating aspects of his fiction lies in its journeys.

If in Stoker's case exile is inseparable from the pleasures of travel, which in turn shade into dreams of empire, what of his relationship to Ireland, his colonial home during the first thirty years of his life? By joining Irving, Stoker took up a life that seemed to position him securely at the center of fashionable English society, feted as a respected figure in the nation's theatrical world. At the time of *Dracula*'s publication, Stoker was described as "a Londoner of nearly twenty years' standing," and it is clear that he regarded the city as "the best possible place for a literary man."[11] But unlike his kinsman Oscar Wilde, Stoker never quite transformed himself into an English gentleman. Instead, he was typed as "a big, red-bearded, untidy Irishman" who "knew everybody worth knowing," a description which marks his success while subtly undermining it.[12]

In a fan letter to Walt Whitman written when he was twenty-four and

*Vampires, Mummies, and Liberals*

working as a civil servant in Dublin, Stoker—"reared a conservative in a conservative country"—praised the poet's *Leaves of Grass* for taking him "away from the world around me" and placing him "in an ideal land," "your own land of progress."[13] Whitman served as a touchstone for Stoker's desire for a wider, less parochial cultural milieu, and while at Trinity College he had on several occasions joined in a public defense of the poet's work led by one of his professors, Edward Dowden, who acquired a reputation for championing a self-consciously "cosmopolitan" approach to literature.[14] According to Dowden, Whitman was "a representative democrat in art," the forward-looking spokesman for a new but as yet "half-formed" egalitarian society, "the comrade of every man, high and low"—in contrast to "the exclusive spirit of aristocratic art" with its constant "striving after selectness in forms of speech."[15] This high valuation of Whitman's progressivism was a consistent theme in his reception among British readers—it can still be found nearly fifty years later in Charles Masterman's *The Condition of England* (1909), for example—and it sheds light upon another component of Stoker's disaffiliation from Ireland: his attraction to the politics of English Liberalism, inspired at different times by such luminaries as John Bright and William Gladstone.[16]

Though Stoker's self-confessedly "hysterical" response to Henry Irving's spellbinding dramatic gifts is often cited by biographers, it is worth noting that he also recorded the thrill of "deep emotion" that he felt upon hearing John Bright's "great oration on Ireland." "To this day I can remember the tones of his organ voice as he swept us all—heart and brain and memory and hope—with his mighty periods," wrote Stoker in his *Personal Reminiscences.*[17] Bright was a radical Liberal speaker renowned for the controlled passion of his popular rhetoric and a powerful prophet of democracy in his own right. In his speeches, and those of Gladstone, the political narratives most characteristic of the English Liberal tradition seemed to open up new horizons that combined social advance and self-improvement, "fantasies of progress" in which virtue was triumphant over vice and darkness was dispelled by light.[18]

Much of the success of popular Liberalism can be explained in terms of its ability to use "the power of exciting stories to move people," creating a sense of identification and purpose.[19] Here the Tory party was represented as the chief obstacle to the onward march of reform and democracy, a reactionary formation founded upon privilege and aristocracy—indeed, "Bright can be understood as inventing the Liberal party by inventing the Tory party."[20] Thus, on the speaking visit to Dublin that so greatly affected Stoker, Bright insisted, to "loud and prolonged cheers," that "whatever there is that is defective in any portion of the Irish people comes not from their race, but from their history, and from the conditions to which they have been subjected." For "it would be impossible to imagine a state of things in which the principles of the Tory party have had a more entire and complete opportunity for their trial than they have had within the limits of this island."[21] Though Stoker's own account of Bright's speech to the Dublin Mechanics' Institute should be read with caution—Bright was, by his own admission, in poor voice and his address was constantly interrupted—the event was a remarkable occasion because of the way in which it simultaneously propounded a radical Liberal solution to the Irish question *and* gave public expression to the nationalist aspirations of many in the audience.[22]

Ultimately, Stoker's most decisive response to what he saw as the backwardness and even the philistinism of Irish life was to leave Ireland to seek his future elsewhere, as three of his four brothers had already done, if perhaps for more immediately practical and financially pressing reasons. When Irving hinted at the possibility of a job in his company, Stoker wrote enthusiastically in his diary: "London in view!"—a comment that speaks volumes about his dreams of a metropolitan life.[23] And once ensconced in London he quickly took on the persona of a man-about-town, joining the city's National Liberal Club and acquiring a great many contacts in British parliamentary circles. One of the first to congratulate him on his new appointment was the cosmopolitan Edward Dowden, who pointedly admonished Stoker not to cut himself off from his friends in Ireland.[24]

Yet, despite this cultivation of a definite emotional and physical distance from his homeland, Stoker seems always to have identified himself as an Irishman, a supporter of its culture and its causes. Notwithstanding his Liberal political credentials, Stoker described himself as a moderate or "philosophical" advocate of Irish Home Rule long before Gladstone had incorporated this demand into his party's platform. During his student days in Dublin Stoker was on close terms with members of the nationalist intelligentsia like Sir William and Lady Wilde, becoming a frequent visitor to their house in Merrion Square, and his support for Irish self-rule was a bone of contention with Irving during their early years together.[25] Though he eventually came to prefer Gladstone's meliorism to the militancy of Parnell, Stoker was sympathetic enough to

*Vampires, Mummies, and Liberals*

Parnell's sometime associate and subsequent critic the combative nationalist MP William O'Brien to try to help bring a dramatization of O'Brien's Fenian novel *When We Were Boys* (1890) to the London stage. Stoker's efforts failed, but O'Brien gratefully wrote to thank him for taking "so genuine a liking" to the book and for his deep interest in the play, whose performance O'Brien believed "would be of priceless value in the Home Rule fight."[26] Set in the revolutionary 1860s and written while the author was imprisoned in Galway jail for making an "illegal" speech, *When We Were Boys* sold well in Ireland, despite the fact that its criticisms of anti-Fenian attitudes among some of the Catholic clergy led to unsuccessful attempts to have the book banned by the Vatican. But "illegal" or not, O'Brien's oratory was extremely influential: Gladstone later maintained that his conversion to the politics of Home Rule grew out of his reading of one of O'Brien's speeches.[27]

O'Brien was not the only Irish writer whom Stoker encouraged. He kept up a wide range of friendships and acquaintances in the Irish literary world both at home and in the metropolis.[28] When "George Egerton" was commissioned to write a series of portraits of Irish men and women of letters in London in 1898, she turned to Stoker as "a representative Irishman."[29] Stoker's nationalist leanings were also reflected in his literary tastes. Always an omnivorous reader and collector, he seems to have admired William Carleton's popular portraits of Irish peasant life, and in his valuable personal library he kept an autographed presentation copy of the young W. B. Yeats's *The Countess Kathleen* (1892), alongside volumes by Stevenson, Kipling, Rider Haggard, and Hall Caine. In a similar vein, Stoker's wife Florence was a devotee of the work of Maria Edgeworth, a writer who boldly foregrounded native Irish dialect in the narration of her first book *Castle Rackrent* (1800) and who is typically said to be the first truly Irish novelist.[30] But perhaps the most commonly cited Irish influence on Stoker's work is that of Sheridan Le Fanu, whose vampire story "Carmilla" (1872) was an important precursor of *Dracula*, and whose influence is openly acknowledged in his short story "Dracula's Guest" (1914). In fact, traces of Le Fanu's distinctive Anglo-Irish Gothic mode are evident throughout Stoker's writing, especially in some of his shorter fiction such as the 1891 tale "The Judge's House," which comes close to pastiche.

So, when Stoker published his first novel *The Snake's Pass* in 1890, just over a decade after arriving in London, it was understandable that he should have chosen to return to an imaginary Ireland for its setting. With this in mind, he went to some trouble to build an audience among those readers who shared his political views on Home Rule, writing to the Irish journalist and protosocialist organizer of the Land League Michael Davitt to secure a favorable mention for his novel in Davitt's newspaper *The Labour World*. On November 29 *The Snake's Pass* received a prominent review, possibly written by Davitt himself, praising it as "a fresh, power-ful, dramatic, intensely interesting story."[31] But perhaps the most gratify-ing response came from Gladstone, "whose magnificent power and abil-ity and character I had all my life so much admired." When Gladstone told him in a private conversation how much he had enjoyed the book, Stoker was extremely touched that the Liberal leader should have found time to read "an Irish novel" at the very moment when his efforts to resolve the "centuries-old Irish troubles" were breaking down, "one of the greatest troubles and trials of his whole political life."[32] Davitt and Gladstone make an odd couple—a former Fenian and a patrician Liberal uneasily making common cause around the question of Home Rule—but together they represent opposite poles of Stoker's imagined compos-ite readership, mingling Irish rural and English metropolitan concerns.

On the face of it, *The Snake's Pass* is a simple romance in which Arthur Severn, a young Englishman who is visiting Ireland for the first time, falls in love with a local farmer's daughter and finds himself caught up in a search for long-lost buried treasure—a chest of golden coins left behind by a French expeditionary force in 1798 and rumored to be hidden away in a hill named Knockcalltecrore. There is a villain to be outwitted, the notorious gombeenman or moneylender Black Murdock, and a lady's heart to be won, the ravishing Norah Joyce with "her beautiful head borne with the free grace of the lily on its stem" (*SP*, 75). And there is also a rival for Norah's hand, Arthur's old schoolfellow and now geologist Dick Sutherland, who quickly becomes Arthur's ally in the adventure.[33] Together with a host of minor rustic characters, these four protagonists struggle to possess and understand the secrets of the land as both a source of their livelihood and a source of wealth.

If myopic English reviewers were sometimes reminded of homegrown writers like Charles Reade, *The Snake's Pass*'s true antecedents can be found in the early-nineteenth-century Irish novelists Maria Edgeworth and Lady Morgan.[34] In their very different ways, novels like Morgan's enor-mously popular *The Wild Irish Girl* (1806) or Edgeworth's more guarded tale *The Absentee* (1812) hinge upon the induction of an absentee Anglo-Irish landlord into the charms and responsibilities of rural Ireland, an

*Vampires, Mummies, and Liberals*

education that is sealed by wedding vows. *The Snake's Pass* follows this cross-cultural marriage plot in outline, but it is far closer to the codes of popular melodrama than anything in Edgeworth and Morgan. Indeed, as Nicholas Daly has suggested, one of the novel's precursors may have been Dion Boucicault's comic melodrama *The Shaughraun* (1874), a play which also unites an English hero and an Irish heroine against a rapacious local moneylender—although, as we'll see in a moment, the gombeenman was already a well-developed fictional type by this date.[35] In *The Snake's Pass*, Black Murdock's persecution of Norah Joyce and her father in order to gain control of Joyce's land and to secure the missing treasure is the driving force behind the novel. Arthur Severn must vanquish Black Murdock if he is ever to win Norah's love: when Arthur asks Norah's father for his daughter's hand in marriage, Phelim Joyce declares that "whin the threasure of Knockcalltecrore is found, thin ye may claim her if ye will, an' I'll freely let her go!" (*SP*, 145).

As in Lady Morgan's *The Wild Irish Girl*, the novel's English hero must fall in love with the Irish countryside before his heart can be stolen by its inhabitants. Both *The Snake's Pass* and *The Wild Irish Girl* contrast what Morgan calls "the embellished labours of art," typified by the English garden, with "the simple but sublime works of nature" found in Ireland: "the stupendous altitude of its 'cloud-capt' mountains, the impervious gloom of its deep-embosomed glens, the savage desolation of its un-cultivated heaths and boundless bogs."[36] Morgan's early description is matched by "the almost primal desolation" seen by Arthur Severn at the beginning of *The Snake's Pass*, "the triumph of nature" in all "her wild majesty and beauty" (*SP*, 9–10). But whereas "the tasteful spectator" who narrates *The Wild Irish Girl* initially finds the Irish landscape lacking and only gradually comes to a full appreciation of it, Arthur immediately feels "exalted in a strange way, and impressed at the same time with a new sense of the reality of things" (*SP*, 11).[37]

At a later point in the story, while looking out from a mountaintop at the "wild moor and rugged coast," Arthur wonders whether "there was some unconscious working of the mind which told me in some imperfect way that in a region quite within my range of vision, nothing could long remain hidden or unknown" (*SP*, 93). From the outset his encounter with Ireland promises to reveal to him a new truth about himself, a truth that is necessitated by his confused sense of disappointment with his own origins. Orphaned while "only a very small boy," Arthur has "been brought up in an exceedingly quiet way with an old clergyman and his wife in the west of England" under "the fiction of my being a schoolboy," the label of "guardian" being exchanged for that of "tutor" as he grew older. Although Arthur has been well provided for by a "wealthy and eccentric" great aunt, he has always been made to feel an "outsider" by his relations, since his father was cut off by his family after having married a woman whom they considered to be his social inferior (*SP,* 11–12). However, at her death Arthur's great aunt leaves him all her property, transforming him from a virtual pariah into one of "the magnates of the county" (*SP,* 13). Daunted by his new-found wealth and status, the "shy" Arthur resolves "to spend at least a few months in travel" in the hopes of "overcoming the negative forces that had hitherto dominated my life"; and, after completing a six months' tour of Europe, he accepts an invitation to visit friends in County Clare, deciding "to improve my knowledge of Irish affairs by making a detour through some of the counties in the west" (*SP,* 11, 13).

## "A land of ruins and of the dead"

Spurred on by the spectacular beauty of rural Ireland, Arthur gains self-knowledge by going out of his way, moving beyond the narrow horizons of his displaced upbringing to receive a romantic education in love and adventure. There is a suspiciously perfect fit between his growing self-confidence and the intoxicating power of the Irish countryside. And if he is thoroughly changed by his experience of Ireland, he in turn expresses his gratitude by changing the country that has changed him. But before following the narrative of *The Snake's Pass* through to its conclusion, I want to interrupt Arthur's story in order to complicate my account of the novel's genealogy. For only when we set the pastoral idealization of Ireland so integral to Stoker's narrative against the complex and contested traditions of nineteenth-century writing in and about Ireland— whether in travelers' tales or in fiction—can we see what is missing.

Side by side with "the Victorian fashion for wild, uncultivated and picturesque landscapes" one may discern a loose counter-tradition that found diverse expression in Thackeray's *Irish Sketchbook* (1843) or William Carleton's literary and sociological documentation of the Great Famine (c. 1847) or perhaps even in parts of Charles Kingsley's hostile Irish journal in *Letters and Memories of His Life* (1877).[38] This counter-tradition sees Ireland as, in Kingsley's words, "a land of ruins and of the dead."[39]

And if that phrase makes us think of *Dracula*, perhaps one can see in Stoker's portrait of an imagined Transylvania some of the features of that other Ireland which *The Snake's Pass* immures in magnificent vistas and a rough-hewn rustic charm. For Transylvania too is manifestly a place of ruins—Dracula himself residing in "a vast ruined castle"—and of the dead—Dracula's hand, we are told, feels "more like the hand of a dead than a living man" (*D*, 24–26). There is, I want to suggest, a curious geographical doubling that passes between *Dracula* and *The Snake's Pass* which hinges upon equivocations in the representability of Ireland and the Irish.

To be sure, *Dracula* also has its roots in other modes of Victorian travel writing, the more so since Transylvania came to Stoker secondhand through the painstaking library research that often characterized his writings, packed with odd correspondences and intriguing references. Significantly, one of several sources for Stoker's descriptions of people and places in *Dracula* is *With "The Unspeakables"; Or, Two Years' Campaigning in European and Asiatic Turkey* (1878), a memoir by the author's brother George which records the latter's experiences as a military doctor during the Russo-Turkish War. There one discovers an account of the Balkans that contains many of the features that later graced Stoker's 1897 novel: the men with their enormous black mustaches and traditional peasant dress consisting of wide baggy trousers and white homespun shirts; the simple, almost superstitious, religiosity of the local people; the packs of wolves coming down from the hills to terrorize the villagers; and the difficult journeys across the snow-clad mountains through precipitous gorges and dangerous ravines.

Yet in the midst of these vivid and unforgettable scenes, and surrounded by the ravages of war and disease, George Stoker could still find odd echoes of his native Ireland among the Bulgarian peasantry as he watched them dancing to the bagpipes, going faster and faster and ending with a climactic shout such as "one hears during the course of an Irish jig." It is as if the land of his birth remains somehow dimly present, still visible through the strange customs and perilous daily lives of the rural populations he encounters. Perhaps, then, it is not so surprising that, upon meeting up with a fellow countryman (bizarrely described as an "Italian from Cor-r-k"), George Stoker is soon singing "The Wearing of the Green" with his new companion, though they take great care to "counterbalance the rebellious sentiments therein expressed," even in these distant climes, by following it up with a loudly "howled" rendition of "God Save the Queen."[40] The reach of the guilty imperial conscience seems to be virtually limitless.

Stoker's brother George was not the only traveler in these regions to be reminded of the Irish. In his 1885 book *On the Track of the Crescent: Erratic Notes from the Piraeus to Pesth*—one of the texts that Stoker consulted while researching *Dracula*—Major E. C. Johnson compared the Szekelys and the Wallachs of Transylvania to "the imprudent Irishman," noting in particular the latter's superstitiousness, as evidenced by "the number of crosses by the roadside" and their fear of the local priest. But Johnson's stereotype of the Irish peasant—"a lazy, pleasant, good-natured, drunken, careless, improvident fellow"—is closer to the kind of figure whose "quaint speech" so amuses and interests Arthur Severn in *The Snake's Pass* (*SP*, 217).[41]

Not that the borderlands between Galway and Mayo are without their dangers.[42] But these are muted, or held in reserve. This is a part of Ireland whose untamed scenery contains only "occasional glimpses of civilization," a land that, like Transylvania, lies on the perimeter of the modern railway network (*SP*, 9). At his hotel, Arthur is warned "against going out too much alone at night" in case he should happen upon "the moonlighters who now and again raided the district," supporters of the Irish National Land League known for attacking their opponents under cover of darkness. And there is always the "more obnoxious" risk that he might be mistaken by the police for "one of these very ruffians" (*SP*, 115). Of course, none of these miscreants ever makes an appearance and the only ruffian to be seen is the sinister Black Murdock.

It is Murdock, standing as a metonym for rural violence, who connects *The Snake's Pass* with a far less cozy branch of Irish fiction. If the novel's marriage plot derives from Edgeworth or Morgan, Stoker borrowed from William Carleton's *Valentine McClutchy* (1845) and *The Black Prophet* (1847) in his creation of Black Murdock, a figure who loudly echoes such villainous land agents or middlemen as Black Donnel or Val the Vulture. Black Donnel's Ireland may be a place of "singular beauty," but it is also a land beset by "wild and supernatural terrors," the residue of years of crime and oppression.[43] Appropriately, Donnel incarnates his country's dualism in his own ambiguous person, so that "at one moment you might consider him handsome, and at another his countenance filled you with an impression of repugnance, if not of absolute aversion."[44] As Terry Eagleton has noted, Donnel "embodies a transcendental evil quite unrelated to his social environs," and this is no less true of Stoker's

*Vampires, Mummies, and Liberals*

reincarnation of him as Black Murdock.[45] In Carleton's writing Gothic sensationalism and a grim, documentary realism are compellingly yet unevenly joined, and, for all his flaws, he was later revived and championed by Yeats as Ireland's "greatest novelist."[46]

In *The Snake's Pass*, Stoker detaches the Gothic component from Carleton's fiction and contains and domesticates it. Yet if we move forward seven years and compare *The Snake's Pass* with *Dracula*, it is possible to see Black Murdock's full-blown melodramatic villainy as anticipating the more radical evil of the Count—even down to the "livid scar" each bears on his face after a potential victim has attempted to fight back (*SP,* 61). And like Count Dracula, Murdock is known as a "human-shaped wolf" (*SP,* 87), as someone who "would take the blood out of yer body if he could sell it or use it anyhow!" (*SP,* 26). At a deeper level, one can also see the Transylvanian topography of *Dracula* as a kind of mirror image of the mountainous Irish terrain of *The Snake's Pass*, and indeed there are brief moments when these twin geographies seem to be indistinguishable. First surveyed under a gathering mass of storm clouds, Ireland offers Arthur "the most beautiful" view that he has ever seen (*SP,* 10), but one that is soon obscured by the darkened sky and gusts of driving rain, making the hills "strange with black sweeping shadows" (*SP,* 14).

Coming as they do at opposite ends of the same decade, a decade of severe setbacks for the Home Rule movement, *Dracula* and *The Snake's Pass* deserve to be read in tandem for the contrasting light they shed on Ireland, its country, and its people. In *Dracula* the opening scenes of natural beauty (so much a feature of *The Snake's Pass*) slide even more alarmingly into the awesomeness of the sublime, and this is of a piece with an instability in the inhabitants of Transylvania themselves, who oscillate between the "picturesque" and the "more barbarian," between rude outdoor health and an uncanny sickliness ("goitre was painfully prevalent"). "Some of them were just like the peasants at home," writes the English solicitor's clerk Jonathan Harker recounting his first trip abroad in a letter to his anxiously waiting fiancée; but we might pause at this sentence to wonder where exactly home was (*D,* 11–17).

## Ethnology and Invective

The close attention that Stoker gives to the physical description of people is especially interesting for the way in which it draws upon the ideas and vocabulary of ethnology, the Victorian "science" of race and the closely related pseudosciences with which it overlapped. For example, one of the discourses that conspicuously left its mark on almost all Stoker's output was that of physiognomy, the belief that there could be a scientific knowledge of a person's true nature based upon the features of their face and upon the outline of their body generally. In his youthful letter to Whitman quoted earlier Stoker happily notes their common interests, calling the American poet "a keen physiognomist," and also declaring himself to be a "believer of the science" and "in a humble way a practicer of it."[47] And as late as 1908 in a newspaper interview with the young Winston Churchill Stoker portrayed the up-and-coming Liberal politician in strict physiognomic terms, drifting off as he so often did into cognate pseudosciences like phrenology and palmistry, giving a detailed account of Churchill's palms, fingers, and thumbs to conclude (quite accurately as it turned out) that "the man with such a hand should go far."[48] Readers of *Dracula* will remember that the Count's hands were an object of great interest too—but that there is a worrying indeterminacy about them: "hitherto . . . they had seemed rather white and fine; but seeing them now close to me, I could not but notice they were rather coarse—broad with squat fingers" (*D*, 28). It is almost as if the signs of the times had gone awry and science is inadequate to the task of reading the character of such hands correctly, defeated by the readiness of appearances to dissolve into their gendered opposite or to dramatically change their class or even their racial connotations. Tellingly, Stoker clung to these "sciences" of faces, hands, and skulls even after they had begun to decline in intellectual respectability toward the end of the century, and their ideas consistently informed his view of the human sciences. As a result, the scientifically precise descriptions which are supposed to provide a measure of stability and certainty often turn out, like Dracula's hands, to be a site of anxiety and apprehension.

The difficulty of interpreting physical types, of sorting out their meanings and effects, lay at the heart of the conundrums of race and nation, and would have presented a displaced and divided figure like Stoker with a peculiarly sharp dilemma. For to be a "believer" in physiognomy who was also Irish, let alone a "believer" in Irish Home Rule—no matter how "philosophical"—was to find oneself torn by a contradictory set of allegiances. Refurbished and given a new Enlightenment imprimatur, systems like physiognomy and phrenology had once aspired to true scientific status as instruments of human progress that might be set

*Vampires, Mummies, and Liberals*

alongside Newtonian physics, but by Stoker's time they were becoming increasingly racialized through articulation with the themes and theories of ethnology and racial biology. In his highly influential 1885 text, *The Races of Britain*, John Beddoe used such variables as hair color and shape of skull to chart the distribution of physical types throughout the country, and attempted to identify the core races that had taken part in the complex processes of migration and assimilation. Drawing particular attention to the "colour-type" found among the inhabitants of the West of Ireland, Beddoe described them as "the swarthiest people I have ever seen" and, noting their flat foreheads, concave noses and prognathous jaws, he speculated on their possible African origins. Of low intelligence, but possessed of "great cunning," "the most exquisite examples" of this race "never would submit to measurement" by the disinterested scientist.[49]

If the recalcitrant Irish were distinguished by their peculiar cranial and facial characteristics, the discourse of physiognomy was one of the main currents feeding into the representation of the Irish as a race apart, lower down upon the evolutionary tree than other European races, the "human chimpanzees" of Kingsley's horrified gaze or the "white negroes" scorned by Carlyle. Not only did physiognomy lend scientific authority to such racist epithets, but, equally perniciously, its descriptive conventions were directly carried over into drawings and sketches of the Irish as a folk. In the abundant caricatures of Ireland in the English press during the troubled 1880s, the Irish were depicted as monstrously subhuman, as creatures of Neanderthal stupidity and cruelty, incapable of civilized life. Among the innumerable permutations generated by artists and cartoonists were Frankensteinian brutes and also vampires, and while the Irish gave as good as they got by quickly reappropriating these images in newspaper caricatures of the monstrous English, they were never able to mobilize the full weight of an intransigently simianizing discourse on so many and varied levels as their adversaries.[50] At best, Irish counterdiscourse merely reinforced a long tradition of political invective against colonial exploitation: the denunciation of landlords as "cormorant vampires" by Michael Davitt, or as "coroneted ghouls" by Fanny Parnell.[51]

Nevertheless, one can see Irish politicians strenuously attempting to counter English prejudices. There is in "the Irish race of to-day . . . no taint of intellectual degeneracy," William O'Brien told an audience in Cork in 1885—as well he might, for as late as 1896 the Irish writer William Lecky was still opposing Home Rule on the grounds that

Ireland's "poor, ignorant, and disaffected peasantry" and "the steady decadence of most of its county towns" ruled out any possibility of manhood suffrage.[52] In a later lecture on "Toleration in the Fight for Ireland" (1892) O'Brien tried to tackle head-on what he called "one of the grotesque assumptions of the opponents of Home Rule": "that the Irish population is composed of two races who have never melted together, and can never by any possibility melt together," namely the English settlers and the Celts. In truth, O'Brien contended, the settlers had repeatedly "defied English statutes to seek the hands of Irish wives" with the result that "in all ages [there] has been the breaking down of the barriers, the identification of the colonists with the natives."

On this view, "Celtic genius" is strong enough to attract, disarm, and absorb its English Other. As we will see, this was not in itself an unusual argument and there were distinguished English commentators who were prepared to argue along very similar lines, albeit with somewhat different conclusions. However, the terms of the racialized discourse in which O'Brien was caught, his tactic of replacing the lie of a rigidly necessary separatism by the truth of good breeding, forced him to invoke a more distant point on the racial hierarchy in order to make his case stick. The aim of "English policy," he says, has "invariably" been "to stand apart from the native population as disdainfully as an English regiment operating in the country of the Hottentots."[53] But as the behavior of the settlers has shown again and again, the Irish are objects of desire, not objects of disdain: they are precisely *not* Hottentots. Unlike the African colonies, Ireland represents no unbridgeable divide, no low Other beyond the pale of civilization, but rather a neighbor of equal status. Fraternizing with the "natives" can naturally only enrich and enliven the two populations as they commingle in what ought to be their parallel but independent national-political spheres. In short, race appears here in the form of an ethnology that has been thoroughly *sexualized*.

Written from his base in the English metropolis, Stoker's two novels of the 1890s cover the same discursive territory as O'Brien's speeches, but without the same confidence, the same élan. *The Snake's Pass* and *Dracula* commence from a shared epistemological standpoint, encapsulated in the figure of the Englishman abroad whose passage into an unknown interior is also a journey of self-discovery. But what is deeply problematic in both instances is any simple "identification . . . with the natives." Even in the least complex of the two narratives, the path to true love in *The Snake's Pass* has to be smoothed by some adroit racial and religious maneu-

*Vampires, Mummies, and Liberals*

vering in order to sanitize and rationalize the stirrings of desire. Not only is Stoker's Irish novel one of his very few books to deemphasize physiognomy's role as a guide to character, but—like O'Brien's 1892 speech—it also predicates sexual attraction on a form of racialized abjection. Norah Joyce, the untutored "peasant girl" with whom Arthur falls in love, is made to inhabit an uncertain zone of sexual exoticism in which the invitational play of race has to be held in check by the dangerous sexuality of miscegenation. In Arthur's male imaginary, "this ideal fantasy" (SP, 51) bears the "traces of Spanish blood and Spanish beauty" that can be found "along the west coast of Ireland," but a beauty brought to perfection by "being tempered with northern calm" (SP, 75). What Norah cannot be, however, as Arthur makes plain while discussing his sexual "ideal" with Andy, his Irish driver, is "all dark," a "nigger," the "Africanoid type" of Beddoe's anthropological speculations (whose dangers are at least symbolically marked by Murdock's "blackness").[54] It is Andy who colloquially draws the essential discrimination, universalizing his and Arthur's own whiteness as constitutive of the heterosexual norm: "a girrul can be dark enough fur any man widout bein' a naygur" (SP, 101).

Up to a point, this attempt to police the phantasmatic site of desire by imagining and instantly disavowing an unthinkable sexual scenario resembles what Judith Butler has called a psychic "logic of repudiation," in which the subject's illicit desires can be homeopathically indulged and exorcised at one and the same time.[55] But even this move is insufficient to secure Norah's nuptial respectability—as if the very thought of her racial impurity were enough to permanently contaminate her desirability. And so a kind of double repudiation must take place. In a land of priests, fairy tales, and the legends of saints, she must also be distinguished as Protestant, and this denomination is then articulated with social class to provide her with the necessary motivation and self-discipline to "try so earnestly to improve," to school herself out of her peasant background so as to rise "higher and nearer to [Arthur's] level" (SP, 157).

The Snake's Pass negotiates Ireland's history of successive invasions and the problem of its colonial status by condensing them into the quest for companionate marriage. In Dracula by contrast, the narrative of invasion is more directly engaged, and in consequence the risks to marital success are at once more lurid and more threatening. The English clerk Jonathan Harker's journey into Transylvania takes him into the heart of a darkness in which miscegenation is deeply inscribed in the country's history as a battleground between the warring tribes of old, and between East and

West. Dracula's land gathers together "every known superstition in the world," making it "the centre of some sort of imaginative whirlpool" (*D*, 10), a place of "many nationalities" (*D*, 14), "the whirlpool of European races," where the Count is the leader of "a conquering race" in whose "veins flows the blood of many brave races" (*D*, 41). When Dracula proudly narrates the bellicose history of his people, the imagery he employs is as much about the mixing as the spilling of blood, interspersed with peasant legends which imagine the savagery of invaders as descended from "the blood of those old witches" who would mate "with the devils in the desert" (*D*, 41). Jonathan Harker discovers a country that is still the victim of its own history, in which the inhabitants are terrified of and terrorized by the barbarian elements in their midst, a condition he soon comes to share. Wandering into the remotest reaches of the Castle Dracula, he sentimentally fantasizes a medieval idyll in which gentle maidens pine for their absent menfolk, only to find himself descending rapidly into nightmare. His chaste bachelorhood promises to be fatally compromised on the very threshold of his marriage as three seductive "ladies" of the night suddenly appear, provoking in him a "wicked, burning desire" that threatens to destroy all hope of respectable domesticity (*D*, 51). Though Jonathan narrowly escapes their clutches, he sees firsthand what these vampire-women are capable of, for he is forced to stand by helplessly as they cannibalize a living child.

Once Jonathan realizes that he has become Dracula's prisoner, the conditions of his captivity are revealed as a microcosm of Transylvanian social and ethnic relations. Helping the Count prepare for his journey to England and effectively guarding the castle are a band of gypsies or "Szgany," "peculiar to this part of the world." They proliferate throughout the region in their "thousands," "fearless and without religion, save superstition," and speaking "only their own varieties of the Romany tongue." Capriciously allying themselves with any powerful nobleman and taking on his name, they are (records the horrified solicitor's clerk) "almost outside all law" (*D*, 55–56). In the crudely racialized ethnology of Stoker's day this migratory way of life was seen as a cause of cultural backwardness and "destined to perish[;] the sooner it goes the happier for mankind." Francis Galton, the statistician and later eugenicist who traveled round Ireland in the 1890s measuring and cataloging the indigenous population, regarded what he called "the nomadic disposition" as quite "alien to the genius of an enlightened civilization," so that "the primary qualities of the typical modern British workman are already the

*Vampires, Mummies, and Liberals*

very opposite of those of the nomad." Alien it may have been, but not so alien that this notion of progress could not contain the seeds of its own potential reversal. The optimism of Galton and others was dogged by a sense of the fragility of such advances, particularly in the light of the hardships of industrial life which were felt to be "crushing [the urban working class] into degeneracy." There was, warned Galton, a very real danger that those "best fitted to play their part on the stage of life" would increasingly be "crowded out by the incompetent, the ailing, and the desponding."[56]

The specter of bad blood and degeneration evoked by *Dracula*'s imaginary terrain and its sinister inhabitants always refers back to an anxiety about the lineaments of national identity, about the health and vigor of a race. Like the vampire in late-nineteenth-century political cartoons, Stoker's narrative shuttles to and fro between settings, never settling into a definitive formulaic set of meanings, but rather exploiting the political resonances of contemporary ethnology to create a generalized sense of social and psychic terror, a sense that includes but is by no means exhausted by "the terror and the trouble of the night" conjured up in *The Snake's Pass* (*SP*, 232). Though shot through with Irish references, *Dracula*'s horror ultimately eludes the deftness of allegory, spilling out in too many directions to be contained by any single racial logic. Indeed, as we'll see in the next chapter, the novel reveals the multiplicity of forms that the ideology of degeneration could take.[57]

Put another way, one can see much of the fear that resides in the pages of *Dracula* as reflecting the underside of the liberalism to which Stoker adhered, a nightmare vision of unruly subjects who are unamenable to its formal democratic calculus. For insofar as liberalism's theory of citizenship is based upon a political rationality that conceives of rights and duties in both highly abstract and highly individualized terms, it seeks to deflect and devalue those collective demands and aspirations that arise out of the solidarities of particular communities. So, for example, the liberal jurist A. V. Dicey argued that the new male voters admitted through British electoral reform would be likely to see themselves primarily as "citizens" or "persons" rather than as proletarians loyal to their social class. To think of political representation in this bloodless way ("irrespective of sex or class" or "regardless of race, colour or creed"—to quote two of the standard formulations) is to be forever haunted by the return of those flesh-and-blood identities that liberalism seeks to neutralize or exclude theoretically.[58]

Thus, according to liberalism's preferred model, citizenship should be based upon rational choice, the achievement of consensus through "the aggregate consent of individual subjects," rather than deriving from one's birthplace or bloodline as in older notions of citizenship.[59] Consequently, a constant preoccupation of liberal thought has been the need for scientific study of the causes of what were seen as society's most deeply irrational currents, epitomized by the ebb and flow of city crowds, those mass phenomena most at odds with liberalism's atomistic logic. By the turn of the century, the fear of degeneration so prominent in the work of Francis Galton had been thoroughly absorbed by modern liberals, and intellectuals like J. A. Hobson could argue that "as the result of urban living," "the popular mind had reverted . . . into a type of primitive savagery dangerous for modern civilization."[60] As always, it is the language of race which names civilization's deepest fears and discontents. Drawing upon Freud and Lacan, David Kazanjian has argued that "the formally equal subject—the abstract subject of classical liberal discourse"—actually requires the existence of "primitivized others" as a kind of phantasmatic proof of its own civility, or as a "means of mastering [the] precariousness" of its own egalitarian claims. Historically, "the aggressive fears" that are projected onto the figure of the "primitive" are closely linked to our "dependence upon the discourses and practices of colonialism."[61] Equally, however, such categories also serve as "an inner condition of modernity," a "fantasy-support" inscribing "an inherent impetus" or will-to-power within the liberal narrative of progress itself.[62]

But by the fin-de-siècle the need to overcome the threat posed by the Other's barbarism had come to embody a second fear: not merely a horror of the uncivilized forces lurking within Britain's borders as well as without (and the Irish could easily be regarded as either), but also a fear that many of its citizens now lacked the moral and physical resources to deal with this threat. Thus, Winston Churchill in his interview with Stoker summarized the current political situation by giving a potted history of liberalism, "the movement for human progress." Churchill—then Liberal Under Secretary for the Colonies—noted that while "the French Revolution" had initiated and "achieved a very considerable measure of political equality—the idea of a national nation—citizens not separated by class prejudice," much still remained to be done. Britain, like many other modern democracies, continued to face considerable social problems rooted in "social and economic injustice," "anomalies" that urgently needed to be removed.[63] In addition to advocating a "more thorough social organization, without which our country and its people will inevitably sink through sorrow to disaster," Churchill was even prepared to countenance more extreme measures.[64] In 1912, when the first International Congress of Eugenics was held in London, Churchill acted as its vice president.[65]

## Criminal Types and Male Hysterics

In keeping with liberalism's gathering mood of insecurity, both *Dracula* and *The Snake's Pass* problematize and even make a mockery of the rule of law, one of the mainstays of the liberal ethos, throwing its agents into crisis. *The Snake's Pass* strongly implies that Ireland's troubles represent a failure of bourgeois legality, since the accusation against the usurer Black Murdock is that (like the English) he has "made the law an engine of oppression" (*SP,* 37). A man who filches other people's lands for his own selfish gain, Murdock is popularly regarded as a common criminal ("that black-jawed ruffian, Murdock") and it is therefore only poetic justice when he is finally swallowed up in an Irish bog, destroyed by his own greed and by the land he tries to steal. Similarly, in the legend of the buried treasure with which the novel begins, when the King of the Snakes is described as looking "mighty evil" he is said to be "as slow an' as hard as an attorney," a sign of the law's disrepute ("I'm the whole govermint here") at the hands of a willful monarch (*SP,* 21).

*Dracula* is also much concerned with legal matters. The novel is after all a quasi-legal narrative of the type popularized by Wilkie Collins in which the various characters, including several scientific experts and "a full-blown" lawyer, offer testimony to the material facts they are supposed to have witnessed. Nevertheless, here too justice is far from certain and the story's heroes are periodically obliged to flout the law in the interests of a higher moral code. At the beginning of the novel the unsuspecting Jonathan Harker is even misled into believing that Count Dracula really "would have made a wonderful solicitor" (*D,* 44). In a sense, this is exactly what happens: Dracula dresses up in Jonathan's suit and carries out his grisly nighttime pursuits while masquerading as a representative of English law.

From his very first appearance, Dracula's "marked physiognomy" is a clue that he will ultimately be assimilated to the condition of a most uncommon criminal, a specimen belonging in the annals of the Italian criminal anthropologist Cesare Lombroso. Once *Dracula*'s protagonists have agreed that "the Count is a criminal and of criminal type"—in other words, that he is merely a creature "of imperfectly formed mind" and can be outwitted (*D*, 406)—the way is cleared for the vampire's defeat.[66] Stoker's explicit references to the emergent criminology of the 1890s is another pointer toward the national-racial context of his writing and to the terrors that lay at its threshold.

Read against its original Italian background, criminal anthropology was intended to be a disciplinary tool of national consolidation, in which the study of crime provided for the diagnosis and the cure of a nation's moral sickness. If the dilemma for postunification nationalists was expressed in the dictum "we have made Italy, now we have to make Italians," then what Lombroso's new science hoped to achieve was to sharply demarcate the eligible body of authentic citizens from its pathological Others—hereditary criminals, cases of atavism and degeneracy, and the criminally insane.[67] By mapping the distribution of criminal acts and criminal bodies onto the new national and regional space, "criminal anthropology constituted at once a political geography, a conjectural history of civilisation, an evolutionary account of organisms and races."[68] *Dracula* speaks to the most troubled point in the whole criminological project: the difficulty of recognizing the criminal by sight. Famous for his elaborate taxonomic use of photography, Lombroso was forced to drastically modify his emphasis upon the so-called "born criminal" whose "natural" pathology was supposed to be clearly legible from the miscreant's face and body type. What is disturbing about the vampire is that he can be so hard to read, altering his "marked physiognomy" and passing as an English gentleman. The terror inspired by Count Dracula is a terror of biological difference both masked and free-floating. When Jonathan Harker sees the Count in Piccadilly in broad daylight, in the heart of the Empire, mingling among London's "teeming millions," what is horrifying is that no one else knows that there is a vampire in their midst (*D*, 215).

The vicissitudes of the law and its ethnological and criminological supports suggest a flawed modernity, a modernity still struggling with the powers of the past, even when equipped with phonographs, telegrams, cameras, newspapers, and typewriters, a world of mechanical and electronic reproduction. When the protagonists of *Dracula* come together to swear a "solemn compact," they are effectively renewing the social contract, pledging allegiance not simply to each other as comrades

*Vampires, Mummies, and Liberals*

in arms but as members of a liberal bourgeois order. Despite the invocation of archaic symbols, the laying of hands on the "golden crucifix," their ceremony is a virtual rehearsal of liberal protocols. The pursuit of the vampire is "serious work," to be undertaken "in as businesslike a way, as any other transaction of life," informed by all the characteristically modern freedoms, itemized as freedom of association, freedom "to act and think," and free access to the "resources of science." "In fact," their leader Dr. Van Helsing reminds them, "so far as our powers extend, they are unfettered, and we are free to use them" (D, 284–85).[69] At the turning point of the novel, therefore, the modern subject is being reconstituted as a prelude to the final heroic climax in which Count Dracula is driven back to his Transylvanian lair and destroyed.

But as we have seen, in Stoker's writing this same subject is hedged about with qualifications, limited by racial, sexual, or religious status. Femininity, for example, is normatively defined by its lack of "the man's desire for action" (SP, 125), so justifying Stoker's repeated polemic against those who defy such norms: the suffragette and the New Woman. On this model, male strength is confirmed by its mastery of feeling, for as Arthur Severn observes when he insistently presses Norah to commit herself to him in The Snake's Pass, "there are times when manhood must assert itself, even though the heart be torn with pity for woman's weakness" (SP, 131). Arthur's naturalization of his own desperate aggressiveness seems conventional enough, fixing the usual binaries—active/passive, strength/weakness, reason/emotion, masculine/feminine—firmly in place. Yet it is important to see that this asymmetrically gendered pairing in turn depends for its appeal upon a pathologized low Other to whom it comes perilously close while always overtly insisting upon its exclusion: thus Norah's "Spanish blood" is "tempered with northern calm" in order to block the delirious slide toward the Mediterranean and the African (SP, 75).

Blurred at their edges, these oppositions start to take on new meaning once Ireland has been fully situated within the already racialized zone of "northern calm." The ordinary Irish "nature" is "essentially emotional" and the sight of oppression will release "a torrent of commiseration, sympathy and pity," even to the point of tears (SP, 37). The spontaneous show of emotion is partly explained here in terms of the rustic simplicity of rural life and is of course being explicitly marked as such by a modern metropolitan gaze, a gaze habituated to the exercise of scientific reason. Hopelessly in love, Arthur's rationalizing reflexes even lead him to speculate that "the wave theory that rules our knowledge of the distribution of light and sound, may well be taken to typify . . . the beating in unison of human hearts" (*SP*, 122). Certainly, as in *Dracula*, *The Snake's Pass* intrudes a logical, procedural eye into a hinterland that is awash with superstition, setting a Protestant discipline against a Catholic worldview with its crucifixes, legends, and stories of saints. But in this imaginary Ireland—whose terrors are only fully unleashed in *Dracula*—there is an almost Rousseauistic reverence for the uncorrupted emotionalism of peasant life, idealized as a natural sign of simple goodness.

Although Stoker's treatment of the Irish national character never strays far from the received categories of his period, his beliefs are compromised by his own cultural affiliations. In *The Study of Celtic Literature* (1867), for example, Matthew Arnold had argued that "the Celtic races" were best defined by their quality of "sentiment": they were "quick to feel impressions, and feeling them very strongly," were "keenly sensitive to joy and sorrow." Celtic "sensuousness" had "made Ireland," yet because "the Celt" lacked "the skilful and resolute appliance of means to ends which is needed both to make progress in material civilisation, and also to form powerful states" its culture and politics were "poor, slovenly, and half barbarous."[70] On these grounds Arnold claimed that the union of Great Britain and Ireland raised the possibility of a racial synthesis of Celtic emotion with Anglo-Saxon pragmatism, taking literature as a model of the higher reconciliation of opposites that might be achieved. Writing over two decades later in the thick of the crisis of Home Rule, the kind of apologetics for the Act of Union represented by Arnold's new imperial subject presented Stoker with a dilemma. On the one hand, as an Irishman born into the Protestant middle class and a former civil servant for the Crown, Stoker was predisposed to make sense of the world through similar categories and oppositions. On the other hand, however, as a supporter of Irish Home Rule, Stoker was compelled to place a different valuation on Celtic sentimentality, complicating the identification of masculinity with strength of character defined against the flood of emotion.

The idea of the Irish as "essentially emotional," when taken together with references to tears as "unmanly signs of emotion," seems to suggest that the unguarded outflow of affect is a source of racial and cultural weakness (*SP*, 90). At least many Victorians in the 1880s and 1890s would have regarded it as such, for by that period ideals of manliness had largely been purged of any open expression of feeling in favor of a self-confident physical robustness that regarded any undue sensitivity with suspicion.

"What was taught and learned," argues Raymond Williams, "was a new and rigid control, 'self-control'—even weak men not crying and being very stiff and proud of it where much stronger men before them had wept when the feeling, the impulse was there."[71] In Stoker's work, however, the point is that the men *do* cry, even if sometimes only "surreptitiously" (*SP*, 90). In vindication of the feminized Irish, the historically dominant version of Victorian masculinity is undermined by reintroducing a complex emotional economy into the male body and psyche. That this is a dangerous and controversial move is shown by the defense of male hysteria in *Dracula*, where an uncontrolled excess of emotion is simultaneously treated as both frightening and reassuring. There are several occasions when male characters succumb to bouts of hysteria while under extreme pressure. The terror that Jonathan Harker experiences as a result of his imprisonment in the Castle Dracula, for example, constantly threatens his sanity, "destroying my nerve" (*D*, 46). But the most elaborate account appears when Dr. Van Helsing breaks down into "a regular fit of hysterics" following the death of a young female patient at Count Dracula's hands. Shocking one of his medical colleagues by "laugh[ing] and cry[ing] together, just as a woman does," Van Helsing explains away his disquieting behavior as a spontaneous release from trauma and distress, a way of "eas[ing] off the strain," which is all the more natural because it comes unbidden. Nevertheless, this emotional self-surrender remains sufficiently sensitive for Van Helsing later to deny "that it was hysterics" (*D*, 209–12).

I have tried to show that Stoker's use of such "sciences" as physiognomy and criminal anthropology—what one might call his ethnological imagination—is closely tied to the question of Irish nationalism in his fiction of the 1890s. The notions of masculinity and femininity, of degeneracy and good breeding implicit in these books all pass through the racialized discourse of moral and physiological difference so critical to late-Victorian conceptions of the social body. Some years earlier, Stoker's hero and fellow physiognomist Walt Whitman had called for the renewal of America, based upon what he had termed a "democratic ethnology of the future," a "science" with protoeugenic overtones.[72] Like Whitman, Stoker invokes an ethnology that also reaches out to sexuality for its assumptions about national character and cultural identity: a sexual ethnology, in fact. Stoker's attempted merger between the expressive man of sensibility and the strong, steadfast man of action has to be understood as ultimately driven by anxieties about the Irish male as subject, just as the fantasy of Irish womanhood requires the careful management of national-racial hierarchies if its desired exoticism is not to be rendered impure and shameful. There is throughout Stoker's texts a fixation with unfixing the boundaries, with the attractions of liminality, in order that the lines of demarcation might be all the more strictly controlled.

In the final analysis Stoker stretches the categories of gender and race to their conventional limits. And this means that he always runs the risk of unseating the familiar logic of difference, sending it spinning down new and frightening paths. For Stoker, I would argue, there is a constant sense that the divide between the stable and the unstable is itself unstable, that the line cannot be held. Subjects and nations seem to oscillate between modernity and atavism, and no science of race or place quite promises to guarantee the former without the latter.

Perhaps it is only fitting, then, that Stoker should be allowed the last emblematic word on this point. In *The Snake's Pass* "a shifting bog . . . high up the hill" is believed to be the site of the iron treasure chest, and at various moments it comes to stand for the Irish homeland and its wom-anhood, the story of its past carrying sediments of the country's history of underdevelopment (*SP,* 42–43). Throughout the novel the bog is a symbolic source of horror and laughter, knowledge and uncertainty, and Dick Sutherland, the engineer who surveys its movements, offers a prog-nosis that is at once bleak and suggestive: "Then with this new extent of bog suddenly saturated and weakened—demoralized as it were—and devoid of resisting power, the whole floating mass of the upper bog might descend on it, mingle with it, become incorporated with its semi-fluid substance, and form a new and dangerous quagmire incapable of sustaining solid weight" (*SP,* 68–69). In this geological forecast "satu-rated" slips too quickly and too tellingly into "demoralized"—a term that is later repeated and redefined as "this silent change" (*SP,* 229)— bringing the sexual or the social body irresistibly to mind as if the decomposition of the land can only be properly grasped by somehow being mapped onto cultural fears. The muddled metonymic relation between the physical and the cultural conjures up a common geography of bodies and land masses, an equivalence still central to so much of nationalist discourse today. But once these raw materials of nations are "weakened," once they become "devoid" of a truly masculine "resisting power," they lose their cultural solidity and identity, becoming "soft and less cohesive." Nevertheless, Arthur's awed response at the prospect of

*Vampires, Mummies, and Liberals*

witnessing such "upheaval and complete displacement and chaos" in the Irish landscape reveals the implicitly sexual fascination as well as the terror evoked for Stoker by the spectacle of degeneration and decline: "Really, Dick, you put it most graphically. What a terrible thing it would be to live on the line of such a change" (*SP,* 67–69).

## Beyond the Blue Horizon

The concluding chapters of *The Snake's Pass* enact a twofold transformation of Ireland's "wild natural beauty" (*SP,* 11). To provide the novel's romantic closure, Norah Joyce is sent off to a Parisian finishing school and two years later she is ready to return home as a lady, after first marrying Arthur in an English church. As a comic tribute to this cultural domestication, Arthur's Irish driver makes a surprise appearance at the wedding specially spruced up for the occasion, "so well dressed and smart that there was really nothing to distinguish him from any other man in Hythe"—until, of course, he opens his mouth (*SP,* 248). Leading the party in a toast, his eyes brimming with tears, Andy blesses the happy couple, "an' yer childher, and yer childher's childher to folly ye" (*SP,* 250). Both Arthur and Norah have undergone a rigorous process of self-development as a result of their experiences: Arthur is no longer the ill-at-ease youth he once was, but the heroic leader of his adopted community, and Norah is now a woman of distinction. "We felt that we were one," concludes Arthur, and the novel's closing words signal the founding of a dynasty (*SP,* 250).[73]

In effect, the novel's finale ties the two countries together in a new kind of Act of Union, rewritten on Gladstonian lines, ratified on English soil to popular acclaim, and looking forward to a line of Anglo-Irish heirs in perpetuity. As in Lady Morgan's *The Wild Irish Girl,* "the distinctions of English and Irish, of Protestant and Catholic [are] for ever buried," but in such a way as to be subsumed under a newfangled Anglo-Irish hegemony—a formula that had long "worked its charm on the liberal Irish Protestant Whigs."[74] The financial condition of Norah's wholly refurbished status, the money for her dresses and her education, resides in Arthur's inherited wealth and his social position. His own good fortune underwrites every aspect of her upward mobility.

At the same time, a combination of luck and business acumen enables Arthur to transform the district around Knockcalltecrore—a corruption of the Gaelic name for "The Hill of the Lost Golden Crown"—into a prosperous community. He sets about buying up all the local landholdings, allowing those who wished to emigrate to do so, and replacing the old cottage economy with modern new farms. Together with his old school friend, the engineer Dick Sutherland, Arthur plans to irrigate the area and use the water to produce a supply of electricity. In the end, however, even the costs of these improvements are defrayed by the discovery of considerable natural resources—first, deposits of pottery clay and, later, when the bog has collapsed and rolled into the sea to expose the land's original topography, a rich vein of limestone. The bog's demise has other beneficial effects too: a search of the area brings to light not only a chest of gold coins brought by the French in 1798 but also the legendary lost crown of gold dating from ancient times.[75] Since the land on which the gold coins are found still belongs to Norah's father, Phelim Joyce, he is the rightful owner of the treasure and Arthur and Dick advise him to keep it for himself, rather than hand it over to the government where it will vanish forever. Nevertheless, Phelim's populist response is to donate this windfall to the community, on the grounds that the "money was sent for Ireland's good—to help them that wanted help, an' plase God! I'll see it doesn't go asthray now!" (SP, 240).

In this utopian fantasy Arthur re-creates his English county seat in the heart of Galway, truly turning Knockcalltecrore into "a fairyland." With his friend's help, he builds an English country house "of red sandstone" for his bride, "with red tiled roof and quaint gables, and jutting windows and balustrades of carven stone" and ornamental gardens, where one can hear "the murmur of water . . . everywhere" (SP, 246). This magical transfer of power, coupled with the district's economic revival, brings a tranche of the most resistant and unreclaimable region in Ireland under the sway of a benevolent British squirearchy, providing it with the independent means and social stability that would enable it to thrive. Stoker's imagined "solution" to the Irish question in this novel is a strange composite, at first glance curiously at odds with the author's avowedly nationalist sentiments, and the terms of its eclecticism deserve to be fully spelled out here. In context, the novel's most significant feature is its break with the increasingly close identification between Catholicism and nationalism following the intense conflict between landlords and tenants during the Irish "Land War" of 1879–82 and the subsequent Home Rule crisis. As depicted in *The Snake's Pass*, the Galway-Mayo borderlands

*Vampires, Mummies, and Liberals*

emerge as a place where Catholics and Protestants can live harmoniously cheek by jowl, under the jurisdiction of "an astute Ulster-born policeman" (*SP*, 116). What ultimately secures this unlikely reconciliation is a model of "national prosperity" that is intimately connected to the land and especially the local bog. For when Dick Sutherland tells Arthur that the future of the bog "touches deeply the happiness and material prosperity of a large section of Irish people, and so helps to mold their political action" (*SP*, 55), he is in fact alluding to an influential tradition of economic analysis best exemplified by Sir Robert Kane's *The Industrial Resources of Ireland* (1844) "in which the utilisation of the peat-bogs, the harnessing of the rivers and the tides and the exploitation of mineral resources was advocated" as the basis for national autarky.[76]

Stoker's political vision is close to the Gladstonian model of Home Rule, a clear preference for devolution rather than complete separatism, expressed at a moment when the Irish branch of Liberalism was a dead letter. This was Stoker's sole Irish novel and after the failure of Gladstone's second Home Rule Bill in 1893 he seldom set his stories in Ireland—"The Man from Shorrox'," published in the *Pall Mall Magazine* in 1894, being a rare exception, a tall tale told entirely in dialect about an English commercial traveler who is tricked by an Irish innkeeper into sharing his bed with a corpse.[77] But beneath the ghoulish humor (at English expense), the signs of political and cultural backwardness are not hard to find: the innkeeper is in fact a beautiful widow whose husband has been murdered by moonlighters who mistook him for another man. Once Gladstone had retired from politics in 1894, the Liberals under Lord Rosebery began to distance themselves from Irish politics, and the Irish parliamentary party, increasingly divided internally, was unable to exert much influence until the balance of power swung in its favor in 1910. Stoker's occasionally mocking references to Irish nationalist movements suggest a certain contempt for what from his standpoint must have looked like markedly illiberal forms of political extremism. In his 1908 romance *Lady Athlyne* the hero's Irish nurse and former foster mother, bemused at her ward's irregular marriage, remarks that "Ireland's changin' fast, for that usen't to be the way. I'm thinkin' that the Shinn-Fayn'll have to wake up a bit if that's the way things is going to go" (*LA*, 326). Nevertheless, the dream of a new kind of polity seems never to have really disappeared, and when in one of his later novels, *The Lady of the Shroud* (1909), Stoker tried to capitalize on the success he had enjoyed with

*Dracula*, what he created was a Balkan imaginary which repeated many of the features of the Irish solution advanced in *The Snake's Pass*. It is here that we find Stoker's liberal utopia in its fullest, most developed form.

Like its Irish forerunner, *The Lady of the Shroud* has been given little attention by critics, and those who have discussed the novel have concentrated almost exclusively on Stoker's recapitulation of his Transylvanian mythology, despite the fact that the question of the heroine's putative vampirism is laid to rest at least halfway through the book.[78] Once it has dispensed with its creaky occult pretext, the novel operates as a simple adventure yarn, though one with distinctly futuristic trappings, such as the strangely noiseless airplanes that can silently rescue prisoners from a tower at dead of night or the mysterious submarine built like "a huge grey crab" which can immobilize a ship by shaking it from side to side (*LS*, 253). However, what motivates these and all of the other stirring and bizarre events in *The Lady of the Shroud*, including the fiction that the heroine is one of the Undead, is the preservation of a small Balkan nation's independence, a country picturesquely named the Land of the Blue Mountains. And so, the climax of the novel is a coronation, culminating in a "titanic picnic," which sets this proud peasant people firmly on the road to modernity, aligning it with the British Empire while maintaining its fiercely cherished status as a free nation (*LS*, 320).

Once again, inherited wealth is a prime mover in the book's final settlement, but, as in *The Snake's Pass*, capital must be seen to be mobilized by scientific and entrepreneurial initiative so as to turn this marginal nation into a commercial and industrial success story. The hero, Rupert Sent Leger, a typically stalwart young orphan from an Anglo-Irish military family who has spent his early years on dangerous expeditions to far-flung corners of the world, finds that he is the major beneficiary of an enormous fortune left to him by his Uncle Roger, a relative whom he scarcely knows. A curious clause in the will promises Rupert even greater riches if he will take up residence in a castle that his uncle owns in the Land of the Blue Mountains for a period of one year. While living in the Castle of Vissarion he meets and falls hopelessly in love with a beautiful young woman dressed in a damp shroud, who appears at his bedroom window late at night, only to hurry away as soon as she hears the cock crow. Though he unhappily suspects her of being a vampire, she is in fact the Voivodin Teuta, daughter and heir of one of the Blue Mountaineers' hereditary princes, and her enigmatic appearance and behavior turn out to be part of an elaborate ruse to prevent her from being abducted by the

*Vampires, Mummies, and Liberals*

country's hostile Turkish neighbors. The couple are married in a secret subterranean ceremony, a hierophantic ritual whose arcane vows and procedures install Rupert at the heart of the nation's intrigues, enlisting him in the struggle against Turkish imperial dominance. By the novel's close, Teuta's shroud, which is also her wedding dress, has become a national symbol, an "emblem of courage and devotion and patriotism" (*LS*, 341).

While *The Lady of the Shroud* resembles *The Snake's Pass* in employing the marriage sacrament as a device for advantageously coupling a rich and forward-looking young man to a beautiful land of priests and mountains, what gives the later novel its distinctiveness is its dialogic relationship to the socioliterary context of the Edwardian period. If *The Snake's Pass* can partly be read as a late addition to the national tales of the early 1800s, a type of text which "habitually presents a regionalist chronotope so strong it can pull cosmopolitan nineteenth-century travellers back into it," then *The Lady of the Shroud* aligns the former's generic elements—"the journey, the marriage, the national character"—with some of the newer strands in utopian writing.[79] For the end of the nineteenth century saw a revival of literary utopias, a trend both inspired by and in reaction against precisely the sorts of spectacular (and sometimes humdrum) technological achievements, like photography or the airplane, that Stoker loved to feature in his novels. At opposite poles, stories of "advanced mechanical civilizations jostled those of simple, back-to-nature utopias," and on this spectrum *The Lady of the Shroud* is positioned neatly in the middle.[80] H. G. Wells, in his influential tale *A Modern Utopia* (1905), criticizes the essentially premodern literary conceit of positing an imaginary secluded space like "a mountain valley or an island" whose perfection depends upon its being sealed off from "the epidemic, the breeding barbarian or the economic power," and asks "what of that near tomorrow when the flying machine soars overhead, free to descend at this point or that?"[81] Stoker's Balkan novel provides one answer to Wells's urgent question.

In a letter Rupert is given by his Uncle Roger's solicitor after he has unquestioningly accepted the provisions of the will, the Land of the Blue Mountains is introduced as "a small, poor nation" which has maintained its national independence for over a thousand years, even overthrowing its own king when he became too "despotic." Impressed by the "unquenchable fire of freedom" exhibited by "the fierce, hardy mountaineers" and keenly aware of the dangers surrounding them, Roger Melton, a businessman who has amassed millions from his commercial ventures in the East, makes a clandestine agreement with Teuta's father to provide the country with the armaments it is unable to afford, and he designates Rupert as his heir to ensure that this work will continue (*LS*, 45–47). As a man whose "reckless bravery is a byword amongst many savage peoples and amongst many others not savages" but who fear "the world of mysteries in and beyond the grave," Rupert possesses impeccable qualifications for such a task. But it is not merely his courage and adventurousness or "giant stature and strength" that are important, or the fact that he has become "inured to every kind of hardship." Rather, it is his capacity to turn his experiences into knowledge that fits him for the role of imperial hero, a rugged investigator of the occult with an "understanding of human nature from its elemental form up" (*LS*, 53).

Rupert's judgment of the Blue Mountaineers (whose name he likens to "a new sort of Bond Street band") is admiring but harsh: "In reality" they are "the most primitive people I ever met—the most fixed to their own ideas, which belong to centuries back" (*LS*, 80–83). His task, then, is to bring this backward nation into the twentieth century while safeguarding their hard-won freedom. From the outset this quest for modernity is invariably conceived in military terms, and is primarily determined by the exigencies of the Blue Mountaineers' geopolitical situation. Despite Wells's criticisms of his contemporaries, one of the most distinctive features of late Victorian and Edwardian utopias (including Wells's own work) was their intersection with narrative fantasies of invasion or mass destruction, beginning in 1871 when Edward Bulwer-Lytton's *The Coming Race* was published on the same day that *Blackwood's Magazine* brought out Sir George Chesney's story *The Battle of Dorking*.[82] So, in *The Lady of the Shroud* the scale of the danger in the Balkans steadily escalates from a fear of local conflict, particularly an attack by Turkey, to a more generalized anxiety about the expansive designs of major powers like Germany and Russia, making it a possibility that "even Turkey" would eventually seek to join the newly founded Balkan Federation which Rupert organizes to defend the region (*LS*, 330).

National security and national prosperity go hand in hand under Rupert's expert guidance, and at his insistence these joint concerns come to be administered under a single government department, "The National Committee of Defence and Development" (*LS*, 297). But in its program of modernization the Land of the Blue Mountains resembles nothing so much as a kind of militarized Knockcalltecrore. Once again, a combination of external capital and natural resources—"our whole mountain ranges simply teem with vast quantities of minerals, almost more precious for industry than gold and silver are for commerce"— transform a small underdeveloped territory into a highly profitable and self-sufficient community, "a mart for the world" (*LS*, 295). Here, however, the explicit aim is "to build up . . . a new 'nation'—an ally of Britain," yet strong and well-equipped enough to stand alone if necessary, its fortified seaboard patrolled by the most advanced warships and its skies defended by "a large and respectable aerial fleet" constructed in Blue Mountain factories (*LS*, 328). More aggressively, by initiating "Balka"— the Balkan Federation—Rupert hopes to create "a new world-power" based on "a lasting settlement of interests," but allowing each unit to remain "absolutely self-governing and independent" (*LS*, 330). By the final chapter of the novel Rupert's ambitions are already a reality, for the signing of the treaty is attended and supported by an impressive array of foreign dignitaries, including the (unnamed but instantly recognizable) "King and Queen of the greatest nation of the earth." Rupert and Teuta have indeed "won empire for themselves" and, in one of the book's most eloquent gestures, Rupert relinquishes his British nationality in order to become the ruler of his adopted country (*LS*, 350).

*The Lady of the Shroud* represents a liberal utopia, but one whose dreams are dreams of empire and whose liberalism is of a very historically specific kind. The operative political catchword throughout the novel is "freedom" and, insofar as democracy exists in the Land of the Blue Mountains, it definitely takes second place to liberty. For reasons that are never fully articulated, the ruling princes decide to replace their own "imperfect political system" with a British-influenced constitutional monarchy, the royal office passing to Rupert after it has been declined by Teuta's father, who wishes to see a younger, more active man become king (*LS*, 200). As his country's new figurehead, Rupert is accordingly legitimized by nationwide festivities that grandly resemble both the St. Louis Exposition and King Edward's coronation, a nice blend of the commercial and the imperial, the military and the religious, and whose music and dancing by torchlight provide a vivid enactment of the erotics of national fantasy. Yet despite this vast expression of national populism, which often seems no more than an extension of the popular militia to which every subject belongs, including the women (under male command), the rights of citizenship are mediated through elected council members who canvass their constituencies on important issues, and competing political parties or factions are completely absent. Moreover, the franchise is explicitly denied to women in accordance with the time-honored "law of masculine supremacy," a principle which Teuta insists on retaining as "an example . . . in an age when self-seeking women of other nations seek to forget their womanhood in the struggle to vie in equality with men!" (*LS,* 309). Rupert's key constitutional innovation precisely encapsulates the liberal populist hybrid of entrepreneurial pa-ternalism, strong state, and carefully demarcated individual entitlements that defines Stoker's preferred futuristic vision. His "Proclamation of Freedom" permits "all citizens to send a deputation to the King, at will and in private, on any subject of State importance" (*LS,* 341).

What finally guarantees the stability of this new system is neither its legal framework nor its popular legitimacy, but rather its racial identity. In a region where conflicts "must be largely one of races" (*LS,* 47), the Blue Mountaineers have successfully fought against assimilation, resist-ing the "shameful slavery" epitomized in gendered terms by the harems of their Turkish aggressors, and they have kept a primitive vitality that has been lost in more sophisticated nations (*LS,* 208). One of the central contrasts in the novel is that between the indolent, landowning English claimants to the Melton fortune and the vigorous enterprise of Rupert and his Uncle Roger, an intrafamilial clash that is then reiterated as a more general opposition between the "rough, primitive, barbarian, ele-mental" Mountaineers and the flippant "high-toned refinements" of such overcivilized Europeans as Rupert's Woosterish English cousin Er-nest (*LS,* 285). But this valorization of the barbarian is significantly qualified by the Blue Mountain's embrace of British expertise and leader-ship, as if modernity could begin again on a new and higher footing, purged of its earlier failings. As part of his occupancy of the Castle of Vissarion, Rupert arranges to have an enormous regiment of retainers recruited from the Highlands both to serve as servants and to be trained as soldiers by his great uncle General Sir Colin MacKelpie, a veritable Scottish plantation from the British semiperiphery. These are the men and women who were historically fitted for the dirty work of empire building, as Sir Colin's own distinguished military career (and the death of Rupert's own father at Maiwand) testifies, but here they meet their mirror image: the Blue Mountaineers "are very much like your own Highlanders—only more so" (*LS,* 80–81). Once again, the ideal of cit-izenship is founded on a "logic of repudiation" in which the abjection of one's deepest racialized fears (here signified by the warlike Turks) is predicated on matching the barbarousness of one's opponents with a primitive energy of one's own. As in *The Snake's Pass* this phantasmatic maneuver creates the space for a new "dominant fiction," a union of men and women who have transformed themselves through their own brave actions.

Whether the end result is the perfection of a Scottish-Balkan "fighting machine" (*LS*, 136) or a unique military-industrial symbiosis, its racial basis lies in a compatibility of national types whose model was first sketched out in *The Snake's Pass*, and later envisaged as a marriage between a more distant North and South. Then the Blue Mountain King joins hands with "the dark Southern Queen with the starry eyes" (*LS*, 350) and they dance to a music that "was wild and semi-barbaric, but full of sweet melody" (*LS*, 321). It has sometimes been said that "Utopia's deepest subject, and the source of all that is most vibrantly political about it, is precisely our inability to conceive it, our incapacity to produce it as a vision."[83] At a new peak of imperialist enthusiasm, yet at a moment when the question of British imperialism in Ireland had temporarily stalled, Stoker imagines that most impossible of utopias, a benevolent colonialism of near-equals in which two marginal peoples come together to create a new world. Many tears are shed by the characters in *The Lady of the Shroud*, tears of gratitude, tears of relief, tears of happiness. But perhaps the most poignant tears of all are those shed by a seasoned London journalist when he hears the national anthem of the Blue Mountains at the coronation's close: "It made me weep like a child. Indeed, I cannot write of it now as I would; it unmans me so!" (*LS*, 323).

# 2 Vampires, Mummies, and Liberals

## Questions of Character and Modernity

Indeed, everything comes alive when contradictions
accumulate. *Gaston Bachelard*[1]

 "In obedience to the law as it then stood, he was buried in the centre
of a *quadrivium*, or conflux of four roads (in this case four streets),
with a stake driven through his heart. And over him drives for ever
the uproar of unresting London!"[2] No, not *Dracula* (1897), but the
closing lines of a much earlier nineteenth-century work, Thomas De
Quincey's bleakly ironic essay "On Murder Considered as One of the
Fine Arts" (1854). De Quincey is describing how in 1812 the London
populace dealt with the body of one of his prize exhibits, a particularly
grisly serial killer who had escaped the gallows by hanging himself in his
cell at dead of night. Yet it is difficult for us to read this gleefully chilling
passage today without thinking of Bram Stoker's classic vampire novel.
The quirky Christian symbolism, the mandatory staking down of the
monster to keep it from roaming abroad, the sense of a busily self-
absorbed London unaware of its proximity to a murderous presence that
haunts its most densely populated byways: together these features seem
virtually to define a basic iconography for the vampire Gothic as it
achieved canonical status in *Dracula*.

In the half-century that separated Stoker from De Quincey the punitive assumptions behind the old suicide laws may have become little
more than a barbaric memory, but the subsequent attempts to view
suicide medically as mental illness, redefining it as an instance of "moral
insanity," offered no easily civilizing consolation. Thus what unites these
two otherwise historically distinct writers is their menacing use of the
buried past to interrogate the present. In Stoker's work the twin poles of
past and present make their appearance through a strangely paradoxical
and crucially modern trope, that of the spectator forced to confront a
horror whose very existence seems to compromise any possibility of
securing the line between the modern and the premodern. This troubling
of modernity's own historical self-consciousness is perhaps especially
marked in *Dracula*, which comes replete with the latest in late-Victorian

consumer goods, many of which function as a means of recording the structure of appearances and hence permit a precise memorializing of the past: cameras, phonographs, and portable typewriters. "It is nineteenth century up-to-date with a vengeance," as one of Stoker's characters so aptly puts it (*D*, 49).

At the same time, in *Dracula* the past extends across space into those zones of arrested development which modernity has not fully reached, where the trains do not yet run on schedule or where the railway lines have come to an abrupt halt. Though no farther from home than a rural Hampstead churchyard, it can be profoundly "humanising" to gaze upon the lights of London and to hear "the muffled roar that marks the life of a great city," despite the knowledge that the capital is simultaneously a site of depravity and danger (*D*, 251). For the routes of communication out of the metropolis may also bring terrifyingly archaic elements back into it, as in that eerie moment when Count Dracula is seen hailing a hansom cab near Hyde Park or when, in *The Jewel of Seven Stars* (1903), the presence of an ancient Egyptian mummy in a house in Notting Hill begins to have strange effects upon everyone who comes into contact with it. Such frightful encounters are imagined as tests of character in Stoker's supernatural romances, moments of truth that will purge the self of its secret weaknesses, ascertaining a person's intrinsic worth in the face of a plethora of social and psychic complications and providing a center of stability in a dangerous world of flux. Hall Caine, the novelist and dedicatee of *Dracula*, once defended the genre of romance as a type of writing that shows "what brave things human nature is capable of at its best."[3] But in Stoker's work, the protagonists are forced to confront their worst, before they can really know what their best might be.

If tests of character are endemic to modern adventure narratives, Stoker's Gothic novels mark a growing sense of difficulty with the notion of "character" itself, a term that was intimately linked to late-Victorian views of modernity. At its most straightforward, "character" designated the self-reliant private individual whose ability to take control of his (quintessentially his) own destiny was the cynosure of social and national progress. This was the brand of individualism espoused by moralists like Samuel Smiles, for whom the display of character was proof that one was living a truly dutiful life. At the same time, in the language of politics, character indicated the rational citizen, the individual property owner of classical liberalism who, by Gladstone's era, was increasingly expected to rise above his own narrow self-interest. What united these different emphases was the belief that character was essentially a function of human willpower, a disciplined effort called into play by the idiosyncrasies of the self and the vagaries of one's situation.

But it was never entirely clear to what extent character was the product of circumstances not of our own choosing. Thus John Stuart Mill, whose *On Liberty* (1859) was the finest defense of the sovereignty of the individual, was also a proponent of "ethology" or "the science of the formation of character."[4] The antinomies of Mill's philosophy are a reminder that throughout the nineteenth century we find arguments in favor of free will and determinism side by side, frequently operating within the same body of thought. Not surprisingly, these inner contradictions helped to make character a thoroughly protean concept, whose meaning could shift radically as it came into contact with newly emergent or smartly revamped systems of knowledge. From the 1880s onward, the assault on the autonomy of the individual subject in fields as various as scientific physiognomy, degenerationism, mental physiology, criminal anthropology, and "psychical research" made the classic liberal idea of character as individual self-mastery harder and harder to sustain. As a corollary, this classic idea began to disappear from liberal political theory during the same period, to be replaced by a new view of character which justified state intervention to actively promote the ideal of individual self-fulfillment by removing the social and material barriers to its realization.[5] For with the expansion of the democratic franchise and further demands for its extension to hitherto excluded groups like women, the question of the moral fitness of a new or aspirant citizenry became a crucial political question. In this chapter I want to argue that one of the remarkable features of Stoker's work lies in the way in which he attempts to hold on to the older notion of character, while being completely transfixed by the findings of the modern sciences and parasciences. This is particularly true of his two most influential novels, *Dracula* and *The Jewel of Seven Stars*, whose narratives press the relationship between science and character toward its most remote epistemological latitudes.

### "Material Facts"

As I have already noted, *Dracula* is a novel that is very much concerned with modernity's strengths and weaknesses, and, understandably, some of Stoker's contemporaries were uneasy with this aspect of the book.

In the *Spectator*, for example, one anonymous critic dismissed *Dracula*'s modern-day trappings, suggesting that the novel would have been "all the more effective if [Stoker] had chosen an earlier period" as his setting, particularly given the essentially "medieval methods" by which the vampire is laid to rest.[6] And, of course, the reviewer has a point, corroborated by no less an opinion than that of Jonathan Harker, the first character to fall into Count Dracula's clutches. Harker innocently worries that "the old centuries had, and have, powers of their own which mere 'modernity' cannot kill" (*D*, 49). The mixture of curiosity and fear recounted by Harker at the opening of the novel as he makes his journey to Count Dracula's castle in order to finalize the mysterious aristocrat's purchase of property in London is a very modern young Englishman's sense of shock at slipping into a premodern world. It is a world that is all too vivid. On his coach ride through Transylvania—his first trip abroad—Harker is fascinated by the sight at "every station" of "groups of people, sometimes crowds . . . in all sorts of attire." "Strangest" of all are the Slovaks, "with their big cowboy hats, great baggy dirty-white trousers, white linen shirts, and enormous heavy leather belts, nearly a foot wide, all studded over with brass nails . . . On the stage they would be set down at once as some old Oriental band of brigands" (*D*, 11). Harker's nervousness is intensified by the "hysterical" reactions that the news of his final destination provokes among the local people. When an old lady offers him a crucifix from her own neck, he hardly knows "what to do, for as an English Churchman" he had been "taught to regard such things as . . . idolatrous" (*D*, 13).

This powerful historical pull back into the past becomes even stronger upon Harker's arrival at his final destination. Thomas De Quincey once observed that the gift of total recall "must be the next bad thing to being a vampire," but it is clear that in *Dracula* total recall is partly what makes the Count who or what he is.[7] Once ensconced at the castle, the newly accredited solicitor hears the Count expatiate with immense pride on his family lineage, tracing it back to Attila the Hun and conceiving time as an endless series of battles and invasions. Harker records that the Count "spoke as if he had been present at them all," his lyrical nostalgia barely disguising the pure immediacy of the good old days (*D*, 40). In a sense, then, Harker must unlearn what he already knows, since *Dracula* is essentially a tale in which Protestant Englishmen and Englishwomen with a healthy respect for facts come to see that, far from being "idolatrous," "such things" as holy wafers, missals, wild garlic, and the rosary are a vitally necessary means of self-defense—despite their medieval provenance.[8] At first glance, the book could be described as a kind of conversion narrative, a return to ancient beliefs motivated by an occult, and truly oscular, dread. From this perspective, *Dracula* can be read as a modern novel that is largely dominated by the stories and specters of the past.

Nevertheless, Stoker's novel does insist upon a very different temporality, a continuous present that is constituted jointly through the procedures of law and science. Jonathan Harker's detailed notes from his Transylvanian journey reflect both his own recently completed legal training and the ethnographic travelogues of the period. If, in purely literary terms, *Dracula* draws heavily upon the legal narratives associated with Wilkie Collins, whose book *The Moonstone* (1868) imagined the novel as a collection of depositions, Stoker's work also invokes more practical nonfictional sources like his own exhaustive compilation of *The Duties of Clerks of Petty Sessions in Ireland* (1879). Written while the author was still employed as a civil servant in Dublin, this handbook was designed to enhance bureaucratic effectiveness throughout "the whole British Empire." In an ambitious attempt to rationalize the mass of "facts and theories resulting from the operations of the last twenty-seven years," Stoker itemized the formal requirements in preparing evidence for use in court proceedings in words that echo those of *Dracula*'s prologue. Thus, "each Information should contain a full and simple statement of all material facts to which the witness can depose" and "should be taken as nearly as possible in the witness's own words, and in the first person."[9] Empirically, therefore, Stoker's novel pretends to the status of "simple fact," assembling an impressive variety of sources, predominantly journal or diary entries, but also including newspaper articles, letters, fragments from a ship's log book, and an alienist's case notes (*D*, 8).

But in *Dracula* "simple fact[s]" are never simple. They are a constant problem for the various professionals who make facts their business. The same opening chapters which depend upon a lawyer's observations also reveal to us the law's fallibilities. After encountering a pack of wolves on his coach ride, Harker confesses that it "is only when a man feels himself face to face with such horrors that he can understand their true import" (*D*, 23). Yet, in truth, it takes him some time to recognize the gravity of his situation. Mesmerized by the vampire's business acumen and reassured by the presence of the Law List among the other English reference books in the castle's library, Harker is unprepared for the Count's nocturnal activities, which include spreading false evidence by putting on the solicitor's own clothes as a disguise.[10] Harker's visit to Transylvania has placed him beyond any legal redress, turning him into "a veritable prisoner, but without that protection of the law which is even a criminal's right" (D, 59). One of the lessons to be drawn from Harker's misperceptions is the need for a thorough scrutiny of the experience of our senses if the true facts are to be known. This gives scientific investigation a special place within the novel.

Insofar as it stands for the accumulation and rigorous testing of evidence, science ultimately provides the key to the novel's construction, offering a master discourse that orders and organizes the disparate empirical knowledges and variously inflected voices contributed by a succession of narrator-witnesses. Still, this investigative stance is not without its difficulties. Private memoranda are not always readily assimilable into publicly intelligible scientific frameworks and there is often an unmanageable residue of testimony that somehow fails to fit. The alienist Dr. Seward's notes on his "life-eating" patient R. M. Renfield, recorded on phonograph cylinders, merge imperceptibly into the doctor's own personal journal (D, 90). Thus, when played back on his "wonderful machine," the heart-wringing tones of Seward's narrative sound so "cruelly true" that its objectification as typescript becomes a way of editing out its emotional expression and protecting the privacy of his suffering (D, 266). Such all-too-human data threaten to overwhelm the explanatory resources available to us, presenting real problems of interpretation. Jonathan Harker's inconclusive speculations as to what makes the "idolatrous" crucifix such a potent force founders precisely on the uncertainty of its ontological or factual status, for he is unable to tell whether "there is something in the essence of the thing itself," or whether the cross "is a medium, a tangible help, in conveying memories of sympathy and comfort" (D, 40). But both of these examples suggest that scientific objectivity is essentially a humanistic ideal. Building upon statements "given from the standpoints and within the range of knowledge of those who made them," science seeks to bring nature under the full control of the human subject (D, 8).

This humanistic focus is epitomized by the quizzically encyclopedic utterances of Professor Van Helsing, "philosopher," "metaphysician," and "one of the most advanced scientists of his day" (D, 137). An austere and sententious figure, he embodies the uncompromising authority of the scientific voice and is therefore the man best fitted to lead the struggle against Count Dracula. "You reason well, and your wit is bold; but you are too prejudiced," he complains to his former pupil and colleague, Dr. Seward. "You do not let your eyes see nor your ears hear, and that which is outside your daily life is not of account to you." And he follows this observation with a baffling list of what the puzzled Dr. Seward rather desperately calls "nature's eccentricities and possible impossibilities" (*D*, 229–31). Science may run counter to the everyday, but the only significant objects of study are tangible, "positively" or directly ascertainable realities, and for Van Helsing—as for the positivist philosopher Auguste Comte—scientific theory is rooted in "the coordination of observed facts."[11] But *Dracula's* "possible impossibilities" point to scenarios both of advancement and of backwardness, revealing an unusually close relationship to the aporias and hesitations of late-Victorian positivism. Van Helsing's supplementary credentials as a "metaphysician" provide an additional safeguard against the unmanageability of these contradictions.

Like Edward Dowden, his intellectual ally and mentor at Dublin's Trinity College, Stoker was gripped by the explanatory sweep of positivist system-building and strongly attracted to the universalizing "power, authority and philosophic certitudes of modern science," even when it threw the traditional claims of "humane culture" into doubt.[12] An avid, if ambivalent, reader of Comte and Spencer, Dowden tried to give "the Positivist in me a fair chance," though as a conventionally devout Victorian he always believed that "in the end that limber transcendentalist in me should take the other fellow by the throat and make an end of him."[13] Dowden's internal struggle highlights one of positivism's key features: its consignment of speculation divorced from observation to the domain of unreality or illusion, a dismissal that for Dowden worked as an incitement to metaphysical revenge.[14] It is precisely this demarcation between the real and the unreal that is at issue in *Dracula*, despite Van Helsing's question-begging complaint against Dr. Seward which amounts to accusing him of not being positivistic enough.

Perhaps because of his training in science and mathematics, Stoker was far more prepared than Dowden to explore and take seriously the outer reaches of positivistic science and to contemplate its starkly problematic edges.[15] Running in and out of science's official claims to steady incremental progress, Stoker descried another, quite discontinuous history of knowledge in which undisciplined and often self-interested experimentation repeatedly confronted the sober, legislative tests of mature theory. Writing of Franz Anton Mesmer, whose "system" combined

*Vampires, Mummies, and Liberals*

an unscrupulous manipulation of his patients with genuine scientific discovery, Stoker noted that "true medical science has always been suspicious of, and cautious regarding, empiricism," and therefore slow to recognize and take up its achievements.[16] From this standpoint, the link between scientific theory and practical knowledge was often problematic and frequently marked by anomalies and gaps, discrepancies which *Dracula* opens up and exploits in ways disturbing to positivist and transcendentalist alike. Coming at a critical juncture in positivism's grand sociopolitical narrative, Stoker's novel seizes hold of that moment and weaves a romance around it, turning it into an adventure story.

## Ideologies of Degeneration

"By the late nineteenth century," Josep Llobera has argued, there were an increasing number of European writers who were "expressing serious doubts about the blessings of Western industrial civilisation," doubts that came to be "articulated around the ideas of race, of the crowd, of violence and of selectionism." Often using "perversions of scientific or pseudo-scientific concepts," these discourses parodied or inverted positivism's normative theory of history.[17] While England was hardly the epicenter of this general movement, it too saw a "sustained and growing pessimism in the 1870s and 1880s about the ramifications of evolution, the efficacy of liberalism, the life in and of the metropolis," and "the future of society" generally.[18] During the 1890s when Stoker was planning and drafting *Dracula*, the human sciences were heavily preoccupied with the pathologies of natural selection—what we might call a case of Darwinism and its discontents. Jonathan Harker's ethnographic diary of Transylvania, the home of "every known superstition in the world" (*D*, 10), offers a foretaste of this discourse which ran across medicine and biology into psychology and social theory.

This fear of a slide back down the evolutionary chain influenced intellectuals at every point on the political spectrum, while posing special problems for those Liberals who had held a strong belief in social progress. By the 1890s the idea of sterilizing the unfit or at least of preventing their reproduction had become a commonplace and "the virtual absence of any protest on liberal or humanitarian grounds" suggests that degenerationism could even be embraced by progressive thinkers who were concerned to set society back on the right course.[19] Consequently Liberals like the political scientist Graham Wallas or the young John Maynard Keynes were not alone in advocating the adoption of eugenic measures, and throughout the Edwardian period there was an extensive debate as to the size of the degenerate population and its likely prognosis. It was, argued the Liberal journalist and future politician Charles Masterman, nothing less than a "blasphemous optimism" to fail to see how "the modern city . . . has choked so many innumerable human lives: a mob moving who are dead."[20]

In the previous chapter I argued that *Dracula*'s elaborately racialized opposition between heartland and hinterland was in part a distinctively Anglo-Irish response to the vicissitudes of the Liberal Party's policy on Ireland. Where *The Snake's Pass* had sought to effect an idealized reconciliation between the two countries, *Dracula* visits a nation that appears to be beyond the pale, a place that seems somehow dangerously close to home yet largely impervious to the appeals of modernity's rational-legal order, at least in its British form. There is a strange duality about Transylvania, "a lovely country . . . full of beauties of all imaginable kinds" that is also "so wild and rocky, as though it were the end of the world" (*D*, 429, 432). At the same time, it is important to remember that *Dracula*, like its author, has a foot in the camps of both colonizer and colonized, and that the terrors and delights of country and city, of periphery and center, are always changing places and identities in the novel, giving rise to phantasms that cloud the confident administrative vision of the imperial agent.

As we have seen, Stoker seems to have had a lively sense of the conjectural theorizing going on in the sciences of his day, and it is remarkable just how thoroughly pervasive the language of degeneration is in *Dracula*, including specific references to such well-known writers on the subject as Max Nordau and Cesare Lombroso.[21] Certainly contemporary portraits of the degenerative condition were key referents for Stoker's depiction of the vampire. For example, the list of identifying traits enumerated in Nordau's controversial book *Entartung* (1893) seems peculiarly applicable to what we know of the Count. In his morbid mix of energy and lassitude Dracula alternates between *extreme passivity*—that "abhorrence of action" which Nordau likened to a state of reverie—and *over-stimulation*, leading to "love of the strange, bizarre, evil, loathsome, and ugly, and to sexual perversions," a condition tantamount to "moral insanity."[22] However, it is important to recognize that *all* the characters in *Dracula* are placed in relation to the conceptual field of degeneration theory. Thus, if the

*Vampires, Mummies, and Liberals*

Count displays his deviant nature anatomically through his "thin nose and peculiarly arched nostrils," "his eyebrows . . . very massive, almost meeting over the nose," and his "mouth . . . under the heavy moustache . . . fixed and rather cruel-looking, with peculiarly sharp white teeth" (*D*, 28), Professor Van Helsing's moral fitness can be discerned from his physiognomic juxtaposition to Dracula: the "face, clean-shaven, shows a hard, square chin, a large, resolute, mobile mouth, a good-sized nose, rather straight, but with quick, sensitive nostrils that seem to broaden as the big, bushy eyebrows come down and the mouth tightens" (*D*, 218–19).

Yet while the ideology of degeneration supplies a semantic matrix for much of the novel's characterization and action, its effects are also complicated by the instabilities inherent in this mode of thinking. "Degeneration" was never a unitary concept, but instead consisted of a relay of representations loosely inscribed in a whole cluster of professionalized disciplines and cultural practices. Because its objects were nowhere consistently or satisfactorily defined, we might best see the various attempts at theorizing degeneration as a set of overlapping hypotheses competing with each other to define the true dimensions of the culture's crisis, its sources and parameters. Hence their broad and often uncertain scope, ranging from worries about the dissipation of natural talent, through narratives of the rise and fall of nations, to moral panics about disease and infection.

Somewhat schematically, these hypotheses and their proponents can be grouped into two general categories. The first group perceived a real decline at the upper end of the social scale, especially though not exclusively within the ranks of the aristocracy: "the tainted offspring of forefathers beggared in their bodies by luxury and riotous living, and of fathers who sapped their manhood in vice," as one moralizing tract put it.[23] Charles Darwin's cousin, the scientist and sometime Spiritualist Francis Galton, provides an exemplary instance of this tendency. "We know how careless Nature is of the lives of individuals," Galton wrote in his 1869 book *Hereditary Genius;* "we have seen how careless she is of eminent families—how they are built up, flourish, and decay: just the same may be said of races and of the world itself."[24] From this postulate Galton argued that inherited titles were no guarantee of innate ability since this tended to decline over the course of several generations, suggesting that, at best, the evolutionary process was prone to breaks and discontinuities. In a subsequent study *Natural Inheritance* (1889), "prompted by questions about traits of notable European families," he developed a statistical model or measure of racial decline which he had initially termed the coefficient of "reversion," later (and less neutrally) referred to as the "regression toward mediocrity," better known today as the "regression toward the mean."[25] Like the Manchester economist W. R. Greg, Galton "used the idea that society could be divided between the 'fit' and the 'unfit' to attack aristocratic privilege and landed property."[26] And Greg, for his part, bemoaned a civilization in which "rank and wealth, however diseased, enfeebled or unintelligent," triumphed over "larger brains."[27] Symptomatically, the reduction of Count Dracula to manageable criminological proportions in the later part of the novel hinges upon the realization that this decadent European aristocrat is "not of man-stature as to brain" (D, 406).

At the same time, Galton also espoused a second perspective on degeneration, most fully typified by the writings of the psychiatrist Henry Maudsley and the zoologist E. Ray Lankester, both of whom were chiefly preoccupied with the threat to the nation emanating from the lower reaches of society. This specifically urban-industrial focus amounted to a kind of rear-mirror Darwinism in which a rapid deterioration in the racial stock was believed to result from the pressure on workers to adapt themselves to a degraded environment, posing formidable problems of social control as the numbers of criminopathic paupers steadily grew. Galton wrote of his distress at encountering "the draggled, drudged, mean look of the mass of individuals, especially of the women, that one meets in the streets of London," "the conditions of their life" destroying any semblance of common humanity.[28] Predictably, Galton took a keen interest in the developing "science" of criminal anthropology and was one of the few British intellectuals to attend the international congresses organized by the Italian criminologist Lombroso. In the same year that *Dracula* was published, Galton presented to the fourth (1897) congress his most enduring contribution to modern policing, a newly devised scheme for classifying fingerprints that was to revolutionize the methods of social control.[29]

Stoker's familiarity with these ideas can be traced to the early 1890s when, in a short story called "The Secret of the Growing Gold" (1892), he writes of "the causes of decadence" in both their "aristocratic" and their "plebeian forms."[30] Despite the manifest differences between them, the one nervous of the traditionally well-to-do, the other fixing its fears upon the new poor, these two accounts of degeneration do find a point of intersection in the threat they each posed to the security of respectable

*Vampires, Mummies, and Liberals*

middle-class society, precisely the world of doctors, lawyers, and teachers that is under siege in *Dracula*. Stoker's depiction of vampirism draws upon and draws together these twin fears of degeneration, fusing them into a single potent compound. Though the Count incarnates a powerful image of aristocratic decadence, falling into a long line of melodramatic rakes and villains, it is crucial that his preferred theater of operations is the heart of the Empire, "the crowded streets of your mighty London, . . . in the midst of the whirl and rush of humanity" (*D*, 31). Both Jonathan Harker and his wife Mina speak of the threat to "London, with its teeming millions" (*D*, 67 and 215), yet it soon becomes apparent that the danger lies not merely in the size of London's population, but in the uneasy coexistence of its social strata, signaled in the novel by the juxtaposition of standard English and demotic or vernacular speech. When the Count's first victim Lucy Westenra has been transformed into a vampire, she is known as "the bloofer lady" among the "grubby-faced little children" on whom she preys, an indication that established social boundaries are being breached (*D*, 213). *Dracula* imagines the Victorian bourgeois family as trapped in a sort of vise (the Count's grip "actually seemed like a steel vice"), under strain from both extremes of the social hierarchy (*D*, 24). Or, transposed into the theoretical idioms of European positivism, the choice of pathologies is between Nordau's "highly-gifted degenerates" and Lombroso's "atavistic criminals."

By vividly dramatizing the horrors of degeneration and atavism, the figure of the Count underscores the sexualized threat that lay at their core, the assumption of "a sexual 'instinct'" capable of turning to such perverse or precocious forms as "homosexuality" or "hysteria." Instructively, in his *History of Sexuality* Michel Foucault traced "the opening up of the great medico-psychological domain of the 'perversions'" in the mid-nineteenth century, showing their interrelation with new ideas about "heredity" and "dégénérescence."[31] His argument suggests that the task of establishing the distinction between normality and pathology required one to work across several different levels.[32] That is to say, the medical expert's attention would move from the minutiae of the sexual act to the classification of various maladies and diseases, and from there to the future disposition of the species, before returning to the sexual act again. In this way the diagnostic treatment of the human body could be connected to a program for administratively regulating hereditary traits, paving the way for the extension of state activity into modern eugenics.

*Dracula* typically follows the same bio-political trajectory, but in a necessarily more anxious key. Thus Jonathan Harker's temptation in a remote wing of the Castle Dracula—one of the earliest episodes in the book—insistently raises the problem of his "biological responsibility," his "obligation to preserve a healthy line of descent."[33] Captured and captivated by "three young women" who cast "no shadow on the floor," Harker finds their "deliberate voluptuousness . . . both thrilling and repulsive" and, though he is unnerved, he is nevertheless consumed with "longing." This ambivalence is heightened by his feeling that one of the "ladies" seems uncannily familiar to him, though he is unable to bring this elusive memory to consciousness. Yet the racialized contrast that triggers his aborted recollection is familiar enough: the woman Harker thinks he knows is "fair, as fair as fair can be, with great, wavy masses of golden hair and eyes like pale sapphires," while her two companions are "dark" with "high aquiline noses, like the Count's, and great dark piercing eyes." Significantly, the role of this blonde Aryan woman is to initiate Harker's fatal seduction, attempting to betray him to the corruptions of the flesh and cut him off forever from respectable domesticity. In "delightful anticipation" of other women later in the narrative, she represents "the enemy within," a source of male hysteria and demoralization, a "dreamy fear" of sexual chaos (D, 51–52). But Harker's rude awakening from this trance promises a different order of terror as the Count interrupts the erotic scene by staking his own unspeakable claim: "This man belongs to me!" (D, 53).

The progenitive powers of the perverse are also at stake in one of the most dramatic episodes in the novel, in which the Count is disturbed while taking possession of *Dracula*'s heroine, Harker's newly wedded wife Mina. The enormity of this scene is all the more intensely rendered by a double narration: once objectively, as an appalling discovery by the four male protagonists Van Helsing, Dr. Seward, the Hon. Arthur Holmwood, and Quincey Morris; and once subjectively, through Mina's own horrified memory. The Count has broken into the Harkers' room and, usurping their marriage bed by reducing the stupefied Jonathan to complete passivity, he has taken Mina by the scruff of her neck, "forcing her face down on his bosom" like "a child forcing a kitten's nose into a saucer of milk to compel it to drink" (D, 336). The extraordinarily dense web of associations evoked by these descriptions—of castration, rape, fellatio, sadomasochism—is held in place by the vampire's bizarrely composite persona, simultaneously that of rake *and* mother, a patriarch who gives birth to monsters. Of all the scenes in the book this was undoubtedly the

*Vampires, Mummies, and Liberals*

one which caused most commotion. For some male readers it offered a fantasy of sexual arousal, a rape that was secretly desired, while for others it was the kind of passage which went against all decency.[34] *The Keighley News*, in an otherwise fairly favorable notice, primly stated that "the nature of Count Dracula's adventure may not be hinted at in this domestic column."[35]

*Dracula* is a novel which excels in reversals of Victorian convention: men become sexually quiescent, women are transformed into sexual predators who cannibalize children, madness seems ready to overwhelm reason, and all of this is charged by a ceaselessly fluctuating economy of blood and desire. But even so, Mina Harker's violation by the phallically maternal Count signals a remarkable development in the vampire's powers. Certainly this episode explodes once and for all any hierarchically gendered division of the cultural field according to which "in one set of works (Poe, Hoffmann, Baudelaire: 'elite' culture)" vampires "are women," whereas "in another (Polidori, Stoker, the cinema: 'mass' culture) they are men."[36] For it demonstrates once again that in *Dracula* it is matter out of place that matters, the contamination and dissolution of the pure and sacred that counts, the transgression of boundaries and borders that is the ultimate horror, just as in theories of degeneration it was the impulsive, the unstable, the unfixed, and the nomadic that were held to be the sign of the savage and the barbarian—those like the gypsies Harker sees at the castle in Transylvania, "almost outside all law" (*D*, 56).[37] In both cases, anxiety around the question of boundaries is always also a demand that there *be* a boundary.

## Faces, Skulls, and the Unconscious

For Stoker, as his contrasting portraits of Count Dracula and Dr. Van Helsing make clear, the "science" of physiognomy served as one of the primary means for making sense of the mutable world of developmental possibilities unleashed by degeneration theory. Physiognomy often figured as a convenient method for ascertaining and depicting character in nineteenth-century novels and, like phrenology, it had been given a widespread currency as a progressive science in such middle-class cultural institutions as the literary and philosophical societies.[38] But in Stoker's fiction its use is unusually explicit and far-reaching. From the inception of his career as a writer, Stoker regarded physiognomy as an eminently practical form of knowledge, and there are countless references to it scattered throughout his work. It has a foundational status in his writing, locating and attempting to stabilize the lines of difference and danger by marking out a highly deterministic order in which some agents can be shown to be so totally other that they pose a threat to human progress. Notwithstanding physiognomy's loss of influence in such diverse fields as painting and medicine once scientists like Charles Bell and Darwin had begun to replace it with a proper psychology of human expression, Stoker continued to be a "believer of the science" and at the time of his death he still owned a five-volume quarto edition of Johann Caspar Lavater's *Essays on Physiognomy* (1789), the book which more than any other had been responsible for the modern revival of this age-old set of beliefs.[39]

In Lavater's exposition, physiognomy emerges as a practice poised somewhat equivocally between the old and the new, an ancient art that he is bringing forward into the modern age by setting it on a proper scientific footing. In true Enlightenment style, Lavater constitutes "Man" as "a grand and interesting subject of investigation," one which can be definitively known through sense-impressions perceptible to "a sound eye." By his own admission, however, Lavater's actual achievements fall short of this lofty ideal. He is able to offer only "a few simple Essays," "*Fragments* which . . . never can compose a Whole."[40] Nevertheless, it is modernity itself which has made this return to the intellectual models of antiquity particularly pressing. Lavater defines his proposed science of surfaces as a necessary form of practical judgment for societies whose basis is changing from inherited status to impersonal contract. As buyers and sellers encounter each other in the market as relative strangers, Lavater argues, they learn how far to extend their trust by reading the characters of prospective business partners from their faces. Physiognomy thus comes to scrutinize and regulate the probity of transactions in a social order increasingly organized on legal-commercial lines.[41]

However, the survival of Lavater's eighteenth-century codification of physiognomic doctrine into the late Victorian era was only possible because of certain crucial but unacknowledged modifications to his original ideas. Without resorting to explicit criticism, later writers changed the whole face of physiognomy by breaking with their founder's virtual silence on questions of race. In predictable pre-Darwinian fashion, Lavater had emphatically denied that there could be any continuity between monkeys and humankind, even in the case of the "savage." Though he had occasionally indulged in idle speculation as to whether "the soul of Newton" could still "have invented the theory of light" if it had "been lodged in the skull of a Negro," Lavater's general working assumption had been that "all men" were created "of one and the same blood."[42] This was a line of reasoning deeply at odds with the focus upon establishing physiological pedigrees of class and nation that was uppermost during the second half of the nineteenth century. From Beddoe to Macnamara, or from Mayhew to Galton, "race" increasingly became a readily identifiable entity both within and between national boundaries, so that by the early 1880s members of the Anthropological Institute could refer to "ethnological physiognomies" or "national physiognomies," terms which would undoubtedly have been quite unintelligible to Lavater himself. But however far their work departed from that of their eighteenth-century exemplar, Victorian physiognomists—including Stoker himself—typically continued to refer to Lavater's treatise as their point of departure.

Despite Stoker's indebtedness to Lavater, the world of *Dracula* is very much a world of "ethnological physiognomies" in which racial identities are assumed to be plainly legible from appearances and can even be used as data from which to extrapolate judgments as to a nation's social and moral well-being. Jonathan Harker's troubled physiognomic description of the Count is immediately confirmed when Dracula tells him "the story of his race" early on in the novel. By proclaiming that "in our veins flows the blood of many brave races who fought as the lion fights, for lordship," the Count is revealing the impurity of the Transylvanian dynasty, as well as that of his "polyglot" state (*D*, 14, 41). His declarations are fateful in another sense, for they also invoke the warrior races of a feudal past in rueful counterpoint to the degraded present, "these days of dishonourable peace" when "the glories of the great races are as a tale that is told" (*D*, 42). The Count's "story" moves rhetorically between stern lamentation and defiant rebuke, telling his own coded tale of degeneration and concluding by asking "where ends the war without a brain and heart to conduct it?" (*D*, 42)—a critical question for those concerned with the preservation of a nation's "fighting spirit" (*D*, 41).

The vampire's chronicle helps to elucidate another closely run antithesis in the novel, that between the use of the term "moral Viking" (*D*, 209) in connection with the American Quincey Morris, the boldest, most adventurous of the book's band of heroes, and the association of Dracula himself with the Berserker hordes (even the Norwegian wolf that the Count spirits away from the London Zoological Gardens is named "Berserker"). Stoker often gives his heroes some kind of Viking genealogy, but nowhere else in his work is this attribute so carefully qualified.[43] Quincey's moral fortitude marks the essential difference between these two frontiersmen, one Texan, the other Transylvanian. Significantly, the phrase "moral Viking" is invoked by a doctor (the alienist Dr. Seward) to describe Quincey Morris's strength of character at the funeral of one of Dracula's principal victims, Lucy Westenra. "If America can go on breeding men like that," confides Seward, "she will be a power in the world indeed" (D, 209). To bear oneself like "a moral Viking" is precisely to display a measure of self-control conspicuously absent among those bellicose peoples who have not yet evolved out of the past. In short, the sublimation of human aggression requires the right combination of birth and upbringing if the march of progress is to continue.[44]

But if the battle lines in Stoker's fiction could consistently be reduced to quite such simple melodramatic binaries, Dracula's anxieties about appearances would be much reduced. For this is also a text beset by the difficulties that haunted physiognomy, the fear that things are not always what they seem. In Dracula, sleeping virgins may really be monsters, dogs may be the agents of demonic powers, and, despite his vivid presence, the Count himself often seems to occupy a space that is virtually beyond representation, an unmirrorable image, a force able to assume a multiplicity of forms, physiognomy's true vanishing point. It is profoundly comforting to place the Count among the classifications mapped out by Nordau and Lombroso—a verdict given toward the end of the novel—since this identification confines him safely within the categorical boxes of one of the most influential brands of medical and sociological positivism. By contrast, the real horror of seeing the Count in broad daylight in Piccadilly on a hot autumn day stems from the realization that so blatant a criminal might not look unusual or remarkable enough to be singled out as he blends with the London crowd. Far from being foolproof, the Lombrosian project of tabulating the various kinds of criminogenic body was coming under increasing strain during this period, even as these ideas were being popularized in England through the publication of Havelock Ellis's The Criminal in 1890 and were beginning to be scrutinized by the Home Office. By the nineties, Lombroso's concept of "the born criminal"—the notion of a natural criminal type recognizable through physical stigmata—was shriveling under a growing weight of evidence, and the criminal anthropologist was forced desperately to modify his theory out of all recognition. Yet, despite this retrenchment, Lombrosian criminology remained influential, its deterministic structure finding echoes even in the alternative aetiology based on "inferior weight, stature and mental capacity" developed by its most incisive English critics.[45]

Just as there were contradictions between Lavater's physiognomy and the newer forms of racial thinking, so the incorporation of physiognomic ideas into criminology came into conflict with established Victorian ideas of individuality and character. In his 1872 letter to Whitman, Stoker perhaps unwittingly put his finger on the root of the problem, by allowing that one's outer appearance and inner life may fail in some ways to meaningfully correspond. After giving a physical description of himself which dwelt upon his facial characteristics, and remarking upon his temperament and disposition, Stoker announced that he was also "naturally secretive to the world," an intensely private self who could choose not to reveal himself to others.[46] Paraded as an advantage here, and idealized in Victorian culture as the character trait of "reserve" or "reticence . . . a quality which a strong man always respects" ( *JSS*, 211), this divorce between the inner and the outer caused the author no end of intellectual trouble and led to some curious disavowals. In the book he wrote—and in a sense could not help but write—on *Famous Impostors* (1910), Stoker revealed a fascination with deception and disguise while also denying its efficacy in some of its "commonest forms." Thus he argued that the impersonation of men by women was "so common that it seems rooted in a phase of human nature," though oddly he then rather inconsistently tried to explain away this phenomenon by relating it to the "legal and economic disabilities of the gentler sex." However, he was also at great pains to deny that men were ever really taken in by this kind of cross-dressing, claiming that the "common dangers" experienced at war or at sea, settings which he took to be typical sites for male impersonation, generated a generous, comradely loyalty that forbore to expose concealed gender differences.[47]

Lavater too had recognized the problem wanton and deliberate secrecy had posed for his system of physiognomy, which, after all, was intended as a highly deterministic science eschewing "arbitrary causes." His ingenious solution was to argue that "the art of dissimulation" was also "founded on Physiognomy" since it was for precisely this reason that "the Hypocrite endeavour[s] to resemble the . . . honest Man."[48] Furthermore, though one might be deluded by the mobile expressions that pass across the face, their interpretation was the province of the adjunct science of pathognomy and therefore a trained physiognomic observer would rarely be deceived. Nevertheless, the question remained as to how one could bracket off the pathognomic component in so complex a signboard as the human face. Lavater suggested a number of remedies: the profile or silhouette was one, and visiting the prison or asylum was another, a proposal which would have gladdened Lombroso's heart, since it was based on the claim that the inmates of these institutions were such visibly marked subjects that the "masks and vizors" of dissemblance would either be altogether absent or completely ineffectual. But the perfect solution was to observe the face after death. For then the features settle and become fixed and the barriers to interpretation are removed. According to this reasoning, in *Dracula* the Un-Dead are especially to be feared because they are able to evade the certain knowledge that death brings, creating a falsely appealing presence in order to lure their victims. Conversely, once a vampire like Lucy Westenra has been exorcised and restored to full humanity, we see her in her coffin "as we had seen her in life, with her face of unequalled sweetness and purity," including all "the traces of care and pain and waste," traces that "marked her truth to what we knew" (*D*, 259).

Stoker's use of physiognomy comes with its historical baggage of contradictions and fallibilities, one of whose effects is to call into play a radically different set of concepts, which serve as a reminder that originally physiognomy performed many of the functions of a scientific psychology. If, by the turn of the century, physiognomy was becoming a far less secure discipline than it once had been, psychology was becoming an increasingly well-established specialism, and selected ideas and technical terms were beginning to filter into ordinary, educated discourse. One of the most widely cited phrases from the nineteenth-century psychological lexicon was "unconscious cerebration," derived from the work of the noted professor of physiology W. B. Carpenter.[49] The term crops up in such otherwise rather oddly assorted texts as Henry James's *The Aspern Papers* (1888) and H. G. Wells's *The Island of Doctor Moreau* (1896), and it appears in *Dracula* too, as well as some of Stoker's other novels. Puzzling over the strange obsessions of his patient Renfield, Dr. Seward obscurely senses that their solution is "growing" from a "rudimentary idea in my mind" by "unconscious cerebration" and will soon mature into a fully conscious "whole idea" (*D*, 88). And later, even Renfield himself shows signs of this subterranean process working "through the cloudiness of his insanity" (*D*, 321–22).

These references to Carpenter's notion of "unconscious cerebration" again show Stoker borrowing from the human sciences, at a point where these overlap with contemporary medicine. And again his use of them brings us up smartly against their limits. The most complete account of "unconscious cerebration" is to be found in Carpenter's *Principles of Mental Physiology* (1874), a text which is a rich historical resource in pinpointing the changing conceptions of the self as agent during the late Victorian period, particularly as these bear on the moral notion of "character." The *Principles* offers both an analysis of the workings of the mind and a "study of its morbid conditions," those barriers to personal autonomy which also define the disturbing mental landscape inhabited by *Dracula*. Carpenter's book was in many respects a polemic, and it is striking that his treatment of the question of free will and determinism takes the form of a dual critique directed with equal ferocity against materialist and Spiritualist views of mental phenomena. Against the materialists, he insisted that "our Moral Nature" (p. 7) was such that human beings ought not be reduced to mere automata whose thoughts and behavior were caused by factors entirely beyond their control. On the other hand, Carpenter attacked nineteenth-century Spiritualists for failing to grasp that the mind could never be wholly divorced from the body, and he believed that their claims to the contrary were largely based on outright fraud.

As his title suggests, Carpenter's *Principles* aimed to demonstrate that the mental faculty was embodied in an economy of nerves and muscles, so that he often used the term *mind* as a synonym for *brain*. In his discussion of unconscious cerebration, for example, Carpenter located the nub of the process in sets of "impressions transmitted along the 'nerves of the internal senses' from the Cerebrum to the Sensorium" (p. 517) or center of consciousness, from which point they could "excite muscular movements" (p. 517). Though we are ordinarily aware of such impressions, there is always the possibility that they may be delayed or stalled and so become lost to "*conscious* memory" but with the result that they subsequently "express themselves in *involuntary muscular movements*" (p. 524). There is, of course, no theory of repression at work in this psychology, but what is evident is a shift toward a heteronomous model of mental life in which the hidden levels or dimensions of the mind can hold surprising consequences for our conscious selves. When he tried to explain away such Spiritualist phenomena as planchettes and table-turning, for example, Carpenter referred to "the records of old impressions, left in the deeper stratum of unconsciousness" which "disclose their existence through the automatic motor apparatus" (p. 525) in a manner entirely opaque to their agent.[50] Carpenter was by no means the only psychologist of this period to arrive at this kind of mental topography; others, like the "psychical researcher" Frederic W. H. Myers, devised far more radically "multiplex" accounts of mind and personality.[51] But what makes Carpenter's work so fascinating is that his virtual decentering of the subject occurred almost by default as he attempted to move between different principles of explanation, despite his best intentions.

On one level, Carpenter placed a high premium on individual independence and self-command, cleaving to a view of the will overtly influenced by the liberal philosopher John Stuart Mill (though, revealingly, he also sometimes cited Mill in support of several of his physiological concepts, including that of "unconscious cerebration"). However, his stress upon what is involuntary and unrecognizable in human action seems to diminish the scope of the will considerably and drew him back toward the materialistic argument he sought to avoid. Thus, because of "the degrading influences of the conditions" in which they found themselves, he denied that "those heathen outcasts of whom all our great towns are unhappily but too productive" could ever be considered "morally responsible" (pp. 9–10)—an argument which gave a new specificity to his assertion that the mind could never be "independent of its Material tenement" (p. 7). More confusingly still, elsewhere in his treatise Carpenter suggested instances in which the operation of the will may lie, paradoxically, quite outside conscious deliberation. In his chapter "Of Sleep, Dreaming, and Somnambulism," for instance, he stated that the somnambulist "differs from the ordinary dreamer in possessing such a control over his nervo-muscular apparatus, as to be enabled to execute . . . whatever it may be in his mind to do" (p. 591). By extension, hypnotism is to be understood as "artificial somnambulism" (p. 601), a relay of impressions and bodily movements which also bypasses the conscious decision of the mesmerized subject.

Hypnotism, somnambulism, trances, unconscious cerebration: these, just as much as a physiognomically grounded "philosophy of crime" or "study of insanity," are the materials from which *Dracula* is constructed (*D*, 405). In their different ways, physiognomy and "mental physiology" were both bodies of knowledge which attempted to put the idea of "character" as it appeared in Victorian social thought on a scientific footing, but because they constantly foregrounded difficult questions of voluntarism and determinism the meaning of the idea continued to be

*Vampires, Mummies, and Liberals*

problematic. So, when Carpenter tries to elucidate the concept of "character" in his *Principles* the result is noticeably inconclusive, since at the same time he depicts it—following Mill—as instantiating an individual's "self-directing" powers, he also presents it as part of a physiologically based causal model, conceiving of character as the "*proportional* development" of "particular *sequences of thought and feeling*" (p. 250).[52] This division was the product of the sharp discontinuity Carpenter had always assumed between the cerebrum as the site of such essential features of the mind as perception, reasoning, intelligence, and will and the lower, automatic sensory-motor centers which are ultimately subordinated to it, a split which replicated the classic mind-body dualism inherited from philosophy.[53] If *Dracula* is positioned on this same fault line, occupying some of the same conceptual space as late-nineteenth-century mental physiology, the instabilities of that paradigm helped to produce a number of incommensurable forms of knowledge, whose emergence can be glimpsed within the novel itself. When Seward fancies that his study of lunacy "might advance my own branch of science to a pitch compared with which Burdon-Sanderson's physiology or Ferrier's brain knowledge would be as nothing" (*D*, 90), he is on the brink of a new view of cerebral functioning—a "knowledge" based upon experimental research carried out within the asylum itself—that was starting to displace many of the old philosophical categories.[54] Alternatively, however, Seward and Van Helsing's interest in Charcot points elsewhere, precisely toward Freud and the study of hysteria, a tradition that would soon leave strictly somatic accounts of mental disorder behind, uncoupling the links with degenerationism which Charcot always tried to maintain.

The "moral Viking," a phrase precisely designed to consolidate the notion of character, in fact teeters on the brink of hysteria. In the case of Quincey Morris, the American's noble demeanor at Lucy Westenra's funeral belies the grief a sensitive observer knows he must be feeling, since, as Seward points out, this disappointed suitor "suffered as much about Lucy's death as any of us" (*D*, 209). Van Helsing's own reaction at the burial, visibly "putting some terrible restraint on himself," underscores the proximity of psychic breakdown, for once the two doctors are "alone in the carriage he gave way to a regular fit of hysterics" (*D*, 209). As I noted in the previous chapter, Stoker is in part attempting to reconcile two ideals of masculinity that had generally become dissociated by the 1890s, creating a bridge between the expressive man of sensibility and the strong, steadfast man of action; and I suggested that this rehabilitation can be read as a kind of Anglo-Irish defense of Celtic emotionalism. Here, however, I want to qualify this argument by stressing the extent to which this sympathetic view rests upon the male subject's vulnerability to forces beyond manly self-control, a vulnerability which can never be entirely free of risk. "King Laugh," observes Van Helsing, is no respecter of persons or occasions—"he come when and how he like"—so much so that Seward feels impelled to pull down the blinds to hide the embarrassment of his colleague's tears and mirth (D, 210).

If such open displays of feeling betoken a lack of propriety or respect, in other cases they may be condemned as dangerous signs of effeminacy, a morally reprehensible weakness of the will and a departure from the heterosexual ideal.[55] This fear of being "unmanned" (by men and by women) underlies the "wild feeling" which engulfs Jonathan Harker when he finds himself trapped in the Castle Dracula at the beginning of the novel (D, 39). After narrowly escaping the Count's advances, and subsequently being reduced to a condition of sexual passivity at the hands of "those weird sisters" (D, 64), Harker chooses to brave the castle's precipice and risk falling to his death in his bid to escape, since "at least . . . at its foot man may sleep—as a man" (D, 69). Ultimately, by artfully negotiating the line between the conscious and the unconscious, and between the voluntary and the involuntary, Stoker recuperates the male hysteria to which both Harker and Van Helsing in their different ways fall victim. In the midst of his terrifying captivity, Harker is surprised to pass an untroubled night of dreamless sleep. "Despair has its own calms," he realizes upon waking (D, 57). But, though the male unconscious seems to possess a self-regulating capacity to return the psyche to a state of balance or equilibrium, its workings remain mysterious, as unfathomable as they are uncertain.[56] "It may be that nerves have their own senses that bring thought to the depository common to all the human functions" (LS, 178), speculates the hero of one of the later novels, producing a kind of muddled pastiche of Carpenter's own scientific language. But the point is that this is something he simply does not know for sure.

In the light of Stoker's highly syncretistic amalgam of conflicting accounts of human behavior, accounts which were themselves internally conflicted, it is hardly surprising that one finds no resolution of these discrepancies in his writings. As a result, the languages of freedom and determinism are always inflected by a variety of accents and sometimes

*Vampires, Mummies, and Liberals*

fall into a confusion of tongues. Thus *Dracula*'s heroes, "our little band of men" (*D*, 449), possess "powers" that "are unfettered," at least "so far as [they] extend" (*D*, 285), while, in a curious parallel, the vampire "is not free" since it must "obey some of nature's laws—why we know not" (*D*, 287). Nevertheless, this unnatural creature that "seems predestinate to crime" (*D*, 405) may exercise a "limited freedom" at "certain times" (*D*, 287). It is the indeterminacy of agency, human and nonhuman alike, the obfuscation of its capacities and limits, that is so fateful for the novel's protagonists. The precariousness of Lucy Westenra's "unconscious struggle for life and strength" is, for example, as much a consequence of the unknown terms and scope of that struggle as it is of the delicately poised balance of power between good and evil (*D*, 192). Reflecting upon Mrs. Westenra's relative calm in the face of "the terrible change in her daughter," Dr. Seward wonders (along classical laissez-faire lines) whether this propensity for self-preservation is not an unintended by-product of "the vice of egoism" that naturally exists in all of us, resulting in "an ordered selfishness" with "deeper roots for its causes than we have knowledge of." Our understanding of "spiritual pathology" and its defenses is far from complete (*D*, 147).

## The Lure of the Mummy

Stoker returned to these questions of knowledge and agency in his 1903 novel *The Jewel of Seven Stars*, an excursion into the orientalist Gothic which forms a kind of sequel to *Dracula*. Like the latter, this text also stages a struggle for possession of the human body, ultimately the body of a woman—necessarily putting the manliness of its heroes under scrutiny in the process—but the general effect is at once more concentrated and more grimly speculative than before. *The Jewel of Seven Stars* was praised by Stoker's occult-minded friends like the Scottish writer J. W. Brodie-Innes, who thought it shed a "clearer light on some problems which some of us have been fumbling in the dark after for long enough."[57] Brodie-Innes (a sometime member of the Hermetic Order of the Golden Dawn) never explicitly names the problems that he felt Stoker had clarified, but the novel is striking in its use of scientific discovery as a springboard for metaphysical conjecture, bringing questions of immortality or reincarnation into the world of radium and X-rays. And once more, to stand at the frontier of scientific knowledge is to become aware of a crisis in how the producer and repository of that knowledge, the human subject, is to be understood.

The book centers upon the resurrection of Queen Tera, a member of the royal Egyptian dynasty that ruled "between [the] twenty-ninth and twenty-fifth centuries before Christ." The queen, a woman of "extraordinary character as well as ability" (*JSS*, 174), is known to have had "power over Sleep and Will" (*JSS*, 175) and to have used her magical gifts to outwit her enemies among the priesthood. In order to investigate "whether or no there is any force, any reality, in the old Magic" (*JSS*, 224), an English Egyptologist, Abel Trelawny, has arranged to have the queen's mummy and burial treasures brought to London for scientific examination. His research culminates in a "Great Experiment" designed to bring Queen Tera back to life, and in Stoker's original version of the novel these efforts succeed, but at a terrible price: all the characters except the narrator suddenly meet their deaths when the subterranean chamber in which the experiment is taking place is mysteriously filled with thick black smoke. In the final pages the storyteller, a young barrister named Malcolm Ross, realizes that he has mistakenly carried the Egyptian queen to safety thinking she was his sweetheart, Trelawny's daughter Margaret. Upon lighting the candles, Ross finds the queen's robe and jewelry where Margaret's body should have been and, returning to the chamber, he discovers Margaret lying on the floor, "her hands before her face" and with a "glassy stare" just visible between her fingers, "more terrible than an open glare" (*JSS*, 337).[58]

However, the story of Queen Tera only emerges very gradually, and much of the early part of the novel focuses upon a bizarre episode involving Margaret's father. The Egyptologist has been found unconscious in his bedroom study, bleeding from a strange jagged wound like the mark of a claw near his left wrist and, despite the intervention of the police and hurried consultations with medical specialists, neither the cause of his injury nor a means of bringing him round can be discovered. The first few chapters function generically as a variant of the locked-room mystery, circling obsessively around the scene of the crime, and the narration seems curiously static, almost deadlocked. Outside influences are carefully shut out, and it is as if the Trelawnys' Notting Hill house has been sealed off from the rest of London except for occasional nocturnal urban sounds, the "roll of wheels" or "the far-away echo of whistles and the rumbling of trains." Like "the Great Experiment" which brings the novel to its shattering conclusion, the midnight vigils over Trelawny's unconscious body are reminiscent of a séance, during which it appears "as though all the real things had become shadows," but shadows "which had had sentience." "It was rather like the picture of a scene than the reality," says Ross; "all were still and silent; and the stillness and silence were continuous" (*JSS*, 44).

Without ever falling asleep, Ross feels that he is seeing visions or dreaming dreams. Indeed, the novel begins in the midst of a dream from which the narrator may never have truly awakened:

It all seemed so real that I could hardly imagine that it had ever occurred before; and yet each episode came, not as a fresh step in the logic of things, but as something expected. It is in such wise that memory plays its pranks for good or ill; for pleasure or pain; for weal or woe. It is thus that life is bitter-sweet, and that which has been done becomes eternal. (*JSS*, 1)

From the outset, therefore, Ross's perceptions are marked as problematic and, if there are hints here of a subjectivity somehow trapped in cyclical time, the novel's mode of address also seems to hover on the edge of a breakthrough to some new order of psychic reality. The narrative spaces of the text are constantly turning in upon themselves, implying that "the logic of things" is coextensive with the enigmatic workings of the mind itself, and the language is always tentative, equivocal: it "was almost as if the light on the white fingers in front of me was beginning to have some hypnotic effect ... and for an instant the world and time stood still" (*JSS*, 160–61).

Reinforcing this heightened sense of interiority, there are repeated references to unconscious states, and one finds the word *unconscious* being employed in practically all its then-current registers. Trelawny's form of "unconsciousness" is said to differ from "the many cases of hypnotic sleep" observable at the Charcot Hospital in Paris (*JSS*, 33); it is a "coma" which shows few "signs ... of ordinary unconsciousness" (*JSS*, 59); and we need to carefully distinguish even the latter from moments of "unconscious self-surrender" (*JSS*, 7) or from those states of unawareness in which one might "unconsciously sink" back upon one's pillow, "lost in memories of the past" (*JSS*, 207). Again, Margaret's "life with her father had had unconsciously its daily and hourly lesson"; yet his influence leaves her unspoiled, "so naive and unconscious; so girlish and simple," with "so little thought of self," a spontaneous femininity preserved within, and perhaps despite, a dutiful, masculine environment (*JSS*, 121).

As in *Dracula*, the "science" of physiognomy underpins a number of key descriptions in the novel, a "habit" of observation which Ross "extends to my life outside as well as within the court-house"—yet here too we see a discreet shift toward a more psychological emphasis in Ross's account of his practice of judging "personality" through people's "unconscious action and mode of bearing themselves" (*JSS*, 30). But, though these various instances of dissociated consciousness may appear as nothing more than a casual collection of merely idiomatic usages, Trelawny's pedagogic exposition of the multiple selves presumed by Egyptian cosmology obscurely suggests that these different facets of subjectivity may be integrated into a grand explanatory system, with a "division of functions, spiritual and bodily, ethereal and corporeal, ideal and actual" that is "guided always by an unimprisonable will or intelligence" (*JSS*, 238).

This stress upon the efficacy and directive power of the will was one of the hallmarks of the late Victorian occult revival and provides an interesting point of comparison with the psychology advanced in Carpenter's *Principles*, from which it otherwise differs so profoundly. When nineteenth-century occultists took up ideas and practices drawn from Rosicrucianism, Buddhism, or the Egyptian mystery religions, they tended to systematize them into highly disciplined programs of rituals and initiations which departed from their original sources in subtle ways. In the hands of organizations like the Hermetic Order of the Golden Dawn, for example, Egyptian magic was always a far more consistent and a far less fatalistic form of knowledge than it was in the disputes among contemporary Egyptologists. According to occult teachings, it was possible for carefully prepared adepts to gain control over the supernatural forces in the world by practicing ritual magic, but an individual's will required rigorous training if this dangerous venture was to succeed. It is no accident, therefore, that Malcolm Ross is at his most vulnerable when he feels something working "on my nerves—on my memory—on my very will" (*JSS*, 41).

Though the systems are diametrically opposed, in both Carpenter's psychological theory and occult doctrine the will was a stronghold of self-mastery (and, in a special sense, of personal autonomy), keeping at bay the materialistic advances of modern science—a science dismissed by one prominent occultist as "ancient thought distorted, and no more."[59] And, just as psychologists like Carpenter were moving toward a complex multidimensional model of the mind, so—albeit for entirely different reasons—occultists were also exploring the hidden reserves and dissoci-

*Vampires, Mummies, and Liberals*

ated states of consciousness revealed during magical rites. One of the commonest ways of making sense of such phenomena was to conceive the mind as a series of levels or strata, an analogy legitimated by the scientific prestige of Victorian archaeology or geology.[60] In *The Man*, published just two years after *The Jewel of Seven Stars*, for example, Stoker places "sexual feeling" on "the bed-rock of our nature," providing a kind of foundation "of our being," however much it may be hidden or covered over by "the slow process of alluvial deposits of experience" (*M*, 169). It might be tempting therefore to see Stoker's exploratory psychology as a version of H. Rider Haggard's notion of a "layered personality," particularly since Stoker was, like his friend Hall Caine, one of the beneficiaries of Haggard's attempt to promote a revival of romance in the late 1880s.[61] Indeed, *The Jewel of Seven Stars* has sometimes been compared to Haggard's *She* (1887), and the resemblances between the two books are striking enough to lead one critic to read the latter as "an inverted version" of the former.[62]

Certainly Queen Tera owes much to Rider Haggard's Ayesha—"She-who-must-be-obeyed"—as the archetype of the immortal Eastern princess, well-versed in the ancient arts and sciences (which turn out to be surprisingly advanced), who poses a threat to British imperial security: the return of the repressed with a vengeance. But, in fact, Stoker's psychology of romance is quite at odds with that of Haggard. Against the monstrous power of the woman, the latter pits the elemental forces of a heroic masculinity that must cast off the encumbrances of polite society if man's original strength and vitality is to be recaptured. When Haggard introduces the trope of the Viking into his fiction, it appears in a starkly amoral form, a violent regression conceived as the release of a submerged and primitive savagery which leaves the protagonists of his novels drenched in the blood of their enemies. Something of a commonplace among defenders of romance, this view of man assumes that civilization is, in Haggard's character Allan Quatermain's phrase, like "the veneer [on] a table," and that just below the surface our barbaric nature survives intact. In short, "man is a fighting animal," as Haggard was to write in his autobiography.[63] By contrast, Stoker is never entirely sure that the "dwellers in the city" can any longer "enter into the feelings of the hunter," to quote Count Dracula's dismissive remark to Jonathan Harker (*D*, 29). For all the strength of character and passion for adventure upon which Stoker's novels depend, there is always a sense that "muscular liberalism," despite its many imperial achievements, will finally be found wanting.[64] And this is exactly what the impact of theories of degeneration would lead us to expect.

Nowhere is Stoker's hesitancy more evident than at the close of *The Jewel of Seven Stars* when the Queen gains the upper hand, despite the fact that Malcolm Ross's devotion to Margaret Trelawny had "brought out all the masculinity in me" (*JSS*, 206). Male strength of character is revealed as conditional at best, even where, "in the conscious sense of it," a man has lost his "baser self"; it is woman whose occult powers remain inexplicably impressive, outside existing knowledge, beyond any possibility of control (*JSS*, 216). And this sense of impotence is magnified, feeding into a Manichean vision of the universe as eternally riven by warring forces. Putting his desire "for love or for love-making" aside, Ross begins to prepare himself for "the Great Experiment," and as he does so his mind soon turns to speculation on the course of world history, reaching conclusions so gloomy that he can hardly bear to dwell upon them. "The more I thought over the coming experiment, the more strange it all seemed," he muses, and rapidly slides into despair: "it was all so stupendous, so mysterious, so unnecessary!" Even if this venture were to prove successful, there might be unforeseeable consequences which would alter the fate of the world forever. Ross reads the terror of the future through a fantasy of the past, imagining the beginning of all life, "when the very air was purifying itself from elemental dross," and he wonders whether the "primal and elemental forces" of ancient days were ever "controlled at any time by other than that Final Cause which Christendom holds as its very essence?" Should this grand séance succeed in resurrecting the dead—precisely the kind of Spiritualist hypothesis Carpenter had been so concerned to combat—"modern mortals" would find themselves "arrayed against the Gods of Old, with their mysterious powers," and the whole cosmic order might be subverted (*JSS*, 250).

Ross's fantasy is predicated upon the breakdown of a strict, almost positivistic separation between the "tangible," scientifically known "world of facts" (in which even Christianity belongs to a system of cause and effect) and those "strange and awful" possibilities which science excludes as unthinkable or mistaken (*JSS*, 252). His secure, taken-for-granted sense of reality is invaded by "strange surmises" that he is powerless to suppress, a "sudden experience of misfitting imagination" characteristic of fantasy's intrusiveness and uncontrollability.[65] Haunted by the thought that there might be "room in the Universe for opposing Gods," Ross fears that "the struggle between Life and Death would no longer be a matter of the earth" but would instead be transformed into a cata-strophic "war of supra-elemental forces" (*JSS*, 252).

The idea of such a terrifying contest was not unknown in occult circles: Yeats, for example, had imagined a "magical armageddon" in the 1890s, believing that "some new civilization [was] about to be born from all that our age had rejected."[66] In *The Jewel of Seven Stars*, however, this kind of mystical self-confidence is wholly absent. R. F. Foster has suggested that underlying both Anglo-Irish (or Protestant) Gothic and Yeatsian occultism is "a mingled repulsion and envy" directed toward the magical elements within Catholicism, a superstitious awe which bred its own esoterica among these "marginalized Irish Protestants."[67] In addition to Le Fanu's Swedenborgianism and Yeats's membership in the Hermetic Order of the Golden Dawn, Foster cites Stoker's *Dracula* (avidly read by Yeats) with its invincible crucifixes and holy wafers wielded by the Cath-olic magus Van Helsing. But, while this provocative thesis sheds light upon Yeats's enthusiastic embrace of ritual magic, Stoker's more nervous, if no less speculative, attempts to bring such phenomena within the ambit of a species of scientific rationalism seem very different.[68]

The pathos of *The Jewel of Seven Stars* lies in Ross's vain struggle to find an explanation, any explanation, that will set his fears to rest. Ross's bleak thoughts immediately give way to Mr. Trelawny's more positive anticipa-tions of his experiment's scientific outcomes, hopes which depend for their plausibility on sliding quickly over the distinction between scien-tific method and the magical arts. His scientific rhetoric at full throttle, the Egyptologist argues that "we are now in that stage of intellectual progress" when we shall soon "have enough of first principles" to make possible "the true study of the inwardness of things" (*JSS*, 254). Then the modern Western and ancient Egyptian sciences are likely to converge, for "the discoveries of the Curies and Laborde, of Sir William Crookes and Becquerel, may have far-reaching results on Egyptian investigation" (*JSS*, 256).[69] Ross is grateful for being "soothed" by "these scientific, or quasi-scientific discussions . . . They took my mind from brooding on the mysteries of the occult, by attracting it to the wonders of nature" (*JSS*, 258). Yet, in spite of Trelawny's inspirational disquisitions, the novel remains torn by its own contradictory deductions, compromising the forward-looking vision it bravely tries to conjure up. If the narrative resolutions to Stoker's novels frequently have a flimsy or contrived qual-ity to them, as though the contradictions that initially brought them to life had proved more intractable than had at first been thought, in *The*

*Jewel of Seven Stars* there is no pretense of a reassuring conclusion. The source of the difficulty lies, as so often, in the insistent question of femininity, the realization of its stubborn irreducibility: "Sex is not a matter of years!" Margaret protests to her father. "A woman is a woman, if she had been dead five thousand centuries!" (*JSS*, 317).

Among the consolations offered by Trelawny's cosmological ruminations is the intimation of a knowledge of origins that might transcend sexual difference, an understanding of "the laws which govern molecular or foetal growth, of the final influences which attend birth" (*JSS*, 254), of the ways in which "nature forms her living entities to flourish on those without life" (*JSS*, 258). But what gives these imaginings their point is the relief they seem to offer from the guilt and anxiety with which sexual relationships are fraught. When Malcolm Ross awakens from his dream of Margaret Trelawny, the dream that forms the novel's starting-point, he depicts this awakening as a kind of token of the Fall, for he sees it as a denial of the possibility of "perfect rest," observing that "even in Eden the snake rears its head among the laden boughs of the Tree of Knowledge" (*JSS*, 2).

Ross's love for Margaret is constituted by the attempt to escape from his fear of the real, "the great world with its disturbing trouble, and its more disturbing joys" (*JSS*, 1–2). Though he idolizes Margaret, Ross is at first "afraid of her" (*JSS*, 82) and Margaret herself seems to move between dream and reality, sometimes in so nightmarish a way that Ross feels all "the horror of a dream within a dream, with the certainty of reality added" (*JSS*, 46). In one early description she is indelibly linked to the occult through the "mysterious depth" of her eyes, which can appear "as black and soft as velvet" yet in the next breath are likened to "a black mirror such as Doctor Dee used in his wizard rites" (*JSS*, 30). Over the course of the novel this antinomy is resolved into a "strange dual existence" as Margaret's old self becomes increasingly submerged under a certain aloofness and reserve, displaying an uncanny prescience regarding all matters Egyptian, as if she were a medium for the ancient queen (*JSS*, 286). We never see the living Queen Tera—though the men in the "great experiment" marvel at the beauty of her unclothed body after they have removed her from the mummy's wrappings—but it is plain that Margaret is her double and that, prior to Tera's resurrection, Margaret speaks and acts as the queen's agent. By the end of the novel Margaret's eyes are blazing "like black suns" (*JSS*, 331). In the original 1903 text, she is sacrificed so that the queen might live.

Queen Tera's final violent onslaught has long been anticipated. In addition to the series of attacks on Abel Trelawny in his London home, there are two accounts of visits to Tera's Egyptian tomb—one from a book by a seventeenth-century Dutch explorer, the other recounted by Trelawny's collaborator Eugene Corbeck—which grimly describe her bloody revenge against Arab grave robbers. Most obliquely revealing of all is the comment by the Dutchman as he gazes at the fabulous blood-red jewel of the novel's title, which had been hidden beneath the queen's unwrapped hand (with its "living flesh") that lies across the mummy. He thinks of "that fabled head of the Gorgon Medusa with the snakes in her hair, whose sight struck into stone those who beheld" (*JSS*, 154).

Trelawny steadfastly maintains that the purpose of his "Great Experiment" is the recovery of ancient knowledge for modern science, and he dismisses Ross's suggestion that what is really at stake is "the resurrection of the woman, and the woman's life" (*JSS*, 290). But Ross has perhaps unwittingly hit upon the truth. For Queen Tera's power and position are quite singular and her magical skills belong to her alone. In her struggle against "an ambitious priesthood" that plotted to bring her down, Queen Tera "had gone further than her teachers" and "had won secrets from nature in strange ways." "Though a Queen" she has "claimed all the privileges of kingship and masculinity," effectively emasculating her opponents by her victory (*JSS*, 175–76). After all, in Ross's eyes it is axiomatic that "a strong man's natural impulse [is] to learn from a man rather than a woman" (*JSS*, 109).

As the novel moves toward its climax, Margaret Trelawny increasingly serves as a reminder of this formidable woman's femininity and her clashes with her father as to how the experiment should be conducted mark out the lines of sexual conflict. Thus when Margaret expresses her revulsion at the idea that a group of men should unroll Queen Tera's mummy, exposing her naked body to "the glare of light," Abel Trelawny replies that the queen would have been embalmed by men: "They didn't have women's rights or lady doctors in ancient Egypt, my dear!" (*JSS*, 317). The contrast and implicit criticism here echo Mina Harker's complaint in *Dracula* that "men are more tolerant" ("bless them!") than the "New Women" (*D*, 110). But it also helps us to see that in an era of growing feminist agitation even an arcane specialism like Egyptology was by no means insulated from the social debates of its time.

One of the most provocative of contemporary archaeological findings was that ancient Egypt was a matrilineal society. According to Flinders

Petrie (one of Stoker's sources for *The Jewel*), "all property belonged to the woman; all that a man could earn or inherit, was made over to his wife; and families always reckoned back further on the mother's side than the father's." Since the general historical trend was toward "men's rights," Petrie argued that "this system" was one which "descends from primitive times."[70] But other writers were less likely to see this as a regressive phenomenon. In her lecture "The Social and Political Position of Women in Ancient Egypt" (c. 1890), Amelia Edwards—one of Egyptology's major fund-raisers and an indefatigable popularizer of the subject—liked to place particular emphasis upon the fact that thousands of years ago Egyptian marriages were subject to a "rule of contract" that gave women far more economic and legal freedom than their modern British sisters. As Billie Melman has noted, "in modern liberal thought and in the liberal jargon of the 1880s and 1890s, the contracting, property-holding man is the symbol of civic and political liberties and the right to vote"—a right that was still denied to women, despite the Married Women's Property Act of 1882.[71] For antifeminist liberals like Stoker the idea that marriage could be a mutually binding contract between equal parties was anathema; and as we'll see in the next chapter, he devoted considerable imaginative energy to its refutation.

To illustrate her theme, Edwards included a history of Egyptian queens, using slides, many of which focused upon the career of Queen Hatasu, who became a female pharaoh or ruler. Like Stoker's Queen Tera, Hatasu is "pictured in man's dress" (*JSS*, 176), and both women are portrayed as leaders and conquerors possessed of godlike status—Edwards depicts Hatasu as a political figure comparable in stature to Queen Elizabeth I.[72] Moreover, both Tera and Hatasu are described as scientists, Hatasu emerging in Edwards's account as the original architect of the Suez Canal, "the scientific ancestress of M. de Lesseps."[73] Finally, one may note that both queens are said to be European in appearance: "the white wonder of [Tera's] beautiful form" resembling "a statue carven in ivory by the hand of a Praxiteles" (*JSS*, 324).

If Margaret/Tera represents the fantasy of the "marvellously strong woman" whose "energy [is] manifest in every nerve and fibre of her being" (*JSS*, 112–13), she invariably embodies the threat of a will strong enough to crush any and all resistance to her. Even to gaze "with irreverent eyes" upon Queen Tera's "completely nude" body with only her face still covered—for at first she cannot stare back—is to begin to become

*Vampires, Mummies, and Liberals*

aware of a physical weakness in oneself, however reassuringly strong and determined one's will might appear to be ( *JSS*, 324). This instability around the subject's sense of self derives from the way in which in fantasy one finds oneself "caught up in the sequence of images," rather than simply pursuing "the object [of desire] or its sign."[74] Thus, "although we might wish to think, even fantasize, that there is an 'I' who has or cultivates its fantasy with some measure of mastery and possession, that 'I' is always already undone by precisely that which it claims to master."[75] When Tera's body is exposed to view Ross confesses to an anxiety as to whether she is dead or alive, and just before the disembalming of the mummy he feels that "the whole material and sordid side of death seemed staringly real" ( *JSS*, 320). Following Freud's interpretation of the Medusa's head, we might say that Queen Tera "isolates" those "horrifying effects" of femininity associated with the "sight of the female genitals," separating them from "their pleasure-giving ones"—just as Malcolm Ross is finally separated out from the glassy-eyed dead as the sole survivor of the Great Experiment.[76]

Freud's Medusa mitigates its own horror by reinstalling and multiplying the missing phallus: in the nest of coiling snakes that serve as the Medusa's hair and in the stiffness experienced by the terrified male spectator. But in Stoker's Medusa—functioning in a sexual economy very different from that of the ancient Greek world highlighted in Freud's analysis—the fear of death and castration is intensified rather than meliorated, as if the strong, willful and desirable woman must ultimately be driven to punish the man who desires her, because he desires her. And so, the aggression that is suppressed in the Victorian idealization of womanhood returns as an ungrateful feminine demand for power, here fantasized as the power to destroy. Queen Tera is Queen Hatasu's alter ego, the woman whose overweening assertion of equality with her male counterparts signals the end of the Victorian sexual order. The only possible avenue of escape lies in the reiteration of the old ideal. Thus, it is in perfect keeping with the logic of the original novel when, in the revised ending to the 1912 edition of *The Jewel*, Queen Tera is absorbed into the more "spiritual" figure of Margaret Trelawny ( *JSS*, 31). There, in the novel's concluding scene, Malcolm Ross marries Margaret, resplendent in Tera's robe and jewelry, returning the narrative to the world of dreams with which it began.[77] But each of these representations bleeds into the other and there is no real contrariety between these two versions of the story, for, as Jacqueline Rose has observed in another context, "the ideal-ization and the aggression are the fully interdependent and reverse sides of the same coin."[78]

## "Our enemy is not merely spiritual"

The extremes of optimism and pessimism that are so strikingly played out in *Dracula* and *The Jewel of Seven Stars* are typical of Stoker's own melodramatic imagination, whether this touches on science or Spiritual-ism, masculinity or femininity, politics or art. At one pole we are pre-sented with fantasies of perfect self-control founded upon a movement toward absolute knowledge in which the operation of the human mind is becoming wholly transparent to itself, the best of all possible worlds; while at the other, everything around us may seem so opaque and uncer-tain that the world lies close to ruin. If we are truly free, if we have mastered the effective exercise of the will, then there may ultimately be a happy ending; but if not, if our lives are determined by forces outside our power, then there is always the danger that we will be caught up in processes that could destroy us. Indeed, one might read the two very different conclusions written for *The Jewel of Seven Stars* as exemplifying opposite ends of a single phantasmatic continuum. At the same time, the carefully placed cultural props that support these fantasies are an indica-tion that they are also always fully social: wherever their unconscious moorings may ultimately be found, Stoker's narratives are symptomatic of a more general malaise in the society in which he lived, a malaise that was popularly perceived as hinging upon the future of the British na-tional character. I began this chapter by emphasizing the way in which tests of character lay at the core of Stoker's supernatural romances, and in this final section I want to return to *Dracula* to explore the kind of future that novel envisages for its new heroes and heroines.

In a sense, the antinomies of freedom and determinism which lie at the heart of questions of character have always been deep and abiding philosophical problems within liberalism, which has consistently wished to presuppose "a single, well-ordered will."[79] As I noted in the previous chapter, the classical liberal model of citizenship was predicated upon the exercise of choice, taking the condition of uncoerced self-control as its highest form. But in Britain in the second half of the nineteenth century, and particularly after 1880, the liberal presumption of individual

*Vampires, Mummies, and Liberals*

autonomy came increasingly to be compromised by the ideas and findings arising from the rapid expansion of the natural and social sciences. Notwithstanding their commitment to a philosophy of the will, both John Stuart Mill and W. B. Carpenter, for example, conceded that this faculty might atrophy so badly that it was possible to imagine will-less automata becoming a reality in certain circumstances. And some of the same worries about the cultural as well as the psychic integrity of the self were also reflected in fears of degeneration at the fin-de-siècle. Thus, one can see in the then Liberal MP Charles Masterman's 1909 description of "the city Crowd" as "little blobs of faces borne upon little black twisted or misshapen bodies" the use of tropes of miscegenation to conjure up and hold at bay the specter of an uncontrollable loss of identity "where the traits of individual distinction have become merged in the aggregate."[80] Moreover, the horror of dependency and violation which are being projected here are essentially the obverse of Mill's classic dictum that "over himself, over his own body and mind, the individual is sovereign."[81] Hence the interest of the "New Liberals" (like Masterman) in actively manipulating and controlling the physical and human environment, an interest they shared with the early eugenicists.

As Masterman's meditations on "the heart of empire" suggest, and as both *Dracula* and *The Jewel of Seven Stars* in their various ways confirm, London was increasingly becoming the symbolic place in the late Victorian and Edwardian imaginaries where boundaries threatened to dissolve. The merest glimpse of Count Dracula in Piccadilly with his eyes on "a very beautiful girl" is enough to turn the convalescing Jonathan Harker "pale and dizzy," precipitating a "relapse" (*D*, 207–8). And, in much of the contemporary literature on degeneration, the city was the site of greatest risk to the proper demarcation both between individuals and between the sexes. It comes as no surprise to learn of Stoker's subsequent affinity for the work of the Viennese philosopher Otto Weininger, who claimed that the predominance of feminine qualities in a national culture could be taken as the main index of its degeneracy. For, as I hope to show more clearly in the next chapter, Stoker splits sexuality into a heavily idealized eroticism and a phobic, virtually hysterical vision of indiscriminate mating in which degeneration is already the normal condition for the majority, for whom sex has become a type of scavenging. In the later novels this self-fulfilling and self-perpetuating cycle of degradation tends to serve as a cautionary backdrop to the central narratives of courtship and wedlock, but when in *Dracula* the Count boasts that he already controls the women in the novel and intends to use them as a lure to unman his hapless male opponents, he conjures up a scenario in which the world is rapidly being populated by indifferently subhuman subjects, "my creatures, to do my bidding and to be my jackals when I want to feed" (D, 365). The first priority of Van Helsing and his associates must therefore be a policy of what was soon to be called *negative eugenics:* to "sterilise" every one of the Count's "lairs" (D, 361).

Only truly strong men can rise to such a crisis, and on one level *Dracula* charts the struggle to define and defend a resourceful and steadfast masculinity that could be seen to win the day. Despite the general confidence in the ideal of sporting manliness in the last quarter of the nineteenth century, this view was not without its difficulties and limitations. One of these quandaries is crystallized through the character of Quincey Morris, the American adventurer who plays a large part in running Count Dracula to ground but who tragically loses his life in the final battle. The Texan's strength and fortitude come in for repeated praise throughout the novel, but when Dr. Seward declares that a race of such "fine fellow[s]" as Quincey would guarantee America's future as a world power, the corollary is a troubling one, at least in its implications for Britain's position in the league table of nations in the 1890s (D, 209).[82] Dr. Seward is reminded of this by his patient, the lunatic Renfield, who in an unusually "rational" moment tells Quincey that he looks forward to the day "when the Pole and the Tropics may hold allegiance to the Stars and Stripes" and "the Monroe doctrine takes its true place as a political fable" (D, 291). Transposed onto the plane of social biology, however, the implicit dangers of interimperial rivalry are lifted once Quincey is dead, since he leaves no heir (having previously been rejected as Lucy Westenra's suitor, who in any case has died despite receiving transfusions of this "brave man's blood" (D, 180). Instead, the Texan's lineage is commemoratively transferred to British stock, "re-born" in the person of the Harkers' infant son who is named after "all our little band of men together" but is always called "Quincey" (D, 449). The story therefore concludes on a resounding counter-note: not only is the vampire's threat to hereditary purity vanquished, but the Harkers' marriage becomes a form of hierogamy which subordinates American energy to the triumphs of British breeding.

Though the late Victorian "code of manly honour . . . echoed evangelical motifs, with its call for self-control and self-sacrifice," it typically "sounded more stoic than spiritual."[83] And in *Dracula* the shoring up of masculinity is made possible by the vampire's gradual diminution in which he is secularized and criminalized at one and the same time. Van Helsing is therefore perfectly right to claim that Dracula is an "enemy" who is "not merely spiritual" (D, 297). The vampire emerges from a world of "traditions and superstitions" into "the midst of our scientific, sceptical, matter-of-fact nineteenth century" to provide stark corroboration of its known scientific laws (D, 285). As the scientist credited with the "discovery of the continuous evolution of brain-matter" (D, 292), Van Helsing well understands the predictability of "this criminal of ours," since Dracula's "intellect is small and his action is based on selfishness" (D, 407). It follows that no matter how cunning or physically strong the criminal may be, the forces of law and order will ultimately have the advantage. Similarly, although the swearing of the "solemn compact" to bring Count Dracula down is a first step in refurbishing manly virtue, a symbolic occasion for abjuring all forms of personal weakness, its subsequent association with criminal anthropology shifts the meaning of the ceremony away from a pre-modern oath of allegiance and places it on a more "objective" scientific footing. Just as eugenics was intended as a science of race improvement, so, once rigorously applied, Lombrosian criminology aimed to weed out the morally unfit with scientific precision, initiating a process of regeneration that would "streamline evolution" and "eliminate the unproductive."[84] Thus, in the curiously mixed idiom that is so persistent a feature of the novel, Dracula's heroic alliance also constitutes itself as an administrative body, resembling "a sort of board or committee" (D, 282) which incorporates and directs its members' energies by giving them a new sense of purpose and a new collective identity, yet which retains links with the sober and very unheroic traditions of Victorian public service.[85]

Another unusual feature of the compact is the way in which it positions Mina Harker as the sole woman among "our little band of men," and the emblematic weight this unique status forces her to bear complicates her femininity considerably. When Mina first enters the story she is an assistant schoolmistress "overwhelmed with work" (D, 70), but her nontraditional appearance of independence is quickly offset by the criticisms she gratuitously lodges against "the New Women" writers for their sexual frankness. Once she has become Jonathan's wife she devotes herself full-time to her husband, while acting as a surrogate "mother-figure to all the other characters in the novel." It might therefore seem as if Stoker was attempting "to show that modern women can combine the best of the traditional and the new."[86] However, several factors make Mina extremely hard to place. For example, it is she—rather than the psychiatrist John Seward—who introduces the names of Nordau and Lombroso into Van Helsing's meditations, to the professor's evident delight at the extent of her knowledge. In the ensuing discussion of criminal peculiarities we learn of Dracula's fatal flaw, that "this criminal has not full man-brain," that "he be of child-brain in much" and so, whatever power he may wield over Mina, he is in reality her inferior (*D*, 405–6). The Count is at a considerable disadvantage against "her great brain which is trained like man's brain" (*D*, 404) and, abandoning her in his haste to escape, he fails to see that in her semivampirized state Mina can gain knowledge of his thoughts and thus effectively bring about his downfall.

By putting herself in Van Helsing's hands and asking him to hypnotize her, Mina becomes both patient and double-agent, serving as a kind of conductor between vampire and man. She is then a curiously mobile figure, one minute an emblem of "the mother-spirit" (*D*, 275), the next mischievously teasing Van Helsing about the record of events leading up to Lucy's death, explaining her "little joke" to herself as "some of the taste of the original apple that remains still in our mouths" (*D*, 220). And this instability in her role as heroine reflects a split between her status and her aspirations. For her transition from schoolmistress to transcriber and chronicler of the book's official history is not simply an exchange of teaching for typing: it contains and expresses her aspirations to be a lady journalist, "interviewing and writing descriptions and trying to remember conversations," aspirations which coexist with her desire to be clerically "useful to Jonathan," even before she is fully implicated in the narrative's events (*D*, 70). Rather than seeing Mina's skills solely as an index of the increasing numbers of women teachers and office workers in the lower-middle-class sector of the labor force, it is instructive to link her to the exceptional cases of upwardly mobile ladies whose contradictory response to the suffrage movement gave them a strategic position in late Victorian society.[87] One noteworthy example might be that of the influential journalist Flora Shaw, also an Irish Protestant like Stoker, who was at the center of British imperial politics during this period, rising to the post of colonial editor of *The Times* in 1893 and later becoming the wife of the governor of Nigeria.[88]

Mina needs to be read as more than one version of the feminine, an unmoored sign of change as well as a firm attempt to hold the line against the New Woman. When Van Helsing pronounces her to be one of those "good women" who "tell all their lives, and by day and by hour and by minute, such things that angels can read," he is in a way providing her with a cover story (D, 221). His eulogy deflects attention from Mina's significant break with that model of the Victorian body politic which identified the middle-class man as its head and the middle-class woman as its heart, the "seat of morality and tenderness."[89] But, paradoxically, while Van Helsing ignores Mina's many doubles as a woman, by repeatedly attributing a "man's brain" to her, "a brain that a man should have were he much gifted—and woman's heart," he extends permission for her to double simultaneously as woman *and* as honorary man (D, 281). Though *Dracula* enacts a struggle for the possession of women's bodies and ruthlessly punishes the least hint of precocious female sexuality (in the figure of Lucy Westenra), it is a novel which temporarily recruits a woman into a man's place, arming Mina "like the rest" with "a large-bore revolver" as our heroes move in for the final kill (D, 423). Ironically, it is only by becoming a man that the woman can ever come to deserve parity of esteem or cease to be other than a problem; but one condition of phallic womanhood is that it is almost immediately abandoned for the overfeminized maternal. Quincey Morris *and* Mina are both described as "brave and gallant" figures, but once she has become the mother of Quincey Harker it is Mina's "sweetness and loving care" that define her as a woman for whom men would "dare much," including risking their lives (D, 449).

With everyone armed to the teeth, the campaign against the vampire ends in true imperial style with a paramilitary raid, a search and destroy mission into the heart of Transylvania. Beneath the Gothic wrapping lies a tale of buccaneering, an adventure story to raise the cheer of civilians in which the *unheimlich* terrors of the home are expelled and then quelled on foreign soil. *Dracula* is situated exclusively within the domain of civil society—the household, the private asylum, the countryside, and the open spaces of the city—and its heroes operate directly in and upon these spheres rather than going through official channels. Policemen, for example, are heard but barely seen in the novel, marked only by the flashing of their lanterns and the off-stage sound of their "heavy tramp" (D, 239). But, as highly privatized as this adventure story is, it is intimately connected to the imperialist's dilemma, one which was shortly to be foregrounded as a result of the Boer War. In 1897 Britain was moving into its last brief climactic imperialist phase and the question that faced her was the same one that was jointly posed by *Dracula* and the theories of *dégénérescence*, and insistently echoed by later writers like John Buchan: can an advanced civilization continue to produce the heroes it needs? Or is "a mature society . . . being assailed by diseased and vicious children"?[90]

To his undying credit Count Dracula recognizes this dilemma from the very beginning. Though his family "can boast a record that mushroom growths like the Hapsburgs and the Romanoffs can never reach," he fears that "the warlike days are over" (*D*, 42) and with them "the pride of his house and name" (*D*, 40). What is finally at stake in *Dracula* is the continuing possibility of racial glory, and consequently questions of birth and reproduction are always close at hand. Hence too the extreme ambivalence concerning those of noble birth so typical of Stoker's texts.[91] Arthur Holmwood, the only true aristocrat on the "board or committee" of heroes, is thoroughly bourgeoisified, indistinguishable from the other Victorian clubmen, and does not even accede to a title until halfway through the book (*D*, 282). Even so, with the death of his fiancée he is effectively denied the opportunity to father a child. But it is the mixture of attraction and repulsion provoked by Count Dracula which best exemplifies the unease associated with an aristocratic mien, at times resisting all comprehension. "There is a reason that all things are as they are," says the vampire to the unworldly clerk, "and did you see with my eyes and know with my knowledge, you would perhaps better understand" (*D*, 32).

In the end, through the medium of Mina's unconscious, Dracula's adversaries do learn to see through his eyes, just as, despite the doubts that the vampire has expressed to Harker earlier in the novel, these "city-dwellers" do finally "enter into the feelings of the hunter" (*D*, 29), transforming themselves into vigilantes—a point made more explicitly in Stoker's draft notes for the novel.[92] There Stoker specifically designates these hunter-citizens as a committee of vigilantes, even making veiled references to lynching which recall both the tacit condonation of this gruesome practice in his 1886 lecture *A Glimpse of America* and the apoplectic racist invective of his last novel *The Lair of the White Worm* (1911), one of whose villains ("Oolanga") is described as a "negroid of the lowest type; hideously ugly, with the animal instincts developed as in the lowest brutes; cruel, wanting in all the mental and moral faculties—in fact, so brutal as to be hardly human" (*LWW*, 36).[93] Stoker's work was never quite able to settle with these racial and scientific issues, nor with the closely connected questions of sexual identity, and they flare up in his essays and fiction again and again. In one optimistic flourish "the note of the unity of the Empire" appears to hold everything together as he euphorically describes the special performance at the Lyceum Theatre for the Indian and Colonial troops that was part of the Queen's Diamond Jubilee in June 1897. This great formal gathering "represented every colour and ethnological variety of the human race, from coal black through yellow and brown up to the light type of Anglo-Saxons reared afresh in new realms beyond the seas." As Stoker wrote of the subsequent stage reception for the 1902 coronation at the Lyceum, such a "magnificent sight" could in "type and colour . . . have illustrated a discourse on ethnology, or craniology," harmonized into a sensational imperial tableau with "the great crown and Union Jack seeming to flame over all."[94] Despite its triumphant conclusion, however, *Dracula* paints a very different picture. Coinciding almost to the month with the Diamond Jubilee, its publication in May 1897 offered a kind of shadow-text to this extraordinary moment of public rejoicing. For at a time when "imperialism" was "in the air" and "all classes drunk with sightseeing and hysterical loyalty," Stoker revealed a more deadly hysteria about race and selfhood at the heart of national spectacle and jingoistic camaraderie, the shape of things to come.[95]

# 3 *Sexualitas Aeternitatis*

I was still lying in bed, and you told me the case history of the woman who had dreams of gigantic snakes. At the time you were quite impressed by the idea that undercurrents in a woman might stem from the masculine part of her psyche. *Wilhelm Fliess to Sigmund Freud*[1]

 Toward the summer of 1906, "one began to hear in the men's clubs of England and in the cafés of France and Germany . . . singular mutterings amongst men." The author is Ford Madox Ford and the muttering men were "serious, improving, ethical, advanced, careless about dress and without exception Young Liberals." Thinking back to a particular night in London, Ford recalled how "extraordinarily angry" one table of such men had become when the conversation turned to the growing militancy of the suffragette movement whose members had recently had the effrontery and "bad manners" to interrupt a speech by the Liberal prime minister, Sir Henry Campbell-Bannerman, at the Albert Hall. But in another moment their anger subsided, for "suddenly all their voices sank low together. I really thought that for the first and last time someone of that circle was going to relate an indecent anecdote. But that would have been impossible. No! They were talking about Weininger." Everyone, it seemed, had been reading Otto Weininger's *Sex and Character*, a book which claimed to prove "that women were inferior animals" and sought to deprive feminism of its legitimacy at a single scientific stroke. Now Liberals no longer needed to worry about the Woman Question. "They were able then and there to throw women over and that was an immense gain for the Party," freeing it to make common antifeminist cause with "the bagman, the music-hall singers and all those unthinking and jovial people who make up the man in the street." As his companions unburdened themselves, Ford noticed the "curious" blend of emotions they expressed, "a mixture of relief, of thanksgiving, of chastened jubilations, of regret and obscenity."[2]

Nineteen six was still a relatively early moment in what was to be a new phase of the women's suffrage movement. The Women's Social and Political Union had been founded by Mrs. Emmeline Pankhurst in October 1903, but despite its rallying cry "Votes for Women," this small organization developed its militant tactics very gradually, initially holding back to see whether the new Liberal government would "give us the pledge we wanted," as their more respectable sisters in the Women's Liberal Federation were predicting.[3] Certainly, the relief and jubilation voiced by Ford's Liberal friends were premature. But what his mocking and frankly polemical memoir captures is a sense of the disturbance around sexual difference that was becoming increasingly pronounced in the Edwardian era, a disturbance to which *Sex and Character* so eloquently, yet so bizarrely, spoke. First published in February 1906 "with a considerable flourish of trumpets," the English translation of Weininger's book was reprinted as a "Popular Edition" the following August and went through several impressions over the next four years.[4] Looking back over this period, the novelist and critic David Garnett remembered that "we all had read Weininger."[5]

For many male readers Weininger reassuringly offered old prejudices kitted out as new knowledge. Like other contributions to the fledgling science of human sexuality which acquired the name "sexology" around 1902, Weininger's book took the highly modern view that "sex" pervaded the whole of a person's being, arguing that "the laws of sexual attraction" depended upon the degree of compatibility between different sexual types. At the same time, however, Weininger upheld the considerably more traditional position that conscious thought was an essentially masculine attribute, deeply at odds with woman's fundamentally sexual nature, so that human history was plagued by an irreconcilable, almost Manichean dualism. This contradictory and wildly speculative blend of empirical biology and philosophical idealism had a peculiar resonance in Edwardian Britain, where there was a growing conviction that questions of sexuality and reproduction were central to the creation of a more rational and efficient social order. Just as new scientific developments would guarantee Britain's undiminished industrial and military power, so it was believed that the application of scientific method to the nation's human and social problems would strengthen the British racial stock. By the early 1900s the nineteenth-century public health movement associated with figures like Edwin Chadwick had been transformed into a national medico-moral program of "social hygiene," which brought ideas drawn from eugenics and psychiatric medicine to bear on such social policy issues as child care and family planning. Social hygiene enjoyed widespread support across the political spectrum, uniting an "amorphous mass of right wing Imperialists, Liberals, Socialists and 'concerned' people" who were worried about the decline of the British race, and it had a significant influence on the Liberal government's legislation in the fields of education and mental health (or "mental deficiency") in the years leading up to 1914.[6] When doctors and politicians blamed military setbacks in the Boer War on the poor physique of recent recruits or when churchmen and journalists attacked the new genre of "sex problem novels" for plunging the nation into the depths of immorality, they looked to social hygiene to provide them with alternatives and solutions.

If the British publication of Weininger's book in 1906 reflected an increasing concern with the sexual and biological health of the nation, the fact that *Sex and Character* was brought out in an abridged and bowdlerized translation, even by so bold a publisher as William Heinemann, shows just how much anxiety the topics of sex and sexuality could provoke. In its uneasy deployment of biological and philosophical idioms, Weininger's work is symptomatic of the difficult transition to a new concept of sexuality in which sexual identity ceased to be "exclusively linked to the internal and external genital organs," and was regarded instead as "a matter of impulses, tastes, aptitudes, satisfactions, and psychic traits."[7] By purporting to outline a general theory of sexual difference, *Sex and Character* seemed to show the scientific invincibility of the antifeminist case, and some of Weininger's most caustic passages were devoted to the denunciation of women's suffrage—what the book's publisher later described as the "superficialities" and "lies" of "the modern feminist movement."[8] We might usefully see Weininger's magnum opus as an instance of what the French philosopher of science Georges Canguilhem has called a "scientific ideology," an explanatory system which draws upon the prestige and resources of existing scientific work, yet "stray[s] beyond" these "borrowed norms of scientificity."[9] In Weininger's case, science serves as a license for a fantasy of erotic mastery, allowing the clear-eyed male thinker to escape from the sexual chaos of womanhood through the power of the intellect alone. By defining the terms of an originary sexual difference, Weininger was thought to have traced the ideal man and ideal woman "back to a final source" with "all the penetrating acumen of the trained logician." For the first time, or so it was said, the secrets of womanhood were revealed "by the voice of a man."[10]

Whether or not Bram Stoker was one of the disgruntled Liberals so vividly remembered by Ford Madox Ford, his writings can certainly be placed within the antifeminist backlash of the period, especially what one might call its pseudoscientific wing. And since Weininger was brought to the British public by Stoker's friend and publisher William

*Vampires, Mummies, and Liberals*

Heinemann, it is perhaps hardly surprising that Stoker should have turned to *Sex and Character* for literary inspiration. In Stoker's 1908 novel *Lady Athlyne*, Weininger is approvingly credited with having hit upon the likely "solution to the problem of sex." "Weininger," the omniscient narrator tells us, "was probably right" (*LA*, 82). In this chapter, I want to try to reconstruct "the problem of sex" as it presented itself to Stoker in order to see how it was that a highly selective reading of Weininger could seem to offer a possible answer. In fact, reference to the Austrian philosopher's curious theories is merely one strand in a complex engagement with sexual questions in Stoker's work throughout the decade, an engagement that necessitated some inordinately tortuous narrative strategies as he set out to create a new dominant fiction for the Edwardian era—one that closely paralleled social hygiene's national-political agenda. The robustly normative heterosexuality adumbrated in his twinned romances *The Man* (1905) and *Lady Athlyne* (1908) places him at the inception of a novelistic tradition in which sexuality forms the core of human self-definition. Read historically, Stoker's convoluted sexual politics make him an unlikely precursor to authors as iconoclastic and as radically different as D. H. Lawrence and Radclyffe Hall.

## Serious Sexual Subjects

By the turn of the century a type of writing was beginning to emerge that brought into view a new and newly sexualized subjectivity, a genre that Dugald Williamson has termed "the serious sexual novel." According to Williamson's genealogy, the conditions for this distinctive cultural form stem from a convergence between literary characterization and the presentations of the self that were being developed in the neighboring disciplines of sexual medicine, sexology, and psychology. These disciplines were, of course, among those branches of the human sciences whose findings seemed to call into question the idea of autonomous individuality or character that had been so central to classical liberal thought. By recasting "sexual knowledges into aesthetic terms," the serious sexual novel provided a fantasy-space within which one could measure oneself against the new norms of sexual health and pathology that were busily being disseminated by popular social hygienist pamphlets and manuals. In these novels readers were required "to take seriously situations in which, beginning from a state of immaturity or moral imbalance, certain characters find spiritual regeneration by discovering sexual vitality and harmony."[11] The individual protagonists of such fictions are each imagined as a site of sexual expression and its moral regulation, of identification and control.

In Williamson's account (as in Foucault's *Histoire de la sexualité*), D. H. Lawrence is taken as the chief exemplar of this trend, a move which directs attention away from sexual medicine's formative period and oversimplifies Lawrence's own literary development. By contrast, Stoker's later romances provide a case study in the genesis of modern sexual fiction, allowing us to trace its cultural and political origins, to track the changing and sometimes contradictory relationship between sexual and spiritual regeneration. What gives Stoker's project its distinctive flavor is that his attempted incorporation of a *scientia sexualis* into his fiction always strives to work within a set of taboos or restrictions whose rationality is constantly being put at risk. In his letters and criticism, Stoker held to a didactic theory of literature according to which fiction was "perhaps the most powerful form of teaching available" and an unrivaled vehicle for moral improvement. But while this stolidly moralistic view of the novel chimes with that of Trollope or even Hall Caine, it differs from theirs in its sense of the constant need to protect fiction from its own excesses. Partly because he believed so strongly in the value of the imagination "as a working factor in education," Stoker also recognized that, once activated, the imagination quickly becomes uncontrollable, a force "no one has power to stop," least of all "the individual whose sensoria afford its source." To take up a difficult or controversial topic— and Stoker claimed that there was "no problem which may arise to any human being" that "need be forbidden to public consideration"— necessarily exposed both author and audience to the dangers of corruption. While Stoker's Liberal suspicion of government made him prefer that novelists police themselves, he argued that the general level of literary "decadence" was so "startling" that a "continuous and rigid" state censorship of fiction was more than justified.[12]

In his essay "The Censorship of Fiction" Stoker praised "the excellences of imagination and restraint," but as the language of sexual medicine began to expand, the balance between these two virtues became ever more delicate. There is a peculiarly involuted reciprocity between desire and convention in Stoker's Edwardian fiction which often produces episodes marked by a kind of sexual brinkmanship. Provisionally, these episodes might be said to court the faint breath of scandal in order to

*Vampires, Mummies, and Liberals*

stage the fantasy of impropriety turned to good account. In Stoker's quasi-supernatural adventure story *The Mystery of the Sea* (1902), for example, the hero and heroine, Archibald Hunter and Marjory Drake, contract a secret marriage in advance of their "real marriage," ostensibly to avert "anything in the way of scandal" that might result from their being seen together at odd hours as they go in pursuit of hidden treasure (*MS*, 209–11). Yet this subterfuge immediately becomes the pretext for a further intensification of the pleasures of secrecy when Archie persuades Marjory to disguise herself as a man in order to conceal her journey to the church in Carlisle. And this masquerade in turn affords a somewhat different pleasure as the couple explore the mysterious cavern under Archie's house in Scotland shortly after their wedding, when our hero confesses his delight at "the ease and poise of [Marjory's] beautiful figure, fully shown in the man's dress which she had not changed" (*MS*, 224). Here, at least, it seems that in desiring a woman the male subject has to partially constitute her as a man, to pass through the man en route to sexual bliss.[13] Stoker goes to quite unusual lengths in placing his protagonists in compromising situations that will permit a carefully rehearsed eroticism whose exploration and celebration entails a delicious affront to the established codes of ordinary respectability. But what makes these moments of rapture peculiarly satisfying is that they suspend, while never ceasing to invoke, the letter of the law.

It is tempting to see these elaborate scenarios of caves and clandestine ceremonies as a purely private species of fantasy, a hollowing out of narrative space so that illicit desires may be both voiced and hermetically sealed. And clearly these moments in the text would have to be among the touchstones for a fully developed queer reading of Stoker's romances.[14] However, the public staging of these fantasies depends for much of its point on the novel's critical relationship to those traditions of writing in which female and male authors sought to produce a self-consciously feminist literature, work primarily associated with the "New Woman" fiction of the 1890s. Under this loose rubric one finds a variety of styles and positions, ranging from the sexual reverie of George Egerton's "A Cross Line" (1893) to the programmatic futurism of Lady Florence Dixie's *Gloriana, Or the Revolution of 1900* (1890), another novel which has a woman dressing as a man, this time in a very successful effort to conquer the bastions of male power by stealth, entering Eton, Cambridge, the military, and Parliament, one after the other.[15] As even this brief synopsis of *Gloriana* suggests, Stoker's own work often contains striking parallels with the New Woman fiction and, as we'll see, the narratives of books like *The Man* or *Lady Athlyne* owe a great deal to the thought experiments devised by writers like Grant Allen, Iota, or Sarah Grand in order to interrogate the institution of marriage. However, Stoker redeployed their tropes and devices, turning them against the women's movement and pressing home sharply revisionist conclusions. No matter how chivalrous or romantic his literary sentiments were, he seldom missed an opportunity to excoriate the presumption of sexual equality.

Moreover, whereas Stoker's own brand of Liberal politics seems always to have been staunchly antifeminist, his convictions hardened appreciably as the decade wore on. Where *Dracula* pokes dismissive fun at the New Women, *The Lair of the White Worm* (1911) back-handedly sums up Lady Arabella March's monstrous feminine resourcefulness as that of "a woman, with all a woman's wisdom and wit, combined with the heartlessness of a *cocotte* and the want of principle of a suffragette" (*LWW*, 206). The gratuitous connection drawn between women's suffrage and sexual promiscuity is quite deliberate here. In 1908, when he republished a rather grim little tale about a stage carpenter who contrives the "accidental" death of his wife's lover, Stoker underscored the moral of his story by adding a jokingly colloquial allusion to those women who "want to be harlequins as well as columbines" in "these days of suffragettes." Chastened by such lethal rough justice, the errant wife henceforth looks toward her husband "with a sort of respectful adoration."[16] In Stoker's nonfiction too the specter of the militant feminist could sometimes bubble dramatically into consciousness at the least appropriate moments. In an otherwise dry essay devoted to a minute dissection of a 1909 parliamentary report on theater censorship, Stoker's silently mounting exasperation at the document's inadequacies suddenly explodes into angry invective: "This is the logic of the Suffragette, not that of the Statesman."[17]

Despite these views, Stoker's letters show him to have been on good terms with several New Women writers, including George Egerton, Elizabeth Robins, and Grant Allen, the controversial author of *The Woman Who Did* (1895). The case of George Egerton (Mary Chavelita Bright) is particularly interesting since, when critics complained of "erotomania" or "perverted emotion" in "certain notorious recent books," her two volumes of stories and sketches, *Keynotes* (1893) and *Discords* (1894), were as often as not cited by name.[18] Nevertheless, some four years after her initial *succès de scandale*, Stoker was in correspondence with her and evidently commenting favorably on her work.[19] Whatever disagreements there may have been between them, the literary terrain of sexuality that Stoker was subsequently to exploit in *The Man* and *Lady Athlyne* was effectively opened up for him by writers like Egerton. It seems likely that he regarded the New Women novelists as moral and ideological competitors—after all, their works were often openly argumentative— just as he later did the authors of the "sex problem novel," whose books he attacked in his essay "The Censorship of Fiction." What made this competition so fraught, however, was the unmistakable recognition that the conceptual resources for understanding the marks and mainsprings of sexual difference were undergoing a decisive shift. Throughout the varied and variable proliferation of books and periodicals on "woman's emancipation," the production of new sexual identities was always at issue—whether in Guglielmo Ferrero's tendentiously scientist assertion that "the emancipated woman" constituted a "third sex" or in Karl Pearson's equally strident claim that the solution to "the woman's question" would change "the very appearance of the streets," sweeping away "the shopping doll, the anti-social puppet, whose wires (well hidden under the garb of custom and fashion) are really pulled by self-indulgence."[20]

In *The Man* and *Lady Athlyne*, more than in any of his other texts, Stoker is preoccupied with what Freud later termed "the riddle of femininity": what *does* the woman want?[21] Published just three years apart, each of these novels revolves around a breach of social convention, the status of which changes radically as the novel progresses, creating the possibility of a more securely gendered order. But while such changes provide the preconditions for narrative closure, their convoluted and constantly shifting character lend them something of an exploratory quality. For in both novels, what are ultimately accepted as foolish errors of judgment are also metonymically hedged about and menaced by the threat of far more serious transgressions whose probable effect would be to drastically undermine society's moral fabric. It is as if, in advocating a model of natural domesticity, the fear of premarital sex, unwanted pregnancy, ruinous debt, and loss of reputation must simultaneously be kept close and kept at bay. The one is always a pretext for the other. And in each case it is the question of femininity which throws the balance of sexual relationships awry, propelling the plot forward, and disturbing everything it touches.

This predicament is given added urgency by the novels' periodization, which points to the special vulnerability of the British nation-state as it entered the Edwardian years. In *The Man* and *Lady Athlyne*, the characters' personal histories are sutured into the larger chronologies of public life by the impact of the Boer War upon their immediate social world. The South African experience, though passed over quickly, is remembered not as a victorious adventure, but is associated here with depletion, catastrophe, and death. Both novels dwell on the early defeats inflicted upon the British army, culminating in the notorious "Black Week" of mid-December 1899, which according to one commentator, plunged the country "into such gloom and consternation as had not been within living memory," producing "a state of emotional tension bordering on hysteria."[22] Though it ended in triumph, the war was a difficult moment for the nation, especially for the Liberals whose ranks were badly split by it. "There never was a case which, among Liberals at all events, could have given rise to more cruelly divided emotions," reflected one commentator in 1902.[23] These internal fissures were also deeply gendered, heightening fears of a debased masculinity encouraged by a "coarse patriotism" among some, while, among others, raising the specter of a masculinity found wanting on the imperial battlefield.[24] Liberal opposition to the war had its own gender divisions too, with the Women's Liberal Federation at the forefront of the movement.

The reverberations from the war's initial setbacks serve as a kind of psychic turning point in Stoker's two books, fatefully and irreversibly coloring the cultural and affective landscape inhabited by the main characters, changing their lives forever. In both cases, the conflict exacerbates and brings to a head a crisis of gender that threatens the integrity of the nation. Played in a comparatively minor key, the war in South Africa is nevertheless represented as an instance of what Kaja Silverman has termed "historical trauma," a set of events resulting in a pervasive loss of male self-confidence and calling into question men's place in the symbolic order.[25] Indeed, the sense of shock and dislocation that the early South African military reversals cause in Stoker's novels sometimes sounds uncannily like a distant echo of the feelings of devastation that were later brought about by the First World War, anticipating the Edwardian era's inglorious close.[26]

## "Let her be indeed our son!"

*The Man*, the longer and more complex of the two novels, was published in September 1905 and apparently "did fairly well."[27] *Punch* placed it "among

*Vampires, Mummies, and Liberals*

the best half-dozen novels of the year."[28] The book is a kind of bildungs-roman about a young woman whose unusual upbringing and circum-stances inadvertently turn her into a highly idiosyncratic and peculiarly ideologically laden representative of late-Victorian feminism. In imagin-ing the harm feminism might do, Stoker has his heroine propose her own hand in marriage to a thoroughly worthless, and at first unwilling, young man—the very same scandalous act used by Mina Harker in *Dracula* to anathematize the foibles of "the 'New Woman' writers" (*D*, 111). This uncomfortable episode forms the linchpin of *The Man*, the shameful event so heavily foreshadowed in the first half of the book. The re-mainder of the novel seeks to explain, excuse, and repair this grievous error, while firmly holding it up as an object lesson on the painful consequences of feminine hubris. Like its companion volume, *Lady Ath-lyne*, *The Man* bristles with misunderstandings and misjudgments which need to be cleared away by the growth of true self-knowledge before a happy ending is possible.

As such, *The Man* is clearly a tract, its romantic narrative larded with obsessive moralizing. But to characterize the novel solely in these terms is to rob it of all literary specificity. As I suggested earlier, this is a novel which needs to be related to, even if it does not quite belong among, the exploratory forms of writing associated with the New Woman in fiction. The disastrous offer of marriage in *The Man* both partially repeats and substantially critiques the same act that Angelica Hamilton-Wells takes it upon herself to perform in Sarah Grand's 1893 New Woman bestseller *The Heavenly Twins* ("Marry me, *and let me do as I like.*").[29] Thus, whereas Sarah Grand's aim was to expose the suffering endured by women be-cause of men's sexual double standard and to explore the possibility of alternative and compensatory social and erotic relationships between women and men, Stoker seeks utterly to condemn all such assaults on the established order by ruthlessly deflating the figure of the independent woman.

However, the construction of a dialogic corrective to the New Women, particularly the need to give a convincing account of why a woman might rebel against her status or why a man might be an unwor-thy object of a heroine's love, forces Stoker onto the same ground as his opponents. This seems to have disconcerted at least some of the book's reviewers. One American reviewer complained of its "grandiloquent moralizings—in which the word 'sex' is unpleasantly frequent," a judg-ment which contrasts sharply with *Punch*'s description of *The Man* as "pure in tone."[30] Moreover, the mimicry that is intrinsic to Stoker's polemic against the New Women writers actually commits him to the use of very similar fictional strategies. Thus in *The Man*, as in Sarah Grand's *The Heavenly Twins*, the image of the degenerate male (already paraded in *Dracula*) serves a critical function in securing the novels' preferred romantic outcomes, invariably underscoring a deadly moral lesson. What typically accounts for the convolutions of plot that are so strikingly common to Stoker and the New Women authors is their shared sense of the mutually reinforcing flaws within nature and society, lapses which force the hapless protagonists of their novels to tack back and forth between an unreliable biological destiny and the arbitrary restraints of social convention. Often, these dilemmas are embodied in the story of a troubled childhood, out of which a strangely hybrid creature will emerge. Iota (Kathleen Mannington Caffyn) gave her rather conservative New Woman novel the title *A Yellow Aster* (1894) in order to symbolize its heroine's artificial upbringing, which leaves her torn between the competing demands of her physical and her social selves.[31] And we find the same sort of dilemmas animating *The Man*, though in the latter case they lead to a far more intractable order of complexity. This too is a narrative of hybrids.

By calling his book *The Man* Stoker seems at first sight to be highlighting the sexual disturbance which the novel exploratively raises and tries definitively to remedy. From the beginning of the story manhood appears as an identity that has been dramatically reassigned and reoccupied, so that the book's opening chapters sometimes sound like an ironic announcement of a woman's presumption in trying to be more like a man and sometimes seem to be hinting at a more permanent fix. In the novel's prologue, for instance, the introduction of the heroine is accompanied by an ominous confusion of signs of race and temperament, revealing "a girl" of fourteen whose "remarkable promise of a splendid womanhood" is undermined by portents of "some trouble which might shadow her whole after-life." Her remarkable beauty is of "a rarely composite" sort, mixing "blue-black" eyes with "thick, massive, long and fine" red hair, while her unusually strong character traits of "pride, self-reliance, dominance and masterdom were all marked in every feature." Strangest of all, she bears a man's name, "Miss Stephen Norman," and her riding outfit displays little masculine touches, "the pocket cut man fashion," the scarf "made in the fashion of a man's hunting-stock" (M, 4–5). In this "fore-glimpse" of the "trouble" that is to follow, Stephen and her nineteen-year-old male companion Harold An Wolf eavesdrop on two young village girls who are sitting in an old churchyard arguing the relative merits of whether it would be better to be God rather than being satisfied with the status of a mere angel.

The subtext of this discussion, promptly picked up by Stephen and Harold and placed at the center of their reprise of the girls' argument, is the question of female agency, the capacity to "be able to do things" (*M*, 5). Taking his cue from a remark by one of the village girls, Harold tells Stephen that what radically circumscribes the kinds of actions a woman may perform are deficiencies in her judgment, amounting to an almost complete inability to be just. When Stephen defiantly insists that justice is a necessary part of "a woman's work also," Harold counters that this may sound plausible "theoretically," but in practice it makes no sense. The putative logic of Harold's case resembles that of the most famous early-twentieth-century theory of sexual difference: Freud's account of the constitutive weakness of the feminine superego. For, like Freud, Harold claims that a woman's interests are so intimately bound up in her own domestic sphere that she is emotionally incapable of taking a dispassionate or objective view of those around her.[32] Harold's last word, his final unanswerable riposte, punitively combines Oedipal retribution with a grim allusion to Irish cultural schism: "Do you think that Sheriff of Galway, who in default of a hangman hanged his son with his own hands, would have done so if he had been a woman?" (*M*, 6–7).

Nevertheless, the text continually insists on the real possibility that there may be no essential difference, that Stephen may be, to all intents and purposes, what her name says she is, identical to a man. After all, her mastery and independence of spirit are visible for anyone to see. What remains uncertain is the source of such masculine traits, the extent of their biological or their cultural provenance. This is the question the novel struggles to resolve, shuttling between quite contrary indications as if the problem were too unwieldy to be fully comprehended, a hesitation that sits oddly with the confident ideological stance so often conveyed through the text's omniscient narration. The "Fore-word" to *The Man* which follows the novel's opening tableau describes a "great book of Life" whose individual pages, though each containing "separate matter," are "so connected that the student goes on straightly with his work." But, even here, the seamlessness of this metaphysical metatext can be deceptive, for the careless reader may skim its pages so quickly that he or she may fail to notice that they are divided into "Pleasures" and "Duties," losing sight of the contrast between "the burnished words" and "the black writing" (*M*, 9–10). The gap between the master-text and its various decipherers also defines Stoker's own authorial predicament: how to ensure that the act of reading will cohere, how to pull the narrative patchwork together into an intelligible moral pattern.

At the outset, the novel stresses the primordial power of the natural world, both in the account of the physical endowment inherited by its characters and in the allegorical description of its initial locale. The churchyard that figures in the opening scene exemplifies "the waste and stress of ages," for it is a "place where culture had once set its hand," but where now "the more elemental forces of cosmic beauty had manifested themselves" (*M*, 1–2). As we'll see, this biological frame recurs in different modalities throughout the novel. But it is culture which provides the main script for Stephen's unusual naming and unconventional childhood as the novel tracks back to the circumstances surrounding Stephen's birth, events which estrange her from any hope of ordinary femininity. Stephen's contradictorily sexed and gendered identity is presented as the product of denial and collusion, the adverse effect of her father's painfully ungovernable desire for a son. Squire Stephen Norman, a wealthy English landowner, faced with a break in the continuity of his family line when his only child turns out to be a girl, is completely unable to cope with his overwhelming feelings of disappointment and frustration. So much so that his wife Margaret, who dies only a few hours after her daughter has been born, turns her husband's deepest wish into her last request, entreating him to let the child "be indeed our son!" (*M*, 16) and be christened with the name of the father, "the name of all the Squires of Normanstand for ages—as far back as the records went" (*M*, 12).

It is important to see that neither the denial nor the collusion that makes Stephen Stephen is a unique action. Rather, they are reiterated across the course of Stephen's childhood, effectively overdetermining the tensions besetting her sexual identity. For, if her time-honored patronymic commits Stephen to the place reserved for the absent son, she must also necessarily occupy the position of her no less absent mother. Consequently, the feminine sympathy which made Margaret Norman complicit with her husband's desires is reenacted by Stephen when she strives to be the child her father really wants. Stephen is so solicitous of her lonely father's happiness, so moved by his predicament, that she seems "to lose sight of her own identity" when she is in his presence. Eager to please and comfort him, Stephen "insensibly" becomes more

*Vampires, Mummies, and Liberals*

and more "like a little boy" in her attitudes and behavior, a spoiled only child with very few friends of her own age and status to distract her from the world of adults (*M*, 24–25). Meanwhile, Squire Norman's "resentment of her sex," heightened by his "growing realisation that his child was a woman," fixes in him the demand that "she must from the first be accustomed to boyish as well as girlish ways" (*M*, 20). And if this were not enough, the Squire's attempt to masculinize his daughter is further reinforced by Stephen's Uncle Gilbert, who makes her the heir to his own estate and insists on calling her "Squire."[33]

The formula for Stephen's difficulties seems brutally simple: feminine essence, masculine overlay. And where the heroine's self-alienation is at stake it is hardly surprising to find a finale which hinges on the recovery of the heroine's womanhood. In order to become "all woman," "at one with the grandeur of nature around her," Stephen must accept "the subjugation of self," learning to be "all patient, and all-submissive" in anticipation of the "coming" of her man (*M*, 434–35). As these concluding words suggest, the novel often implies a psychic structure in which an authentic sexual essence conflicts with a false self, perhaps the dominant paradigm for erotic awakening in "the serious sexual novel." From this perspective, *The Man* has unexpectedly close parallels with a number of later and more explicit treatments of sexual liberation. Mutatis mutandis, there are several instructive points of contact between Stoker's novel and Radclyffe Hall's classic lesbian bildungsroman *The Well of Loneliness* (1928), a far more troubled text, the name of whose heroine, Stephen Gordon, even rhymes with that of the earlier Stephen Norman. Here too we find a father's desire for a son resulting in "a caricature," and a daughter whose intrinsic biological destiny is unhappily at odds with her upbringing.[34] If this sounds like a direct inversion of *The Man*, the combination of Stephen Norman's "peculiar training" (*M*, 78) with her "peculiar nature" (*M*, 118) suggests that there may be deeper affinities between the two books than is at first apparent, at least insofar as they are both thoroughly saturated with the new diagnostics of degeneracy and perversion. Yet, whatever lines of convergence unite these novels, I want to argue that to speak of Stephen Norman's latent sexual identity purely as a kind of essence is much more problematic than the similarities with *The Well of Loneliness* would lead us to believe. Instead, despite the novel's own periodic use of the language of essences, it is its unsettled quality, its oscillation between different sexual and psychological paradigms, that makes *The Man* such an extraordinarily indeterminate text.

Stephen's emergent sense of self is driven by a paradox. The more she is emotionally engaged by her father's solitude and loss, the more she feels impelled to take the place of the missing son. In short, the more feminine she is, the more masculine she must become. Her boyishness grows in direct proportion to that strength of feeling for her immediate kin which is supposed to render a woman unjust, to make her unfitted to play the role of the Oedipal father who will slaughter his own offspring if duty so requires. Not surprisingly, then, her attempts to live up to the masculine ideal lead her toward the law and lead her into contradiction. For, on the one hand, her claims to equal access and equal opportunity are based upon the abstract liberal notion of equality before the law, irrespective of such contingencies as gender or class. So, when Stephen convinces herself that there is no reason on earth why she should not offer her hand in marriage to the man of her choice, her rationale is basically a formal and legalistic one. If, she argues, marriage "is in the eye of the law a civil contract," then it follows that "either party should be at liberty to originate the matter" (M, 90). On the other hand, however, the specific cross-gender identification that motivates her claims tends to undercut the cogency of her liberal rhetoric. One early sign that she has begun to take her father at his word is her decision to join Squire Norman when he attends the local Petty Sessions court where he serves as a local magistrate. But her actions cause an outcry, particularly from her Aunt Laetitia, who, voicing the concern of the traditional woman, insists that to sit in court is quite inappropriate to Stephen's class *and* gender, since it involves her listening to "low people speaking of low crimes . . . cases of a kind" that she is "not supposed to know anything about" (M, 83). By literally trying to follow in her father's footsteps, Stephen only succeeds in foregrounding the very difference her male identification seeks to disavow.

When her self-willed entitlement is denied, Stephen vigorously re-sists. She defends her visits to the local rural courts as preparation for her future position in the squirearchy, she redoubles her efforts to win over the object of her affections when he tries to shrug her off, and she decides that she will forgo a university education after a visit to Oxford reveals that the men there look at her only "as a girl," "not as an equal" (M, 78). Rather than become a Somerville girl, Stephen chooses instead to attach herself to the University Mission House, studying its charitable work among the urban poor, the "submerged tenth" in London's East End (M, 88).[35] Her experiences in the metropolitan slums are "bitter" ones and

*Vampires, Mummies, and Liberals*

lead to the most dangerous identification of all. Stephen shocks her aunt by praising those "bad women who seem to know men best, and to be able to influence them most," because "*they* never hesitate to speak their own wishes; to ask for what they want" (*M*, 92). In Stephen's eyes, the worldliness of such women and their disdain for social convention gives them a power that is unfortunately all too rare among their sisters in polite society. By giving utterance to such heresies, Stephen is not only overstepping the established boundaries of morality and class, she is also siding with her social inferiors against her own family and peers in her zeal to prove that men and women can coexist as equals. At the same time, when she returns from London, Stephen also shows "a new gravity," "a new toleration" in which "pity was tempered by reason," displaying exactly that sense of justice which her friend Harold had earlier denied her. Harold himself draws her attention to this surprising change as he becomes aware that she "was beginning to look at things more from a man's point of view than is usually done by, or possible to, women"—without, in the slightest degree, "losing any of her womanhood" (*M*, 88–89).

## Saracens, Vikings, and Crusaders

So, according to one logic of identification, an imaginative leap across gender and class lines can create a new citizen-subject untrammeled by accidents of birth and condition. By achieving this personal and political goal Stephen would become a living proof of liberal feminist egalitarianism, a vindication of her own independently developed "theory of sexual equality" (*M*, 391). But, of course, this is not the novel's last word on the subject, nor is it the first. If we return to the opening scene in the country churchyard, the signs of a counterlogic, immanent in the substance of nature, human and nonhuman, are immediately legible. We are offered another perspective, one in which the struggles between men and women are inseparable from, and ultimately subordinated to, the question of national renewal conceived as a drama of contending racial selves. The state of the graveyard mirrors the state of the nation, evoking a complex temporality in which past, present, and future coexist symbolically. Though the now "decrepit" tombstones tilt and slant "in all directions," there are still at least "a few stately monuments, rising patrician fashion amongst the crowd," in somber contrast to the ancient yew trees, "so worn and broken and wasted with time and storm." But this melancholy scene is already being observed retrospectively from a standpoint in the future which reveals a kind of nostalgia for its prelapsarian innocence. In the narrator's world, "noise" has become "the measure of strife" and "shrieking shell and the fierce crackle of far-extending rifle lines make sport of the puny sounds of angry voices or the bitter silence of tears" (*M*, 1).

The unmistakable reference to the trauma of the Boer War here is confirmed at a later moment in the novel when Stephen inherits an aristocratic title. She is alone: her attempt to initiate a marriage has ended in miserable failure and, through a misunderstanding, she has fallen out with Harold, the one man who truly loves her, and as a result of their estrangement he has quit the country. Since his departure the South African war has begun in earnest and, before three months have passed, "nearly every great house in the kingdom was in mourning," the families of the aristocracy sustaining losses "so numerous that whole entails were changed." The army's well-born officers were slow to see that "the old British system of fighting" had been rendered obsolete by the modern long-range rifle, and when they gallantly led their troops into battle they became easy targets for "a nation of sharpshooters" (*M*, 324).[36] Stephen's good fortune is therefore contingent upon the heavy concentration of casualties among the officer corps. It is an index of the generalized sense of crisis that so strongly permeates Stoker's writing in *The Man* that a woman should take the place not merely of an earl but of the head of a distinguished military family.

This loss or lack is made good in the final, climactic reconciliation between Stephen and Harold, by which point the reader knows that the crisis of succession is rapidly being brought to an end as Harold, having transformed himself into an extremely wealthy man, prepares to take the Lady de Lannoy, as Stephen has now become, for his wife. The years of their tragic estrangement have given them time to undo the error of their ways and when at last they again confront each other they are not only older and wiser, but subjects who have remade themselves. By the novel's closing chapters Harold and Stephen have become model partners locked in a long and intricate pas de deux which gradually brings them closer and closer together as they painfully learn to correct the misperceptions that have kept them apart. The inevitability of their union is seemingly confirmed when Harold is shipwrecked off the northeastern coast, coincidentally close to the de Lannoy estate. Yet the upliftingly heroic rescue scene that ensues provides the occasion for another flurry

*Vampires, Mummies, and Liberals*

of misunderstandings and miscues—partly symbolized by Harold's temporary loss of sight due to his courageous actions in saving the ship. Harold's blindness (or lack, or castration) is reminiscent of that of Mr. Rochester in Brontë's *Jane Eyre* (1847), a text whose conclusion Stoker evokes and revises. For if *Jane Eyre* struggles to arrive at "a final union of relative parity" between hero and heroine, the perfected companionate balance extolled in *The Man* is conditional upon a wholly one-sided suspension of criticism, requiring Stephen to renounce any last vestige of a "militant or even questioning attitude" toward her man (*M*, 400).[37] In her new aristocratic identity as the Lady de Lannoy, and as Harold's future wife, Stephen is forced to acknowledge to herself, "as every true brave woman does," "that she had found her master" (*M*, 421).

What makes the couple such a fine match? Given the moral and psychological rehabilitation that the two star-crossed lovers undergo, the novel might be thought to turn upon the solidly Victorian rhetoric of character building and self-possession, to enact a kind of triumph of the will. And there is much to support this reading. Harold's exemplary acquisition of newly minted imperial and entrepreneurial credentials could be drawn directly from the work of Samuel Smiles, as could the novel's opening references to "the golden pages of Duties" in the "great Book of Life" (*M*, 7–8).[38] What Harold learns in the Alaskan wilderness through a life of "danger and strenuous toil" is the "power of self-control," the Smilesian virtues of "self-reliant manhood" (*M*, 352–55). As a gold prospector, he gains new wealth and a new maturity and his intrepid efforts are further rewarded by the honor of having a frontier city named after him—ironically immortalizing the alias he has been using to cloak his identity. At the same time, however, Harold's rugged individualism is also placed under another, markedly less voluntaristic explanatory schema, one which gives his choices a far more circumscribed role.

On the voyage out to America, Harold finds that the fortitude with which he faces a storm at sea "seemed to come quite naturally to him," that he is "tuned to the war-note of the deeps." As the ship pitches and tosses, his racial history is half-consciously rekindled in him, for the "rough voyages of his forebears amongst northern seas" a thousand years ago "had left traces on his imagination, his blood, his nerves!" Infused with "the old Berserker spirit," Harold momentarily forgets "his sadder self" and begins to glimpse a world of possibilities that his quiet upbringing in a village rectory had concealed from him (*M*, 279–80). Up until this point, the novel has traced a spiral of misrecognition that reached a peak in Stephen's embarrassing proposal to her childhood friend Leonard Everard and the difficult aftermath it provokes. But the Atlantic storm marks a change of course, the turn to a narrative of reparation in which misunderstandings can be cleared away. At the height of the gale Harold gains the undying trust of a six-year-old girl whom he bravely saves from drowning. Her name for him announces that it is Harold, not Stephen, who is the true bearer of the book's title, "The Man" (M, 280). And, once he has arrived in Alaska, his battle against the wilderness's "vast primeval forces" merely reconfirms and amplifies the deeply rooted inner identity of this humble clergyman's son, revealing him to be "essentially a man" with an "adventurer's instinct" (M, 350).

There is a move toward a truncated version of naturalism here, a naturalism whose uneven relationship to the novel's religious sentiment lends the "great Book of Life" a palimpsestic quality in which different discourses can be seen to merge or stand in relief depending upon one's angle of vision. Harold's unceasing "strife against nature" teaches him self-reliance, yet another lesson of his Alaskan interlude is that he too belongs among the "primeval" phenomena upon which civilization is superscribed (M, 345). Threaded into the double helix of misperception that weaves its way through so much of the narrative are indications of a very different economy of forces, less malleable, less yielding to the determination of human will, and considerably complicating the workings of ordinary consciousness. For while the struggle for mastery over the elements serves as the crucible of self-development, the lives of humankind also exemplify and fulfill the regularities and teleologies of the natural world, whether its motions are conceived in terms of spiritual destiny or cosmic law. Hence the vicissitudes of human psychology, such as the tormented mood swings Harold must endure during his self-imposed exile, alternating between amnesic release and "bitter remembrance of the past," are the product of "a scientific law which knows no exception," stipulating that "action and reaction are equal and opposite" (M, 304–5). More significantly still, "the laws of sex"—"as strange as they are strong"—are governed by the selfsame principles, as the earlier dialectic of attraction and repulsion between Stephen and Leonard Everard has so graphically shown (M, 261).

"The process of nature," according to the novel's metacommentary, "is one of shocks" (M, 20). In choosing the wrong man as her desired mate, Stephen is effectively refuting "her own theory" and unwittingly demon-

*Vampires, Mummies, and Liberals*

strating feminism's impasse. It is therefore crucial to the experimental format of *The Man* that she regard her proposal to Leonard, her first truly independent act following the sudden death of her father, as a practical "test" of her ideas (*M*, 109). But Stephen's folly also allows the reader to grasp the full measure of the contrast between two divergent forms of masculinity by giving a scientific exposé of their natural dispositions. As the subsequent clarification of its title suggests, Stoker's book is as much about the meanings of manhood as it is about the position of women themselves. Indeed, one of the important ways in which Leonard and Harold differ is precisely in their attitudes to the opposite sex, for Harold's idealization of women is almost the exact reverse of Leonard's undervaluing of them. Leonard is a young man who prides himself on knowing how to use "the whip with the weaker sex" and habitually looks down on what he has always regarded as women's frailties (*M*, 260). His brutal will-to-power is driven by a "hard, natural, voluptuous, unscrupulous egotism" which is quite indifferent to the feelings or sufferings of others (*M*, 144). By the time Stephen proposes to him, Leonard has turned into an irredeemable ne'er-do-well, constantly in debt, and a philanderer whose cynical lovemaking has already brought about the suicide of a pregnant servant girl.

At first sight, Leonard appears as an attractive, Oxford-educated English gallant: tall, good-looking, blue-eyed, curly-haired, and "clean-skinned, sun-burned with the delicate sun-burning which comes to a skin habitually clean" (*M*, 134). This description reveals Leonard to be a distant cousin to his more subtly ambiguous namesake Everard Barfoot in George Gissing's *The Odd Women* (1893), another tall, brown-haired Etonian with a disreputable sexual history who is also notable for "the warm purity of his skin."[39] In both men an easy, well-groomed presence betrays a less salubrious nature. Thus the phrenological or physiognomic criteria employed by Stoker (and by Gissing) show Leonard to be wholly the creature of his own physicality, a sensualist for whom "animal instinct" or low cunning invariably substitutes for intellect (*M*, 207). If Harold's nature or "race" has resulted in his being "essentially" an adventurer, Leonard's heredity has made him "essentially a voluptuary" (*M*, 264). The passages that depict Leonard in altercation with his father about his debts and dissolute living represent a stylized portrait of that slide into degeneracy which the eugenicist Francis Galton famously termed "regression towards mediocrity" in families of "a poor stock."[40] To be sure, Mr. Everard is of a "higher" type than Leonard, a cold, ungenerous banker who is pitilessly fastidious in his business transactions. But, since the "children of such a man seldom improve on their father," Leonard's rapacious hedonism is merely Mr. Everard's own more austere brand of egotism in degraded form, or what is here dubbed "the voluptuousness of cold natures" (M, 196–97).[41]

Stephen is aware of none of this. In her ignorance, she is prepared neither for Leonard's flippant and ungentlemanly rejection of her love nor his scornful dismissal of her aggressive femininity. The meeting she has engineered in order to broach the question of marriage swings painfully between Leonard's jocular evasions and Stephen's intensified efforts to overcome his blithely disingenuous incomprehension, each parry forcing her into more and more compromising self-revelations. Leonard's blunt rebuffs—"You're too much of a boss for me!"—are accompanied by Stephen's uncontrollable blushes and speechless humiliation, "hiding in her hands her face which fairly seemed to burn" (M, 131–32). When, at last, she cools and becomes aware of her mistake, finally realizing "that she had never really loved him at all," and peremptorily discharging him with all the hauteur "of an empress to a serf," the couple are beginning to change places. Silenced and "outclassed," Leonard no longer regards Stephen as the little "girl whom he had played with," but starts to see her as "a woman," one who had never looked "so attractive" (M, 138–39). From this moment, he has metamorphosed into the ardently opportunistic suitor she cannot accept. Stephen's spirited resistance merely succeeds in rousing "the natural man" in Leonard, that side of him which "is fierce in his moments of sexual recognition, and strong, and assertive, and dominant, and merciless." Indeed, "with every moment of denial, his desire towards Stephen grew more and more," inducing in him "something like the intoxication of sex" (M, 261–62).

Perhaps the greatest difficulty for the project of reimagining wholesome relations between men and women in *The Man* lies in the slippages and ambiguities surrounding the meanings of "sex" and the "natural" self, a problem which continued to preoccupy Stoker in *Lady Athlyne*. As Stephen discovers to her cost, "sex" may come to be "a dominating factor" in one's thoughts, "consciously or unconsciously," precipitating a desperately "feverish condition" (M, 108–10). Before they can live happily ever after, Harold and Stephen have to reach a new understanding of themselves, which means that they each have to realize the truth of their sexual beings. The subtle contextual shifts in how the word *sex* signifies, its slide between the domains of fantasy and instinct, while constantly

*Vampires, Mummies, and Liberals*

straining toward a notion of sexual identity which indefinably suffuses the entire person, are central features of Stoker's discourse in *The Man*, implying a principle of characterological intelligibility which the novel struggles to bring into focus. Despite assertive references to "the laws of sex," it is the enigmatic character of sexuality that is really at issue. In the narrator's generalizing consciousness the "mysteries of sex" hover at the threshold of our knowledge, opaque as yet to "Science," but glimpsed "now and again" by "true-lovers, in their moments of communion, when the desire of each is to unfold to the other the most inmost secrets of their souls" (*M*, 103). So, in the end "Nature" will reign "sweet and simple and true" once "the dross and thought of self" has "passed away," restoring a pristine and timeless harmony to the world, a transcendental "epoch" which "crowns sex," a *sexualitas aeternitatis*, (*M*, 434–35).

The model of sexuality that is being embraced in these and other passages in the novel is at once expressive and naturalistic, recalling the phraseology of a Havelock Ellis or an Edward Carpenter. Contrary to the Smilesian ideal of self-control advanced elsewhere in *The Man*, here "the body rather than the mind is in this matter the parent of thought" and one represses its promptings at one's peril (*M*, 106). With the tragic death of Stephen's father, Harold longs to comfort her and declare his love, but instead he resolves to "put his strongest restraint on himself," ignoring the urgings of his sexual nature and remaining resolutely silent so as to give her "time to choose a mate" on her own. Stubborn in his self-denial, Harold's private "martyrdom" causes him to suffer "the tortures and terrors of the night, the longings and outpourings of heart and soul and mind which seemed to quiver through the darkness out into space." Yet, far from being held up for admiration, it is made painfully clear that Harold's vow of silence is a sign of weakness, "a weakness coming from his want of knowledge of the world of women." What he fails to see is that "love requires a positive expression," that to take the initiative would be to engage Stephen's newly awakened passions, "her growing instincts," "the vague desires of budding womanhood . . . trembling within her" (*M*, 104–6). Unwittingly, Harold's effective recognition of her right to free choice, his reluctance to let his sex speak, his refusal to act masterfully, brings Stephen closer to the point where she will put Leonard's name to her own inchoate yearnings.

But it is in the figure of Stephen that the variegated strands of naturalism and willfulness, race and character intersect, calling each other into question and pressing the different principles of explanation as far as they will go. Appropriately for someone whose mind is usually to be found "running all at once into extremes" (M, 79), Stephen's temperament exhibits many contrary facets, so that at one moment it is her sense of hospitality or etiquette which is "knit in the very fibres of her being" (M, 133), the next, her "raging incessant desire" (M, 340). Her attraction to diametrically opposed men is partly due to the fact that her ancestry mixes elements from both racial types, as well as other, more remote forebears. When we first meet her in the village churchyard, a fourteen-year-old girl in a riding outfit, the racial hybridity that defines her beauty is her most distinctive quality. The "high descent from Saxon through Norman" may be read in the line of her jaw, nose and forehead, and these, especially when combined with her thick red hair which reveals "the blood of another ancient ancestor of Northern race," align her with Harold (M, 3). Yet, despite her noble lineage, Stephen is "essentially an egoist" like Leonard, and her recklessness can also be traced to physical causes (M, 114). Her "purple-black" eyes, "raven eyebrows," and finely curved nostrils indicate that she has "the Eastern blood of the far-back wife of the Crusader" (M, 3).

Though the text assumes a pre-Freudian childhood innocence, this early description already begins to inscribe the core of Stephen's sexuality as a fantasy of imperial and erotic conquest, and it is later playfully linked to her pseudomasculinity when her Uncle Gilbert persuades her to entertain her father by masquerading as a young oriental male with mustache and fez. "Daddy!" she delightedly informs Squire Norman, "your Stephen isn't a girl at all! She is a boy—a man. Look!" (M, 45). When she has grown into a young woman her extraordinary eyes take on a new intensity, containing "something tropical," "something of another land and another time," for in them are preserved "the very eyes of that Saracen maid who had cheerfully left her glowing sunlight for the chilly north to be with her lord" (M, 119–20). Stephen combines the "up-to-date twentieth-century girl" (M, 120) with the exoticism of the odalisque, her graceful movements carrying a charge of sexual danger which always has "Eastern" origins, glimpsed when her black eyes become "fierce with passion and blood-rimmed as a cobra's" (M, 176). Such contrasts indicate a highly mobile and intense sexual nature, sometimes conveyed in a series of shades of red, from her "rich red" hair to "the carmine of her lips and the slumbrous warm pink of her cheeks," a coloring which also suggests the intermingling strains in her blood (M, 120).

Stephen's headstrong actions, her courage as well as her impulsiveness, can readily be interpreted as those of a subject within whom a number of different racial selves have been yoked together. But as we have seen, this is by no means the only possible interpretation of her beliefs and behavior, though it undoubtedly had its place in Stoker's own sexual ethnology. On another level, Stephen's oddly overdetermined character underscores the extremely heterogeneous construction of human agency across the novel. There simply is no single unambiguous model of embodied selfhood whose full presence is compatible with the range of various types of agents who figure in the text. In some instances, a character will appear to be locked into a relatively fixed set of possibilities and to have little option but to act out his or her own biological script. In the case of Leonard Everard, the most glaring example of this kind of determinism, the facts of his hereditary involution are so overwhelming that he is virtually doomed at birth. Indeed, it is a cardinal point of Stoker's use of the codes of physiognomy that the deviant propensities of an adult can be read in the face of a child. Hence, the "seeing eye" can easily discern the "great and inevitable danger" awaiting the "swarthy, large-mouthed, snub-nosed" Susan Mings, the little village girl who wishes she were God, and who will subsequently become the young servant whom Leonard seduces and abandons. Yet, what troubles this bleak diagnosis, and what ultimately haunts the novel, is the overlap, the partial equation between Susan and Stephen, both of them sharing the same dark eyes, the same "stubborn," "impulsive," and "assertive" natures (M, 4–5). Even Susan's misplaced social ambitions, the restlessness that has been induced "by an education beyond her class," hint at parallels with Stephen's "peculiar training" beyond her own gender, so that when Stephen speaks up for those unmarried mothers among the poor whom her aunt categorically condemns, it is Susan that she is unknowingly defending (M, 111).

That Stephen lacks awareness of her position is more than an incidental narrative irony. Notwithstanding her lively, if wayward, intelligence, the novel seems to imply that she is excluded by her youthfulness and, more poignantly, by her gender, from a proper grasp of the temptations and limitations that hedge her path, as if real self-knowledge were almost completely denied her. Before the mirror she can gaze with "a certain sense of triumph" at her own beauty (M, 119), but, without access to the kind of secure judgments available to the omniscient narrator's "seeing eye," her confidence quickly begins "to ooze away" (M, 121). Moreover, it is in the nature of her emergent sexuality that she cannot be fully conscious of the forces that are at work within her as she approaches true womanhood. While Stephen is never less than "the very incarnation of grace," an eroticism permeates her movements, especially during "those languorous moments when voluptuous fancy unconsciously swayed her thoughts, and through her thoughts, her body" (*M*, 107).[42] Yet insofar as this is not only a body with a checkered, racialized history, but also a body commanded by the "primitive strength" of her will, a will which can sometimes fail her, Stephen's womanliness becomes fragmented and ambiguous, moving in unexpected and disturbing directions. Far from her sexuality being an innate disposition into which she matures, Stephen's "sex" is perhaps best understood as the theater within which she enacts multiple and competing desires, the site of an unstable, conflictual, and emphatically modern psychic life.

## Weininger's Sexual Types

Though *The Man* ends happily ever after, secure in Stephen and Harold's blissful union, the riddle of femininity remains. Or, more precisely, two unresolved versions of femininity are proposed by the text, and neither is entirely discounted. On the one hand, the main business of the novel is to overturn Stephen's challenge to the ideology of women's subordination by showing that no good can come of it. Nevertheless, she retains her father's name and position and her conduct receives at least one significant, if carefully conditional, defense from Mr. Stonehouse, the American businessman and father of the little girl whose life Harold saves on the voyage to New York. Upon hearing Harold's story, Stonehouse—one of the many purveyors of fatherly wisdom who turn up so frequently in Stoker's books—warns our hero against his youthful tendency to over-idealize women. What Harold has failed to appreciate is that women "are human beings" with "the same passions, the same faults, the same weaknesses, the same strengths" as men, "the same in all things *except* where the influence of their sex works radical changes of thought and purpose and action" (*M*, 320, my emphasis). The qualification is crucial, taking a sideswipe at precisely the kind of liberal egalitarianism to which feminism appealed. But the scope of Stonehouse's caveat remains uncertain, unelaborated, and indefinably limited—after all, Stephen's own "outrage on convention" is, as her aunt acknowledges, merely "foolish," "nothing which anyone could call wrong" (*M*, 250).[43] Despite his reservations, then, Stonehouse's minimization of the disparities between men and women tends to produce a line of argument that exonerates Stephen.

On the other hand, this partial vindication is more than offset by a considerably less accommodating stance, visible throughout the novel, which insists upon a series of absolute and typically invidious oppositions. Thus, "men are tolerant of ideas," whereas "women are tolerant of persons" (*M*, 134); men are more systematic thinkers than women; women will become caught up in matters of detail; men are much more frank than women; women cannot develop a logical argument with the same skill as a man; "a woman's anger is not always reasonable or well directed, or true in its ultimate purpose" (*M*, 317); it "is part of the nature of all women" to "desire to play with fire" (*M*, 422). The list is hardly exhaustive and there is no necessary consistency between one binary and another. But in each case the alleged difference is held to be intrinsic, "of the very essence of her sex," and closely related to questions of power and authority—a woman is debilitated by not being "cool at a really critical time," for example (*M*, 124). And one female trait has an especially pointed bearing upon the novel's title, since, unlike a man, a woman is said to seek love in the abstract, rather than the love of a specific person: " 'Man,' not 'a man' " (*M*, 106). A woman may therefore be thought to advance toward sexual maturity to the degree to which she willingly submits to the mastery of a particular male.

As a table of gendered differences, *The Man* offers an inventory or catalog of the stock prejudices, the most reactionary opinions, of an era. But, despite specific references to "the laws of sex," the novel fights shy of theory, relegating the "analysis of character by the sexes, each to each" to "a later age" (*M*, 262). Less than a year later, with the English publication of Otto Weininger's *Sex and Character*, the new age had begun. Notwithstanding the many contradictions in his arguments, Weininger's treatise provided a way of rationalizing the kind of the tensions that had plagued *The Man*, while at the same time spurring the language of naturalistic sexuality toward a greater directness and vigor. In attempting to theorize the parameters of human sexuality, Weininger also provided a critique of those trends in the relationships between men and women that he regarded as particularly insidious. It was this aspect of Weininger's work that earned him the gratitude of discontented Liberals like those remembered by Ford Madox Ford. Such men were probably only too happy to overlook Weininger's claim to have demonstrated the moral superiority of state socialism, conceived along suitably masculine lines, as a logical corollary of his antifeminist case.[44] In fact, irrespective of its author's avowedly modern political allegiances, *Sex and Character* actually drew much of its vocabulary from an older and thoroughly romanticized philosophical individualism, whose major propositions it then rewrote in the most lurid of gendered terms.[45] Announcing that he hoped "to place the relations of Sex in a new and decisive light" (p. ix), Weininger produced a curiously potent amalgam of German Idealism and medical science and one of the most bizarrely misogynistic texts ever written. Before considering Weininger's impact upon Stoker, I want briefly to summarize some of *Sex and Character*'s main theses and ideas.

Weininger's study revolves around two poles, bisexuality and genius, which in strange ways both attract and repel. In the first part of the book, devoted to "sexual complexity," Weininger presents a tangle of biological evidence, ranging from embryology to entomology, to show that among most living things a clear separation between males and females cannot be made, since "only the intermediate stages" exist (p. 7). But these composite forms are inherently unstable, so that the sexual identities of human beings fluctuate to a greater or lesser degree ("for instance, many men feel more male at night"), depending upon the conditions in which they find themselves (p. 54). Against this muddling middle, Weininger pits the extremes of sexual development, generating a series of antinomies in the second part of the book which focuses on the elucidation of "sexual types." Indeed, it is when individuals wrestle with their corporeal, sexual being that the highest peak of human achievement is reached. Far from being the result of inherited intelligence or talent, genius represents the triumph of mind over body, of masculinity over femininity, "a conquering of chaos, mystery, and darkness" through "a supreme act of the will" (pp. 183–84). Thus, what distinguishes a great artist or philosopher as a genius is his attainment of a special clarity and comprehensiveness of thought, a universality of consciousness, a transcendental freedom from ordinary finitude through the exercise of complete self-mastery. However, the creative leaps of genius are, at best, fitful, precarious, and historically unpredictable. Not only is it impossible to know when great men will appear among us, but we can never be sure how long the manifestations of their genius will last. Theirs is an elusive, transient form of perfection, and "even the greatest genius is not wholly a genius at every moment of his life" (p. 116). There is a constant danger that the burden of genius will become unendurable, tragically degenerating into madness, where "the ruin is greater in proportion to the success" (p. 184).

*Vampires, Mummies, and Liberals*

By contrast, the female of the species is so immersed in her sexual nature, so continuously "engrossed by sexuality" throughout her life, that she can know nothing of this. Instead, her "only vital interest," her true, base desire is that "sexual unions," whether her own or those of others, shall occur as widely and as frequently as possible (p. 258). The prostitute, "the mother type," the match-maker, or the female voyeur are all only special variants of this "generalised, impersonal instinct" (p. 260). Psychologically, woman's innate preoccupation with what Weininger calls "pairing" means that she conspicuously lacks the willpower which allows men access to the lucid heights of individual genius, and consequently whereas all men have some trace of genius in them, the notion of "a female genius is a contradiction in terms" (p. 189). In a new twist to a now familiar argument, women are denied insight into or distance from their own condition, precisely because they are said to be unable to develop clear, objective ideas or "henids." As one of Weininger's aphorisms "bluntly" puts it: "man possesses sexual organs; her sexual organs possess woman" (p. 92). Other dualisms follow thick and fast. The "male lives consciously, the female lives unconsciously" (p. 102) and therefore she cannot achieve a stable individual ego or self; she lacks a sense of logic or morality, and even a continuous, orderly memory seems an impossibility for a woman. In Weininger's crushingly dismissive summary, "mind cannot be predicated of her at all" (p. 253). And this is, of course, deeply threatening to the masculine ideal. For, given the theory of bisexuality, it must follow that "man contains woman," since "he contains matter." So, a man must choose whether to allow his femininity "to thrive and enervate him" or rather to "recognise and fight against it" (p. 295).[46]

Similarities between many of the cruder contrasts animating Weininger's theory of "sexual types" and the catalog of gendered differences which can be extracted from *The Man* are not hard to find, though there is little in the novel to suggest a concordance on the question of bisexuality or "sexual complexity." Yet it is just this aspect of Weininger's work which is approvingly cited in *Lady Athlyne* as the likely "solution of the problem of sex." In that novel Stoker uses a version of "the laws of sexual attraction" outlined in *Sex and Character* to underwrite the intense physical passion passing, at times like an electric current, between the novel's Irish aristocratic hero Lord Athlyne, "a very masculine person," and the young woman he loves, Joy Ogilvie, an American colonel's daughter "in whom the sex-instinct was very strong" (*LA*, 82). Unlike Weininger, however, Stoker is concerned to celebrate carnal passion, so that the division between the spiritualized male and the hopelessly sensual woman drops out of sight and is effectively replaced by an ideology of natural selection. According to Weininger's laws, the maximum of sexual affinity occurs when partners are drawn together by each one's instinctively matching her or his individual mix of sexuality with that of the other like the torn halves of a letter, a predominantly feminine woman finding the missing portions of her femininity and masculinity in the man and vice versa.[47] But, in Stoker's rendering of Weininger, the latter's stress on "the universal presence of sexually intermediate conditions" as the basis for a wide variety of complementary sexual types lapses into a simple restatement of degeneration theory (pp. 12–13). Though the narrator recognizes a "scale between the highest and the lowest grade of sex," this continuum is resolved into an opposition between "the ideal" man or woman and "the great mass of persons who, having only development of a few of the qualities of sex, are easily satisfied to mate with any one" (LA, 82).[48]

## Red-blooded Passionate Natures

Lady Athlyne offers us the perfect couple, pursuing the signs of their perfection from South Africa to London and from New York to Gretna Green as the impediments to their glorious consummation are gradually peeled away. A kind of comedy of errors, it is the story of Lord Athlyne's protracted wooing of the vivacious Joy Ogilvie, against her proud father's misguidedly hostile wishes. Beyond the novel's contrived confusions of identity and intention, Stoker attempts to supply a more consistent and intensive anatomy of sexual desire than had been possible in The Man, enlarging the sphere of sexuality while remaining securely within the bounds of convention. In scene after scene, the deceits and encumbrances of polite society are set over against a fiercely urgent "natural impulse," only to be delicately guided into relatively "safe channels" and so defused or disarmed (LA, 181). The effect is the buildup of a tension between inner and outer nature, conceived not simply as a split between private selves and public decorums, but as "the whole mechanism and paraphernalia" of an "emotional and speculative psychology" (LA, 171) whose workings are seldom fully available to consciousness, and are sometimes presented as a theological wonder, through "an analogy to the Seen and Unseen worlds" (LA, 249). For, clearly, one of the problems posed by Stoker's sexually explosive brand of naturalism is the need for a moral or philosophical justification which would lend it some measure of respectability. *Lady Athlyne* therefore contains a number of substantial digressions which ransack the popular literature on modern physics to find "the occult root forces"—electrical, magnetic, or protoplasmic—that might dignify and even spiritualize Stoker's account of appetite and desire (*LA*, 112).[49]

Nevertheless, in this intermingling of the languages of sexuality and metaphysics, it is sexuality that ultimately calls the tune. Thus, if "the meeting of the two forces of sex may create a new light," it will be "a light strange to either sex alone" or perhaps a "music . . . which is more potent in the end than the forces of winds or seas" (*LA*, 112–13). In these moments of fusion, mind, soul, and body are joined in a transcendental embrace, yet however elevated the consciousness such unions evoke, it is the nervous body—the "different sets of nerves" commanded by the various "phases" of passion—that is set in motion (*LA*, 111). There is no point, not "even its very highest," at which the love between a woman and a man is "devoid of physical emotion," so that ultimately the embodiment of desire is what matters, the animation of bodies whose mechanical parts are in smooth working order, whose flesh is suffused with the glow of sexual arousal (*LA*, 169). The mechanisms of attraction and response, the physical sensation of rapture, the promise of sexual bliss are all located in bodily functions and processes that primarily operate outside the conscious control of the agents themselves, but which belong to an exemplary natural order. The chapter in which Lord Athlyne begins to feel that he must stop at nothing if he is to win Joy's love is symptomatically entitled "Instinctive Planning" and it traces the course of his desire from a chaotic, tumultuous state of wordless, thoughtless sensations through the gradual mobilization of "all his faculties" (*LA*, 168) to the conscious formulation of a soldierly plan of battle, on the understanding that "a woman's heart is oftener won by assault than by siege" (*LA*, 175). In keeping with Stoker's habitual use of mechanical imagery, the unnamable experience of sexual excitement is displaced onto the thrill of speed as Athlyne whisks Joy away on a clandestine ride through the Lake District in his fine red motor car. Yet, at first, it had scarcely occurred to him "that with such machinery at his command he might try to carry her off, either without her consent or with it" (*LA*, 168).

The unintended outcome of the couple's drive in the country and the novel's central tableau occurs when Joy and Athlyne, who have become temporarily separated after he has been taken into custody by the police for speeding, find themselves quite inadvertently to be sharing the same suite of rooms at a small Scottish hotel, the "Walter Scott." Waking in the morning, both of them in their underwear and lying in "a sort of languorous ecstasy" induced by memories of the previous day, they are suddenly reunited when Joy discovers Athlyne to have been sleeping in the adjoining room (*LA*, 250). They immediately fall into each other's arms, only to be surprised a few moments later by Joy's father, Colonel Ogilvie, who has driven pell-mell across the Scottish border in order to prevent what he suspects is their elopement and so save his daughter from dishonoring the family name. But glimpsing "the bed with clothing in disarray" through the half-opened door to Joy's bedroom, the Colonel at once imagines the real event whose phantasmatic presence hovers around the entire scene, yet which cannot be allowed to happen (*LA*, 258). There can be only one solution: "the old laws of Honour" passed down from father to son in Kentucky require that the Colonel challenge Athlyne to a duel, in order to exact full Oedipal retribution (*LA*, 8).

While these events depend upon a wildly improbable order of coincidences, the artificial character of the obstacles to Athlyne and Joy's union only reaffirms the naturalness of their infatuation with each other. Still, it is important for the moral authority of the novel that some semblance of feasibility be sustained, particularly if the lovers' plight is to be ameliorated. In fact, *Lady Athlyne*'s conclusion is based upon an odd, but historically accurate, legal anachronism. One of the peculiarities of nineteenth-century Scottish matrimonial law, researched by Stoker with his usual zeal, was that a man and a woman could claim full marital status simply by making a declaration in the presence of witnesses or, in some circumstances, a couple's actions or statements could be interpreted retrospectively as evidence that they were de facto husband and wife.[50] Through the use of another of Stoker's avuncular father figures, a local sheriff (or magistrate), as *deus ex machina*, legal chapter and verse are quoted to show that under "our law Mutual Consent constitutes marriage" and, because the couple had sought to disguise their unchaperoned liaison by pretending to the arresting officer that they were husband and wife when he stopped them for speeding, they are now genuinely married (*LA*, 291).[51] Moreover, since it has been made abundantly clear throughout the novel that Athlyne and Joy's romance is a case of love at first sight, the reader knows that their hearts and desires are true. It only remains to question the hotel staff to ascertain that no impropriety has taken place, by proving that Athlyne had arrived long after Joy had retired for the night and was in complete ignorance of her presence. And yet . . . the entire *mise en scène* is framed by a commentary that rationalizes and eulogizes in equal measure, extolling the couple's near-orgasmic potency and holding them out as a model of positive eugenics.

Legally covered, Athlyne and Joy exemplify the peak of heterosexual naturalism as they move through the carefully coded stations of proto-coital intimacy. Though they are only half dressed and have acted in flagrant disregard of Joy's father's commands, they run to embrace without hesitation, forgetting everyone and everything around them and feeling no shame, since shame is, after all, merely "a conventional ordering of the blood" (*LA*, 255). The flimsy and unwitting fig leaf of legality serves a dual function: it simultaneously shields the two lovers from opprobrium by putting them technically within the law, and it also draws attention to the purely sexual nature of their union, to which this paltry quasi-official sanction is entirely irrelevant. Thus begins "the hour of life which is under the guidance of Nature" (*LA*, 256). Taking Adam and Eve as precedent, the narrator suggests that "Dame Nature has her own church and her own ritual," an instance of the same hidden hand of "Cosmic Law" Stoker had described in his 1908 essay on censorship in fiction, "that systematised congeries of natural forces working in harmony to a common end" (*LA*, 254). In a sense, the couple's desire is self-legitimating, and as manifested in their physical energy and vitality it can readily be translated into the vocabulary of moral hygiene. Here are "two young people" who are "both healthy, both red-blooded, both of ardent, passionate nature," "drawn together each to each by all the powers that rule sex and character" (*LA*, 170). The final Weiningerian flourish is, for once, entirely apt. Just as Weininger located the presence of sexuality in every human cell, so Stoker imagines Joy and Athlyne in the full flood of eroticism. As soul calls to soul and sex calls to sex, Athlyne is "lover all over; nothing but lover, with wild desire to be one with her he loved" (*LA*, 181).

In spite of its stilted language and creaky plotting, the sexological substructure of *Lady Athlyne* brings it very close to the sexual epiphanies associated with the modern novel. If we compare Stoker's romance with D. H. Lawrence's early novels which began to be published just three years later, some interesting parallels emerge. In *The Trespasser* (1912), a book almost suppressed by the author on the grounds that it was "pornographic" as well as "bad art," Lawrence writes of "the one long kiss, in which man and woman have one being" and of the soft enticement of the soul "from its bondage."[52] Lawrence's erotic lexicon is notorious for its mediation between "blood" and "soul," later idealized in the call for "a new blood-contact, a new touch, and a new marriage," already anticipated in this, his second novel, as well as in its predecessor, *The White Peacock* (1911).[53] But while it is possible to see the outlines of a future sexual utopia in Lawrence's writing from this period, his sense of the sharp antagonism between the sexes prevents its realization, even though his characters already appear as fully sexual subjects. What finally dooms the two ill-starred lovers in *The Trespasser*, for example, is an incompatibility of sexual character that might almost be read as a partial inversion of the typology of gendered differences proposed by Weininger. In Lawrence's novel it is the woman Helena who rejects "the 'animal' in humanity" and whose "dreams are abstract, and full of fantasy," while Siegmund's dreams are "melted in his blood, and his blood ran bright for her."[54]

In fact, this erotic impasse points toward a more general cultural malaise. As the domain of sexuality underwent rapid expansion, the question of its proper regulation became a pressing concern. The fear of an unregenerate sexuality that inspired the emphasis in social hygiene upon "training" and sex education can also be glimpsed both in the young Lawrence's writing and in the responses of his critics. Though the *Nottinghamshire Guardian* attacked *The Trespasser* for its "philosophy" of "animalism, which is human animalism," the idea of the "animal" is always fraught with difficulty in Lawrence's early work, from *The White Peacock* through to *Women in Love* (1920).[55] In the latter novel, for example, Rupert Birkin is caught in a "violent and directionless reaction between animalism and spiritual truth" which "would go on in him till he tore himself in two between opposite directions, and disappeared meaninglessly out of life."[56] As David Trotter has forcefully argued, one of the ways out of this dilemma involves recognizing that "primitive voluptuousness" is a form of "regression," a species of "collective degeneration" represented by characters like Gudrun and Loerke.[57] Similarly, the degraded virility associated with Leonard Everard's "animal instinct" serves as the moral catalyst for Harold and Stephen's reconciliation in *The Man* (M, 207). And in Stoker's *Lady Athlyne*, the vibrant sexual health enjoyed by Joy and Athlyne also has its abjected counterpart. Athlyne's manliness is positivized in a passage which conjures up the pathetic spectacle of rampant masturbation, the "hundreds, thousands, of half-pulseless boys, flabby of flesh and pallid with enervating dissipation," looking on with their cynical smiles, a description which also shades into post-Wildean stereotypes of the homosexual (*LA*, 176).[58] The self-disqualifying sexual absorption of these effete specimens lacks the one quintessential component of imperial masculinity, that rugged fortitude in adversity that is the making of the true soldier: "grit" (*LA*, 176).

Athlyne is a man so steeled by combat that he automatically thinks of courtship as a military engagement, and the line dividing his roles as lover and fighter is quite deliberately blurred. His prowess on the battlefield at de Hooge's Spruit when his intrepid horsemanship saves a battery of artillery from the enemy is duplicated by his gallant rescue of Joy on her runaway pony in Central Park. Another context in which to place those dissipated youths is, therefore, the agitation around the quality of army recruits, culminating in the Physical Deterioration Report of 1904. While this investigation failed to find any evidence of physical degeneracy, its reiteration of the grim facts of working-class poverty, malnutrition, and disease did little to convince eugenicists like Karl Pearson or Sidney Webb that their views on national racial decline were mistaken.[59] Returning to England immediately after the Boer War, Athlyne finds a country marked by a "full tally of loss; of death and decay." His former companions are now gone, their places taken by unfamiliar faces, and the society circles in which he once moved have become trivial and insular, completely absorbed in the new craze (or "fetish") for playing bridge. Worse, a "new order of 'South African Millionaires' had arisen who by their wealth and extravagance had set at defiance the old order of social caste," altering "the whole scheme of existing values" (*LA*, 53). It is as if the war had been fought in vain, its sacrifice and heroism betrayed at home by an erosion of the trusted certainties of class and status.

Athlyne's lack of either a function or a future is linked precisely to a crisis of reproduction. What especially marginalizes Athlyne is the absence of a marriageable young woman, since all those to whom he had previously been attracted have found husbands for themselves while he was fighting at the front. And so, a distinguished family that can be traced back to twelfth-century Ireland is threatened with extinction. The preferred solution, matrimonial alliance with a rich American family, refers to a practice that became increasingly common in English high society in the years before the First World War, often undertaken purely for financial reasons—though Stoker disingenuously fudges the issue by making his hero an independently wealthy man.[60] Among the British ruling classes this type of exogamy was a controversial matter, but Stoker used it repeatedly to frame a new dominant fiction of sexual difference, a series of myths of national regeneration, underwritten by sexological principles and combined with the residual trappings of a kind of natural religion. The search for a new national hybrid, or an interracial marital diplomacy, consistently figures as a defining characteristic of Stoker's writing, from the cross-class Anglo-Celtic marriage in his very first novel *The Snake's Pass*, through the symbolic naming of the Harkers' son in *Dracula*, to the dynastic union between a Scottish carpetbagger and the peasant queen from the Land of the Blue Mountains in *The Lady of the Shroud* or the marriage between Archibald Hunter and the American Marjory Drake in *The Mystery of the Sea*. And it also occurs in Stoker's last novel, *The Lair of the White Worm*, a truly Weiningerian extravaganza in which Adam Salton and the half-Burmese Mimi Watford join hands against that epitome of decadent English femininity, the green-eyed snake-woman Lady Arabella March.

The regeneration narrative, often paired with a parallel and caution-ary story of degeneracy, was hardly unique to Stoker. It can be found in E. M. Forster's *The Longest Journey* (1907), for example, as well as in Law-rence, and as Stoker knew, some of its most powerful statements, fusing spirituality and eroticism, had come from the New Women novelists he wished to contest. Stoker's own distinctive contribution to what became the serious and self-improving sexual novel lies in his thoroughgoing racialization of the ideal of domestic harmony, a preoccupation with blood mixing and blood intimacy that stalks the pages of his Gothic adventure stories and modern romances alike. At a moment when the relationship between citizenship and civil society seemed to be entering a new period of crisis, and when the proponents of formal liberal rights felt increasingly troubled by the particularities of gender or race or other stubborn "questions of fact," Stoker sought to reimagine the bio-political basis of the nation-state by working through the categories of social hygiene, sexology, and eugenics.[61] Couples like Harold and Ste-phen (part-Viking warrior and part-Saracen maid) or Lord and Lady Athlyne (Anglo-Irish and American) unite distinct national-sexual types in a libidinal bond whose function is to iron out the antagonisms of race and gender and turn these lovers into exemplary citizen-subjects. In the imaginary settlements envisioned in Stoker's Edwardian romances, the

*Vampires, Mummies, and Liberals*

woman must learn to replace the "abstract creation" of "her own unconscious desires" with "a definite individuality," "to accept" the power of
real men, rather than merely idealizing "the Man" (*LA*, 26–27). But in
their most intimate encounters these fictional creatures of flesh and
blood look into each other's eyes only to see the future of the nation.

# *Coda* Travels in Romania—

# Myths of Origin, Myths of Blood

Thus does the régime, in vampire-like fashion, feed off blood spilt in the past, while proceeding to spill fresh blood. *Branka Magas*[1]

 Vampires, according to a recent essay in *Le Monde*, are currently making a big comeback. "With the crisis of rationalist thought," wrote Edgar Reichmann, "Dracula and his rivals are returning in force." Thanks to the retreat in Enlightenment philosophy and the failure of utopian politics ("l'échec des utopies matérialistes") "a certain romanticism" has reappeared and with it all manner of "creatures of the night"—"gnomes, goules, striges et vampires."[2] Reichmann's bestiary has its familiar human counterparts, running from Vlad the Impaler to Nicolae Ceauşescu and ending with references to the Balkan killing fields, so that his article becomes an extension of his own thesis in which real and imaginary monsters are indistinguishable. In spite of its rarefied cultural generalities, Reichmann's staunchly Cartesian perspective is certainly correct in pointing to the vampire's increasingly frequent incursions into political discourse, and I would suggest that it is this feature which provides a bridge between Stoker's work and contemporary vampire myths. Where a nineteenth-century image like "the Irish vampire" was once unusual enough to cause comment, today we find its descendants are well-nigh ubiquitous, invading our quotidian dreamscapes and demonologies at every turn. "Bush and Reagan. Took your money. Drank your blood" was one graffito added to the posters for Francis Ford Coppola's film of *Bram Stoker's Dracula* in the New York subway during the final run-up to the 1992 election.[3]

At the same time, one of the most striking aspects of the current vogue for vampire stories in popular culture has been its enduring fascination with ethnic difference, a preoccupation it shares with the previous fin-de-siècle. Throughout this study I have argued that Stoker's writing was driven by a many-sided bio-politics whose racialized fears and desires preyed upon every aspect of his work from its hesitant nationalist yearnings to its theories of sexual fulfillment. In this coda, however, I want to consider the cultural legacy of Stoker's work in our own era, the parallels and adaptations that return us conceptually to the continuing dilemmas faced by the liberal tradition. For just as the bio-political questions with which Stoker grappled were seen as a stumbling block for the type of liberal individualism he espoused, so today's "tribal" solidarities and interethnic conflicts are often conceived as archaic obsta-cles to the advance of liberal modernity, the terrifying obverse of civility and rational choice. This is because, in liberalism's narrative of progress, human biological and cultural differences have tended to be regarded as ephemeral and inessential modes of variation destined to be superseded by "a single form of life, a universal civilization" in which intractable rivalries and divisions would fade before the spread of humane and rational political principles.[4] But, as Jean Baudrillard has observed, the corollary of this extraordinary faith in the future has been a widening system of exclusions in which "the progress of Humanity and Culture are simply the chain of discriminations with which to brand 'Others' with inhumanity." Those who fall outside "the sign of a universal Reason" find themselves "pushed to the fringes of normality" or consigned to a zone of refractory, but ultimately malleable, entities that includes "inanimate nature, animals and inferior races."[5]

The vampire stands at the threshold between the human and the subhuman and it is entirely appropriate that Dracula and his kind make their mark through their shifting affinities with a variety of nonhuman forms: wolves, lizards, bats, and dogs. "There is much to be learned from beasts," the Count tells Mina Harker, his victim-lover in Coppola's re-cent film adaptation.[6] And there is a lesson here. For while the vampire's peculiarly perverse polymorphousness is the source of its resistance to representation, making it notoriously difficult to pin down—throwing no shadow on the floor, leaving no footprints in the dust, casting no reflection in the mirror—its polymorphous perversity is what allows it to proliferate. Though, in Stoker's imagination at least, Dracula's likeness cannot be captured either by painting or photography, the vampire con-tinues to reproduce itself in a seemingly endless series of copies, always resourcefully different from previous incarnations, often revising the rules of the game in order to secure a new lease on life, without ever finally being laid to rest.[7] This protean durability of the Undead is un-doubtedly what confers true immortality upon them and it is also what qualifies their incessant returns as *myths*, those potent cultural stories we listen to again and again and never tire of retelling. "Love never dies," announced the slogan for Coppola's movie, and because vampires never simply fade away, we need to ask why, to explore the links between myth, representation, and repetition that explain this busy cultural traffic.

Before looking in detail at what is at stake in some of our contemporary vampire narratives, real and unreal, I want to begin by reexamining the concept of myth's usefulness for questions of popular culture. If popular culture is, as Stuart Hall has recently reminded us, "an arena that is *profoundly mythic* . . . a theater of popular desires, a theater of popular fantasies," then one way in which a myth may be defined is as a structure of repetitions, as a story whose essential features are always already known by its audience.[8] Part of the appeal of a novel like *Dracula* lies not only in its spectacular depiction of the return from the dead, but also in its deathlessness *as* narrative, a story that never seems to come to an end, that never quite drops out of circulation.[9] Moreover, this very persistence of myth is echoed by its static or recursive mode of construction, making it tempting to see myth as a virtual negation of history and, more strongly still, as an impediment to social change. So, for example, in the work of Roland Barthes and Claude Lévi-Strauss, two of the most influential analysts of myth, their otherwise divergent accounts concur in seeing myths as "machines for the suppression of time," whose codes are "constituted by the loss of the historical quality of things."[10] Nevertheless, to view this opposition between myth and history as an irreconcilable split would be to overlook their complex interdependence. Myths need to "ripen," Barthes conceded: the extent to which they dehistoricize our grasp of things is really a matter of degree, their largely conservative political function notwithstanding. And Lévi-Strauss, who strongly believes that the recurrence of the same mythic elements over and over again can be traced to universal structures of the human mind, once argued that since most myths clearly do "tell a story, they are in a temporality." What matters, then, is that "this history" is "closed in on itself, locked up by the myth" rather than "left open as a door into the future."[11]

A history "closed in on itself": for a mythic narrative as claustrophobic as *Dracula* with its profusion of locked or sealed interiors—castles, asylums, chapels, mausoleums, coffins—this phrase sounds peculiarly apt. But what history? And how is it secured? A partial answer can be found in a new definition of myth advanced by Jean-Jacques Lecercle which realigns history and myth, using Stoker's novel as one of its key examples. Lecercle follows Barthes and Lévi-Strauss in suggesting that myth should be read as a species of ideology which provides an imaginary solution to real and insoluble contradictions. But, unlike these earlier

*Vampires, Mummies, and Liberals*

writers, he argues that this phantasmatic solution is accomplished not so much by occluding or minimizing history as by drastically altering its form.[12] History is compacted into myth through a kind of chiasmus, a double movement of ideological inscription in which, just as the historical conjuncture is sexualized (or "familiarized"), so conflicts within the family structure are projected out onto the wider public sphere. That is to say, for Lercercle, *Dracula* (like *Frankenstein*) is simultaneously a sort of historical romance and a family romance "au sens freudien," and it is as a mythic fusion of "the personal and the historical that it is able to persist and to feed into new conjunctures."[13]

Schematically, Lecercle argues that *Dracula* belonged to ("il reflétait") a difficult historical moment in which the beginning of Britain's decline was signaled politically by setbacks during the First Boer War (1880–81), economically by the Great Depression between 1873 and 1896, and culturally by a pervasive sense that the high point of the Victorian era was now past and the signs of decadence were plainly visible for anyone to see. These anxieties are condensed in the threat the vampire poses to London, the heart of the empire and center of the civilized world. Yet, at the same time, the novel's topicality is displaced onto an eternal struggle between good and evil, repeatedly embodied in fears of sexual possession through the flagrantly sexualized motivations that give the vampire's actions their bite. In *Dracula* scenes of seduction are just a breath away from rape, and defenselessness is a precondition of pleasure, whether in the vampirization of Victorian children, young women, or eligible bachelors. However dated Stoker's book may appear, the undying appeal of his nosferatu depends upon a confusion of temporalities in which ancient folktales, medieval legends, and modern obsessions may all be instantaneously present, coalescing with horrifying effect. Reaching back through time in order to immure us in a mythological past, *Dracula* appears as the very paradigm of what Lecercle calls a "mythe réactionnaire," a narrative that immobilizes history.[14]

What makes *Dracula* a reactionary myth in Lecercle's eyes is precisely its pull back into the past, "vers l'origine," insisting on the primeval thirst for blood that is imagined always to be lurking just below the civilized surfaces of the psyche and the social fabric. But, as I have suggested throughout this book, the contrast between civility and barbarity takes many forms in Stoker's work, depending upon the kinds of knowledges that are being invoked. Nevertheless, Stoker's various attempts to promote a science of origins invariably place the liberal citizen, the ideal of the rational, fully autonomous agent, on one side of the equation and everything that is excluded by it on the other. One might say that Stoker's project is to settle the question of origins scientifically, to transcend the limitations of a traditional or mythic past by bringing it within the scope of rational comprehension. Stoker's heroes and heroines come to know their own rationality—and even seek to achieve a revitalized sense of reason—through their immersion in a kind of mythical prehistory, an encounter which provides the raw materials for a vigorous counter-myth. To the extent that this counter-myth triumphs over and displaces its primitive substructure, *Dracula* may be a somewhat less reactionary species of myth than Lecercle supposes. Yet insofar as this vision of liberal reason depends upon or is constituted through an excluded other, it inevitably risks becoming ensnared in the logic of its own construction. And Lecercle is surely right to stress the ways in which historical and sexual discourses are inextricably intermingled and intertwined through the endless work of mythic signification.

The complications that arise from the two-way street between history and sexuality so neatly articulated by Lercercle's theoretical definition become clearer when we consider two recent versions of the *Dracula* myth which appeared in 1992: Francis Ford Coppola's film *Bram Stoker's Dracula* and Dan Simmons's novel *Children of the Night*.[15] Each of them invokes the 1897 *Dracula* only to rewrite it by returning to the mythologized history that formed Stoker's original starting point. It is as if the Dracula myth can only be renewed by disinterring more of its folkloric past, an extended movement perfectly captured by the subtitle given to the published script for Coppola's film: *Bram Stoker's Dracula: The Film and the Legend*. As the director observed in one of his postproduction interviews, "You could make a movie on Dracula even without the Stoker, it would still be fascinating."[16] And Dracula-without-Stoker exactly describes Dan Simmons's project—except, as might be expected and as his novel's title duly indicates, shades of Stoker are never very far away.

Paradoxically, while Coppola and scriptwriter James V. Hart expand and enhance *Dracula*'s mythic content, the net result of their innovation is thoroughly to demystify the narrative, reducing the vampire's pure unmotivated evil to rational proportions from the very beginning. In Stoker's story vampirism figured as an unknowable given, a challenge to established scientific modes of thought—"there are always mysteries in life," says the scientist and metaphysician Professor Van Helsing (*D*, 230)—and it is not until fairly late in the novel, when Dracula is finally on the run, that the vampire can be dismissed as a mere criminoloid aberration "of imperfectly formed mind" (*D*, 406). By contrast, not only does Coppola use his opening shots to reveal the historical source of vampirism, by revamping the life of Vlad the Impaler, but the few loose ends and misconceptions that still remain are diegetically dispatched almost as soon as they arise. "The vampire, like any other night creature, can move about by day," Van Helsing helpfully instructs the unenlightened viewer, but "it is not his natural time and his powers are weak." Where the central device of Stoker's novel was the slow accumulation of evidence and testimony as the characters struggled to make sense of experiences that pushed them to the limits of their reason, Coppola's *Dracula* substitutes fast cutting, abrupt transitions, and shifts of style to create a dazzling tangle of scenes and surfaces that tends to conceal the film's underlying narrative order, whose meanings are only overtly spelled out in the omniscient voiceover.

This is perhaps clearer in James Hart's screenplay, which begins and concludes with Van Helsing's offscreen commentary, considerably reduced in the final cut. Fully unpacked, the film's metanarrative most resembles a kind of rational theology, for it reveals the origin of Dracula's condition in the tragic alienation of this fifteenth-century warrior-king from God, following the suicide of his bride who mistakenly believed him to have died in battle defending his church against the "Moslem Turks." It is therefore the vampire's redemption that is at issue here, not his exorcism. At root, Coppola's *Dracula* is a tale of spiritual exile, of an apostate prince who is given a second chance by the reincarnation of his lost princess in a circular story of sacrifice and salvation through undying human love, hinting at "a definite Christ parallel, oddly enough."[17] From a generic point of view, the film's achievement is to transform Gothic horror into religious melodrama; in short, to prefer *The Robe* over *The Fly*, however much our sympathy with the devil may be engaged.

Dracula's erotic power is given a new genealogy, but one which renders him curiously innocent, a monster who has been wronged, a victim without redress. By providing him with a traumatic personal history, Coppola not only romanticizes the vampire, he also sentimentalizes him and, as a corollary to this, effectively removes him from the realm of sexual polymorphousness so insistently evoked by the novel—where, in a strangely prescient moment, the endangered Jonathan Harker complains of "all sorts of queer dreams" (*D*, 10).[18] Dracula's sartorial outrageousness merely adds a camp veneer that is directly proportional to the normalization of his desires, now stabilized inside a firmly heterosexual frame. Indeed, one sign of just how solid the vampire's heterosexuality has become is his adherence to an all-too-conventional double standard, remorselessly pursuing the sexually precocious and "positively indecent" Lucy Westenra with her "free way of speaking," while devotedly and conscientiously withholding his full vampire nature from the straitlaced Mina Harker, who has failed to realize that she is a reincarnation of his former bride. Yet, before his entry onto the streets of London in the romantic guise of a young and somewhat eccentric Continental gentleman, the Dracula who welcomes Mina's fiancé Jonathan to his Transylvanian castle seems to epitomize the sexual and cultural uncanny: an unsettling otherness which is hauntingly familiar, insinuatingly intimate but always somehow deeply foreign.

"The impression I had was that we were leaving the West and entering the East." Jonathan Harker's journal, quoted directly from the 1897 *Dracula*, is superimposed over the lower part of a wide shot of the Orient Express traveling into the sunset and simultaneously added as a voiceover by actor Keanu Reeves. Preceded by a train's-eye shot of the railway tracks emerging from a tunnel in the Carpathians, moving toward a fading red sun, this juxtaposition of colors and images establishes Transylvania as a nightmare land of mists and shadows, unrelievedly nocturnal and ill-lit. Where the foundational Christian narrative prologue suggested a world at once feudal and Byzantine, in which stone crucifixes and religious iconography dominate the visual field, this return to Transylvania radically expands the orientalist elements of the earlier *mise-en-scène* to create an effect of alterity and menace. Dracula becomes a bizarre figure of indeterminate age and sexuality, with high-coiffed Kabuki hair and dressed in a long red silk tunic embossed with golden Chinese dragons and trailed by an enormous cloak "designed to undulate like a sea of blood."[19] And, though the elongated fingers with their sharp pointed nails are staple vampire fare, in this newly orientalized context Dracula's hands and costume conjure up another popular Eastern villain, the ageless Dr. Fu Manchu.

Symptomatically, the film's designer Ishioka Eiko refers to both Dracula's "aura of transsexuality" and "the androgynous quality of his character," confusing these terms as if they were synonymous—but the real point here is that the film provides no basis for telling one from the other.[20] Gary Oldman's performance teasingly alternates between belligerence and camp, his dandyish swishiness of gesture suddenly giving way to the hiss of his sword. However, these nods toward vampiric transgression only serve as a temporary screen and are rapidly resolved into an avowedly heterosexual object choice once Dracula catches sight of Jonathan's pocket daguerreotype of Mina/Elizabeta. As if to underscore this sexual closure, Jonathan's subsequent seduction by the Count's three "brides" becomes an occasion to display the unbridled nature of vampire eroticism which also allows Dracula to answer their reproach against his interference ("you yourself never loved") with the softly introspective reply "Yes—I too can love. And I shall love again." At the same time, by leaning heavily toward orientalist fantasy, this scene reinforces Dracula's identification with the mysterious East, for it is modeled on the conceit that the influence of Turkish culture on Vlad the Impaler, following his youthful days in Istanbul, would have led him to keep a harem. Hence the Turkish cymbals on the soundtrack, the diaphanous gauzy dresses partly copied from Bombay shrouds, and the attempt to cast the "brides" as identifiably "ethnic types."[21]

The sense that sexuality is being produced through race, that the function of racial difference is to key in and give definition to the fear and fascination of sexual excess gains added impetus from the scenes at the country house at Hillingham, which are intercut with the Castle Dracula episodes, providing a chiaroscuro of English daylight and Transylvanian night. Hillingham too is an unmistakably orientalized milieu: from Mina's tightly buttoned high-collared silk tunic, to the turbaned servant who accompanies the arrival of Lucy's suitor "Lord Arthur," to the Byzantine influences on the decor of the conservatory and drawing room, the house and its occupants are steeped in the plush acquisitions of a well-developed imperialist culture. The linchpin of this anxious infatuation with the East occurs in the first scene at Hillingham when Lucy discovers a shocked Mina looking at an erotic illustration to Sir Richard Burton's *Arabian Nights*. Mina's question "Oh, can a man and a woman really do—that?" implies that desire is constituted *as* desire by first being staged as an exotic aberration that needs to be policed. From this perspective, the afflictions of those who have returned from Transylvania— Jonathan's male hysteria and his predecessor Renfield's madness—serve as warnings of cultural contamination, the risks of "going native," especially evident in Renfield's case, for since his return he "is now obsessed with some bloodlust, and with an insatiable hunger for life in any form." He remains confined to an asylum cell throughout the film.

Here the ghostly traces of an earlier Coppola film begin to intrude. As

the script slyly suggests, the journey "through the magnificent Carpa-
thian Mountains" takes "us into the heart of Transylvanian darkness,"
and, if this is so, then Dracula's struggle to defend the West against the
"sensual Orient" has turned him into a kind of Kurtz.[22] At the same time,
we can also begin to see some of the ways in which Coppola's Dracula
blurs into other (post)modern vampire stories, helping to nourish a
different but related type of cultural myth, and one which goes right to
the heart of Dan Simmons's gory Romanian thriller *Children of the Night*.
One of the legendary depictions of horror for our own era can be found
in those popular and journalistic histories of Romania which deploy
Nicolae Ceauşescu as a dead ringer for the vampire himself, "the communist Dracula."[23] According to London's *Sunday Times*, Ceauşescu was "like
a character from a Transylvanian fairy tale": "the demon cobbler" became
"the evil emperor who cast a seductive spell on the Western world while
he violated his own people."[24] Yet such narratives often reveal a certain
ambiguity, an equivocation around the intentionality of evil: "was it the
monster, or was it the swamp?"[25] Thus in his book *The Life and Evil Times of
Nicolae Ceauşescu*, cheek by jowl with folk rumors that Ceauşescu sucked
the blood of infants in order to gain strength, John Sweeney portrays
Romanian political culture as a tight combination of submissiveness and
authoritarianism explained by the country's history of incorporation
into the Ottoman empire, symbolically clinching his argument with the
observation that Turkish style coffee is the preferred drink in Bucharest:
"dark, impossibly sweet and disgustingly gritty."[26] As one critic has
noted, underlying this sort of account is a "concept of 'Europeanness' "
which forms "the dividing line" between the civilized and the primitive, a
racialized separation that is reduplicated throughout the region, pitting Serbs against Croats, Czechs against Slovaks, or Bulgarians against
Pomaks.[27] Small wonder, then, that Jonathan Harker has an acute sense
that Western rationality is slipping away from him as he crosses the
Danube and moves "among the traditions of Turkish rule" (*D,* 9). In his
Transylvanian journal he records his dismay at having "to sit in the carriage for more than an hour before we began to move," complaining "that
the further East you go the more unpunctual are the trains." "What ought
they to be in China?" he asks, not altogether rhetorically (*D,* 10–11).

The amplification and primitivization of difference by local prejudices and sensationalized reportage can also be found in more serious-
minded analyses of East European ethnic politics, and it reaches a peak
in the rival myths of ethnogenesis which stake out official nationalist

claims to particular territories or provinces. Transylvania is a stark example of just such a "contested terrain," the subject of competing histories of autochthonous peoples that also offer models of racial purity and continuity. In the Romanian state myth evidence of indigenous Daco-Roman tribes has been used to assert that Transylvania was "the original homeland of the Romanian people for more than two thousand years," and the rival mythology of a Hungarian Transylvania based upon claims that such ethnic groups as the Szekelys should be recognized as true Hungarians has been hotly disputed.[28]

Moreover, the promulgation of this nationalist myth of origin was closely linked to the Ceauşescu regime's bio-politics, since its programs of community resettlement, ethnic dispersal, and sweeping demolition of the traditional built environment sought to undermine local ways of life that were held to impede the "true" unity of the Romanian people. One fear, for example, was that "the 'pure' Romanian birthrate" was falling behind that of the country's ethnic minorities, putting "the 'special' character of the Romanian genetic pool" at risk.[29] When Ceauşescu took over the leadership of the Romanian Communist Party in 1965 he committed the nation to raising its population from nineteen to thirty million by the year 2000. Since giving birth was designated "a patriotic duty," abortion was banned for women under forty-five and with fewer than five children, monthly pregnancy tests were required of women under thirty as a condition for receiving free state medical or dental care, special taxes were imposed on couples who remained childless after two years of marriage, and, in 1985, contraception was outlawed.[30] Ruthlessly enforced, Ceauşescu's policy had succeeded in raising the Romanian population to twenty-three million by 1977, but the additional strain it placed on ordinary families already suffering considerable economic hardships led to large numbers of dangerous illegal abortions and the dumping of tens of thousands of unwanted and abandoned children into state orphanages. More gruesome still, the archaic practice of giving micro-transfusions of blood to these malnourished orphans in the belief that this would boost their immune systems created an AIDS epidemic resulting from the use of unscreened blood banks and recycled syringes. But the idea that the nation's stock could be in any way polluted was unthinkable within the Romanian myths of racial purity, and until Ceauşescu was deposed in 1989, AIDS officially did not exist. It was a disease belonging only in the non-Communist West.

Since, both at home and abroad, Ceauşescu has popularly been coded as a political monstrosity of vampiric dimensions, preying upon and perpetuating a backward nation, it was but a further twist of the cultural myth to use the enormities of Romanian bio-politics as raw material for a new Transylvanian Gothic. Dan Simmons's *Children of the Night* is a novel that maps the linked crises of AIDS, abandoned children, and Romanian autocracy onto more traditional vampire themes, crossing Bram Stoker with the kind of ultracontemporary post-Communist thriller associated with Martin Cruz Smith. The book posits an inbred vampire strain with a weakness in their immune systems which can only be offset by ingesting human blood, since an inherited retrovirus allows them to rebuild damaged tissue even to the point of "cannibalizing" their own blood cells when "host blood" is inconveniently out of reach.[31] This physiological mutation confers extraordinary powers of recuperation and longevity, releasing the vampire from the phantom space beyond the mirror and turning its thirst for blood into a genetic peculiarity. This peculiarity permits an eternalized Vlad the Impaler to figure as one of the novel's central characters, just as he does in Coppola's film. Historically and scientifically, then, "the myth has its origins in reality" (p. 136). And so "reality" turns out to be another variant of the vampire myth.

As I noted earlier, part of the work that myth performs upon narrative is to make its component actions conform to some timeless design, classically the battle between good and evil, which transcends immediate historical interests and dilemmas. In Coppola's *Dracula* this opposition is mediated by race, using orientalism as a visual repertoire for marking out the exotic and alluring thresholds of transgression. *Children of the Night* shares this use of race as the primary means by which evil is made tangible, but the vampire's distinguishing traits are remarkably unexotic, its ethnic hallmarks "secrecy, solidarity, inbreeding," and a strategic desire to pass unnoticed and unremarked (p. 136). Ethnicity here is unostentatiously clannish and insular, as furtive, conspiratorial, and patriarchal as a Mafia family. Nor is it too far-fetched to see traces of a *Godfather*-type narrative through the Romanian Gothic haze, since the clash between good and evil manifests itself in the book as a battle over the custody of a child, none other than Vlad Dracula's successor. When Kate Neuman, an American doctor—and possibly the first hematologist heroine in the history of the vampire novel—discovers an "abandoned, nameless, helpless" baby boy in a Romanian isolation ward "who responded to transfusions but who soon began wasting away again" from some undiagnosable immune disorder, her decision to adopt him brings her up against the *strigoi*, the legendary vampire caste that has dominated the country for generations (p. 53). Symbolically the stakes are extraordinarily high: for Kate's experimenting with the child's unusual retrovirus offers hope of "a cure for cancer, for AIDS" because of its similarity and resistance to HIV, while, for the *strigoi*, restoring this boy she calls Joshua to the bosom of the clan promises to preserve the original Dracula lineage intact (p. 337). The clinical and genetic rarity of the virus makes this a zero-sum game of survival on both sides. Unlike traditional vampires, the *strigoi* are only able to reproduce themselves infrequently because of the unusual double recessive nature of the virus, and they typically produce normal human offspring. True-born *strigoi* are therefore highly prized and their more commonplace brothers and sisters are treated with contempt and abandoned. This disregard toward ordinary human life is closely related to the *strigoi*'s chronic craving for power and, although they need human blood in order to live, it is their callousness that makes them so wholly pernicious. In the lore that passes among their potential victims Gothic imagery and political rhetoric combine in a single register, feeding on each other like the parasites they name: "these animals bleed my people dry and lead our nation into ruin" (p. 223).

Behind the novel's detailed evocation of a troubled post-Ceauşescu Romania is a view of history as an immense conspiracy stretching back through Communist and Fascist regimes to at least the fifteenth century, depicting "a nation which has never taken a breath outside of totalitarian madness" (p. 336). The *strigoi*'s pure will-to-power has no time for those features which make some systems of rule more tolerable than others, interesting itself in political institutions solely to exploit them for their tactical advantage. In contemporary Romania "we've got the government versus the protestors versus the miners versus the intellectuals, and the *strigoi* seem to be pulling most of the strings on each side" (pp. 301–2). Part of the paranoid logic of conspiracies is that it is impossible to fathom how far they stretch, and in *Children of the Night* this impenetrability is compounded by Vlad the Impaler's own mysteriously elided history. He appears in the novel as an aged and decaying tyrant who has survived for over five centuries, and whose bloodcurdling memories dwell on his younger days, on the uncompromising sadism of his military exploits, which are interspersed throughout the narrative as sinister "dreams of blood and iron," warnings of the terror that may still be to come. This is a figure who despises "Stoker's idiot, opera-cloaked vampire" for having done "nothing but blacken and trivialize the noble name of Dracula," but who confesses to being irresistibly drawn to one of Stoker's own phrases when boasting of his own achievements: "I have bred and led a race of children of the night" (pp. 277–78). The significant addition to Stoker's original phraseology here is the word "race."

Curiously, however, he is first introduced to us in the persona of "the Western billionaire, Mr. Vernor Deacon Trent," a corporate magnate whose transnational commercial operations give his work a global reach and influence, though we never learn how he managed to fabricate this impressive new identity (p. 10). When he and Kate finally meet on the evening before Joshua is to be initiated into the practice of drinking human blood, Vlad tells her that "the vast and varied affairs of the Family" are dispersed across "a hundred-some cities in twenty-some nations" and that he plans to take advantage of the AIDS epidemic to move into the "market for safe transfusions," estimating its worth at over two billion dollars per year. Far from the *strigoi* being mere Eastern European revenants who "keep orphanages stocked for our needs," Vlad makes clear that for his kind "it is not the addiction of blood that is so hard to break," but rather "the addiction to power" (pp. 318–19). In this he is our most ancient contemporary: hypocrite vampire—mon semblable—mon frère.

Despite disclaimers to the contrary, *Children of the Night* does actually parallel "Stoker's abominable, awkwardly written melodrama"—at least, up to a point (p. 277). The expeditionary journey into Transylvania, the vampire invasion of the West (here substituting Boulder, Colorado for imperial London), the kidnapping of babies, the role of contemporary medicine in the power-knowledge standoff against the "Family of Night," the cathartic narrative finale at the Castle Dracula—all recognizably transpose key elements from the original story into a modern idiom. Similarly, at a more episodic level, Kate's desperate climb *up* the walls of the castle to rescue her adopted child at the novel's climax is a neat textual inversion (a mirror image, one might say) of the Count's sinister climb *down* them in one of *Dracula's* opening chapters, a climb also motivated by the pursuit of babies. Yet, in common with Coppola, Simmons's rewriting of Stoker is also heavily rationalized, straining toward a verisimilitude that almost makes too much sense for a tale of "nature's eccentricities and possible impossibilities" (*D*, 231). In the end, Vlad the Impaler is a monster whose aspirations turn out to be entirely rational (or, as he says, "more progressive"), the calculative ambitions of the corporate entrepreneur (p. 319). Conniving at the destruction of the majority of his diseased blood relations, he converts to a newly manufactured "hemoglobin substitute" and plans to return to "the States, or at least the civilized part of Europe." But, perhaps remembering his oriental past, his thoughts also turn East and he contemplates a visit to Japan, "an intriguing place, filled with the energy and business that is the lifeblood I feed on now" (p. 379). Soon he is imagining once more that he might live forever.

In this eerily happy ending one can see what is perhaps the most distinctive feature of the modern vampire myth, at least as currently narrated: the tormented humanization of the nosferatu, which reverses the emphasis on the monstrous in texts like the original *Dracula* and brings them closer to us.[32] Indeed, in Stoker's work the vampire is essentially mysterious and much of the novel's psychological interest stems from the struggle within the victims between their good and demonic selves. Here, however, it is the vampire himself who is torn between conflicting forces, who is looking for a way out. And clinically this turns him into something of a borderline case.

If Simmons and Coppola offer us *Dracula*'s doubles, these are doubles with a difference. Less concerned with containing and destroying the vampire, they pose—often in the vampire's own words—the pressing question of his cure, the remedial treatment that would expel his worst self while still allowing him to remain unmistakably Other.[33] What a cure might mean in such a context is always ambiguous and liminal, sliding uncertainly between moral and medical metaphors. Hence in Coppola's film, the sympathy engendered by Dracula's plight produces a demand that he receive absolution ("give me peace"), that his condition be ameliorated. This is accomplished by Mina Harker in the movie's final frames when she cuts into her lover's heart and then cuts off his head, simultaneously purging herself of her adultery and laying Dracula's soul to rest in a renunciation of her deepest, most contradictory desires. In so doing she is ensuring that her "prince" dies as a human being.[34] Similarly, in *Children of the Night* the *strigoi* baby Joshua, who is physiologically identical to the other members of the "Family," is saved from exposure to the corrupting practice of drinking human blood by Kate's intrepid efforts, a victory that is echoed by Dracula's own more questionable conversion to the virtues of private enterprise. But in each case, the part played by female agency in forcing the narrative to a conclusion should not blind us to the way their own actions restore them to conventional family life as wives and mothers, Mina returning to Jonathan Harker, Kate to a new romance with Mike O'Rourke, the ex-priest who has been her companion in these adventures. After all, when Jonathan Harker announces at the end of the film that "Our work is finished here . . . hers is just begun," he is publicly underlining his wife's duties. In a sense, at least in these two texts, the ambivalence we feel toward the familiar, the homely, and the intimate, an ambivalence which Freud locates at the sexual heart of those fearsome Gothic fictions he calls "the uncanny" (*das Unheimliche*), seems to be dissolving back into the coziness of hearth and home, of kith and kin, even if home is no longer quite what it once was.

I began by drawing attention to the fabled insubstantiality of vampires, but the trouble with these more recent specimens is that they are altogether too real, their reality a little too easily explained. They come to us saturated in a history whose living presence is encoded in the racialized markings they bear, signs which lend these vampires substance, whether as oriental despots or members of ethnic clans. It is precisely this stain of particularity that torments the vampire and that his opponents must evade or disavow if they are to prevail in the struggle against him. Thus Mina Harker's moral imperative compels her upright Victorian persona to slough off her ethnic past, forcing her to part company forever from her reincarnated Romanian forebear, Princess Elizabeta. And in a revealing passage in *Children of the Night*, Kate, escaping with Mike O'Rourke and the vampire child from the ruined Castle Dracula, looks down from a stolen helicopter at the country below and experiences a moment of freedom and relief from the ties of blood and birthright, the glimpse of an escape from the messy contingencies of history: "There was no sense now of national boundaries, or of nations, of the darkness that lay below those clouds" (p. 375). These words recall the "internationalist" expedition against Count Dracula in Coppola's film, with its Dutch scientist, English aristocrat, and American adventurer, in which Stoker's Western imperial alliance is supplemented by Japanese corporate backing and global distribution. So it might seem as if the new myth that is on view holds out the promise of a transcendence of petty historical and ethnic differences, subsuming them into a new liberal cosmopolitanism, a universalistic identity in which everyone can find their place. But before accepting this promise too quickly, it is worth stressing the dangers to which this humanism, its eyes upon the ever-improvable future, is sometimes blind.

In an important essay on racism and nationalism, Etienne Balibar has drawn attention to the way in which "the classical myths of race, in particular the myth of Aryanism" imagine purity or superiority to reside

*Vampires, Mummies, and Liberals*

in a phantasmatic collectivity "which transcends frontiers and is, by definition, transnational." There is, he suggests, "a racist 'international-ism' or 'supranationalism' which tends to idealize timeless or trans-historical communities such as the 'Indo-Europeans,' 'the West,' 'Judaeo-Christian civilization' and therefore communities which are at the same time both closed and open, which have no frontiers or whose only frontiers are . . . inseparable from the individuals themselves or, more precisely, from their 'essence' (what was once called their 'soul')."[35] The ideological operation that chiefly constructs these myths is that of sepa-ration, the sifting of an ideal humanity from the detritus of history, safeguarding it from an animal or tribal or degenerate past. Vlad's con-spiracy to destroy the bulk of his *strigoi* entourage in *Children of the Night* perfectly exemplifies this process of ethnic cleansing, "purifying the Fam-ily of its decadent branches" (p. 378). That this narrative aggression is sexualized through and through, not merely in the virility of its heroes and heroines but in the preoccupation with heredity, interbreeding, and the erotic bestiality of the Other, is entirely in keeping with the racist metatext to which these vampire tales are closely articulated. Hence the profusion of animalistic representations around and within Coppola's vampire, the mark of the beast that must be purged, are of a piece with one of the cornerstones of racist doctrine, the "discovery of which it endlessly rehearses, . . . that of a humanity eternally leaving behind and eternally threatened with falling into the grasp of animality."[36]

Of course this is very much Stoker's own paranoid rhetoric too. For him it is axiomatic that even the most evil white European shows "traces of the softening civilization of ages," whereas the top-hatted African factotum Oolanga in *The Lair of the White Worm* (looking "like a horrible distortion of a gentleman's servant") is without doubt "the lowest and most loathsome of all created things which were in some form ostensibly human . . . in fact, so brutal as to be hardly human" (*LWW*, 35–36). It used to be said that the fantastic tropes of nineteenth-century Gothic fiction were "nothing but the bad conscience" of a "positivist era."[37] If, as Cop-pola's Count Dracula suggests, there really is a lesson "to be learned from beasts," perhaps it is that the compassion for the vampire that many of today's texts elicit has its roots in the bad conscience of a racialized humanism.

At the beginning of this book I began to sketch a picture of Bram Stoker as a writer whose work and public persona were caught in a series of unresolved dilemmas: between Victorian romance and Edwardian modernism; between the discourses of medicine, literature, and the law; between Irish nationalism and metropolitan English liberalism; between a moralizing fin-de-siècle antifeminism and the uneven and exploratory disciplines of sexology and sexual psychology. In each case, Stoker's texts are ambiguously placed in relation to these conflicting currents, clinging to the gentlemanly ideal of good character as they desperately seek to exclude or regulate the very terms that haunt that cherished identity. It is an ideal which goes to the heart of Stoker's liberal politics. For the notion of the rational citizen-subject securely positioned among a community of equals—what Homi Bhabha has called "the homogeneous, horizontal claim of the democratic liberal society"—has too often been predicated on a certain cultural distance, suppressing or explaining away whatever disturbs its serene accomplishments.[38] But in Stoker's imaginative world, a world in which the lines between inner and outer, conscious and unconscious, home and abroad all turn out to be surprisingly thin, the fears and desires of the self-consolidating Anglo-Irish outsider multiply almost as fast as the theories that are advanced to make them seem harmlessly (though sometimes also thrillingly) intelligible. If, in the end, Stoker remained trapped between the hopes of liberal modernity and the racial, sexual, and political forces whose challenges could never quite be accommodated within its ambitious protocols, his predicament contains uncanny echoes of our own as we struggle to imagine a more humane world amidst the wreckage of a once-confident liberal order.

# Notes

## Introduction

1. Quoted in Suzanne Moore, "Flying the Flag of Convenience," *The Guardian*, July 20, 1995, p. 5.
2. Yukio Mishima, *Sun and Steel*, trans. John Bester (1970; New York: Kodansha, 1980), p. 7.
3. See Harry Ludlam, *A Biography of Dracula: The Life Story of Bram Stoker* (1962; reprinted as *A Biography of Bram Stoker, Creator of Dracula*, London: New English Library, 1977); Daniel Farson, *The Man Who Wrote "Dracula": A Biography of Bram Stoker* (London: Michael Joseph, 1975); and Alain Pozzuoli, *Bram Stoker: Prince des Ténèbres* (Paris: Librairie Séguier, 1989).
4. Stoker's self-confessed secretiveness is one of the revelations contained in his February 1872 letter to the American poet Walt Whitman. See *With Walt Whitman in Camden, Vol. 4*, ed. Horace Traubel (Carbondale: Southern Illinois University Press, 1959), p. 183.
5. David J. Skal, *Hollywood Gothic: The Tangled Web of Dracula from Novel to Stage to Screen* (New York: W. W. Norton, 1990), p. 40. In the same sentence in which Skal mentions Stoker's possible "sexless marriage" he refers to another enigma, the mystery behind Stoker's "lodgings," which "on one of his trips to America" as business manager to Sir Henry Irving's touring theater, "he kept oddly separate from those of the Lyceum company."
6. Dan Simmons, *Children of the Night* (New York: Putnam's, 1992), p. 277.
7. Brian W. Aldiss, *Dracula Unbound* (New York: HarperCollins, 1991). The phrase "the ginger man" is, of course, also an affectionate reference to J. P. Donleavy's bawdily picaresque novel from the mid-fifties.
8. See, for example, Joseph S. Bierman, "Dracula: Prolonged Childhood Illness and the Oral Triad," *American Imago* 29, no. 2 (Summer 1972): 186–98, and Seymour Shuster, "Dracula and Surgically Induced Trauma in Children," *British Journal of Medical Psychology* 46, no. 3 (1973): 259–70.
9. See Maurice Hindle's introduction to his edition of *Dracula* (Harmondsworth: Penguin, 1993), p. xvi. For a similar argument, see Nina Auerbach, *Woman and Other Glorified Outcasts* (New York: Columbia University Press, 1985): pp. 269–70.
10. See "Mr. Bram Stoker: A Chat with the Author of 'Dracula,'" *British Weekly*, July 1, 1897, p. 185. For suggestions concerning the links between Stoker's life and work, see Phyllis A. Roth, *Bram Stoker* (Boston: Twayne Publishers, 1982).
11. For this and much more in a similar vein, see Talia Schaffer, "'A Wilde

Desire Took Me': The Homoerotic History of *Dracula*," *ELH* 61 (Summer 1994): 381–425.

12. In his 1872 letter to Whitman, for example, Stoker wrote: "How sweet a thing it is for a strong healthy man with a woman's eyes and a child's wishes to feel that he can speak so to a man who can be if he wishes father, and brother and wife to his soul." *With Walt Whitman in Camden, Vol. 4*, p. 185. On Stoker's reputation as a "womaniser," see Daniel Farson, *The Man Who Wrote "Dracula*," p. 212. Examples of letters to "Uncle Bram" include those written to Stoker in the 1890s by the American actress Ray Rockman and also his correspondence with the artist Pamela Colman Smith (illustrator of *The Lair of the White Worm*). Smith's card to Stoker, Christmas 1903, was inscribed to "Mr Uncle Bram from Pixie Pamela." Brotherton Collection, Leeds University Library. For a cautionary note on the question of queer readings, see Alan Sinfield, *Cultural Politics—Queer Reading* (Philadelphia: University of Pennsylvania Press, 1994), esp. ch. 1; also Joseph Bristow's thoughtful commentary "Post-sexuality? The Wilde Centenary," *Radical Philosophy* 71 (May/June 1995): 2–4.

13. Ken Gelder, *Reading the Vampire* (London: Routledge, 1994), p. 74.

14. Mrs. A. M. Boyd-Carpenter to Bram Stoker, July 11, 1897 (The Deanery, Windsor Castle), Brotherton Collection, Leeds University Library.

15. *The British Weekly*, July 1, 1897, p. 185. The interviewer's question was prompted by "a recent leader on 'Dracula,' published in a provincial newspaper" suggesting "that high moral lessons might be gathered from the book."

16. Stuart Hall, "Cultural Studies and Its Theoretical Legacies," in Lawrence Grossberg, Cary Nelson, and Paula Treichler, eds., *Cultural Studies* (New York: Routledge, 1992), p. 278. Hall's remarks are taken from his address to the April 1990 conference "Cultural Studies Now and in the Future" at the University of Illinois at Urbana-Champaign, whose proceedings reflect many of the disagreements and uncertainties surrounding the occasion, including a healthy skepticism as to the value of cultural studies per se.

17. W. L. Burn, *The Age of Equipoise: A Study of the Mid-Victorian Generation* (London: Allen & Unwin, 1964).

18. Stuart Hall and Bill Schwarz, "State and Society, 1880–1930," in Mary Langan and Bill Schwarz, eds., *Crises in the British State, 1880–1930* (London, Hutchinson, 1985), p. 11.

19. Raymond Williams, *The Long Revolution* (1961; Harmondsworth: Penguin, 1965), p. 86.

20. I owe this term to Manthia Diawara's essay "Canonizing Soundiata in Mande Literature: Toward a Sociology of Narrative Elements," *Social Text* 31/32 (1992): 154–68.

21. Michel Foucault, "Truth and Power," in *Power/Knowledge: Selected Inter-

*views and Other Writings, 1972–1977*, ed. Colin Gordon (Brighton: Harvester, 1980), p. 131.

22. Bram Stoker, application to The Royal Literary Fund, February 22, 1911, Royal Literary Fund, File No. 2841, British Library, London.

23. *The Lair of the White Worm*, originally entitled *Rushing Wings*, manuscript dated February 29, 1911, to June 12, 1911, Fales Library, New York University.

24. See Ludlam, *A Biography of Bram Stoker, Creator of Dracula*, p. 27, and Farson, *The Man Who Wrote "Dracula,"* p. 18.

25. Bram Stoker, *Personal Reminiscences of Henry Irving*, Rev. ed. (London: William Heinemann, 1907; originally published in 1906 in two volumes), p. 303.

26. In his recent survey "Ireland 1850–70: Post-famine and Mid-Victorian," R. V. Comerford notes that both the number of publications and their total sales were increasing significantly in these years. By 1871 twenty-two newspapers were being published at least once a week in Dublin, eight of them daily, and local periodicals were the site of "varied and vibrant literary activity." See his chapter in W. E. Vaughan, ed., *A New History of Ireland, Vol. 5, Ireland under the Union, I: 1801–70* (Oxford: Clarendon Press, 1989), esp. p. 376 and p. 391.

27. Richard Dalby, *Bram Stoker: A Bibliography of First Editions* (London: Dracula Press, 1983), p. 73.

28. Stoker, *Personal Reminiscences*, pp. 8–9.

29. Bram Stoker, *Seven Golden Buttons*, manuscript dated from March 22, 1891, to April 10, 1891, Brotherton Collection, Leeds University Library.

30. Letters from Geneviève Ward to Bram Stoker, June 29, 1875 (Manchester) and July 27, 1875 (Paris), Brotherton Collection, Leeds University Library. See also the letter to Stoker from Miss Ward's mother, Lucie Leigh Ward, September 22, 1875 (Leicester). Geneviève Ward may well be the mysterious "Miss Henry" for whom Stoker claimed to be writing a play at this time, but whose identity he declined to reveal. See Ludlam, *Biography of Dracula*, pp. 42–43.

31. W. H. Kendal to Bram Stoker, March 2, 1908 (London), Brotherton Collection, Leeds University Library. Kendal did express (possibly diplomatic) admiration for the play, and the two men remained on good terms. Stoker sent Kendal a copy of his *Personal Reminiscences* early in November 1909.

32. A variety of readers commented on his manuscripts, including his friend the hugely successful novelist Hall Caine—see, for example, Caine's letter to Stoker, July 12, 1894 (Peel, Isle of Man), in the Fales Library, New York— and the landscape painter David Murray and the artist and cartoonist Bernard Partridge, both of whom he asked to comment on his use of dialect. See David Murray, R.A., to Bram Stoker, July 19, 1894 (Reading), and Bernard Partridge to Stoker, December 4, 1892 (St. John's Wood), Brotherton Collection, Leeds University Library.

33. See James MacArthur, "Books and Bookmen," *Harper's Weekly*, February 20, 1904, p. 276.

34. Bram Stoker to Mr. Ham-Smith of William Heinemann, October 13, 1907 (Burley-in-Wharfedale, Yorkshire), and Bram Stoker to Ham-Smith, January 27, 1909, and to Sydney Pawling, February 3, 1909 (Chelsea, London), Octopus Publishing Group Library, Rushden.

35. Bram Stoker to William Heinemann, February 27, 1906 (Chelsea, London), Octopus Publishing Group Library, Rushden.

36. Jennifer Wicke, "Vampiric Typewriting: *Dracula* and Its Media," *ELH* 59 (summer 1992): 467.

37. See the anonymous review of *Lady Athlyne* entitled "An Irish American Comedy" in *The World's Work* (London) 12 (July 1908): 174.

38. "Mr. Henry Irving's *MacBeth*" (1875), in Henry James, *The Scenic Art: Notes on Acting and the Drama*, ed. Allan Wade (New York: Hill & Wang, 1957), p. 36.

39. For information concerning the Stoker brothers, see Sir William Thornley Stoker's obituary in *The Times*, June 3, 1912. None of the biographies reveal much about Stoker's sisters, Matilda and Margaret, but according to Sir William's obituary, at least one of them married into a medical family, since it is noted that his "younger sister is the widow of Sir William Thomson, of Dublin, who also served in South Africa as Surgeon-in-Chief of the Irish Hospital." There is an entry for Thomas Stoker in the first edition of *Thom's Irish Who's Who* (Dublin: Alexander Thom & Co., 1923), p. 239.

40. See Stoker's *Original Foundation Notes and Data for "Dracula,"* Rosenbach Museum and Library, Philadelphia.

41. Bram Stoker, "The Work of William De Morgan: An Artist, Manufacturer, and Inventor Who Began Writing Novels at the Age of Sixty-Four," *The World's Work* (London) 12 (July 1908): 160–64.

42. John A. Hall, *Liberalism: Politics, Ideology, and the Market* (London: Paladin, 1987), p. 9. See especially ch. 1, "Knowledge and Morality."

43. These notes are written on the back of an envelope addressed to the actor Sir George Alexander, Brotherton Collection, Leeds University Library. In his *Personal Reminiscences* (p. 18) Stoker commends Bright as one of the most moving orators he had ever heard.

44. These men include Stephen Gwynn, Henry Labouchère, the Hon. Harry Lawson, Sir Henry Norman, and Sir Edward Russell. Labouchère, a Liberal MP who supported Irish Home Rule, is most famous for his amendment to the Criminal Law Amendment Act of 1885 which made acts of gross indecency between men punishable by imprisonment. Stoker's contact with him dates back at least to 1890 when he sent Labouchère a copy of *The Snake's Pass*, and it continued into the Edwardian era.

45. Bram Stoker, "The Censorship of Fiction," *The Nineteenth Century* 64 (July–December 1908): 479–87. This essay originated as a much-criticized

talk at the Author's Club on November 18, 1907. See the report in *The Times*, November 19, 1907. It should be added that, like many Liberals, Stoker could sometimes see the individual as vulnerable to group pressure; see his reference to Dean Farrar's phrase "the mysterious sympathy of numbers" in *Personal Reminiscences*, p. 18.

46. For a good introductory survey, see Grenfell Morton, *Home Rule and the Irish Question* (Harlow: Longman, 1980). In his excellent book *The Making of Modern British Politics, 1867–1939* (Oxford: Basil Blackwell, 1982), Martin Pugh argues that Home Rule radicalized the Liberal Party by forcing the secession of the old Whig elements. He notes that "of the 73 Liberal Unionist MPs who survived the 1886 election only 20 were radical supporters of Chamberlain; by 1892 only 11 of the latter remained and several had rejoined the Gladstonians" (p. 35).

47. The idea behind devolution was that a separate legislature would be set up in Dublin to deal with Irish, as opposed to "Imperial," matters. Parnell, the dominant figure in the Irish nationalist movement, was a very critical supporter of Gladstone's plan, but some Liberals like John Bright opposed Home Rule on the grounds that Ireland's problems could be solved by "a wide franchise and a Liberal government," since Ireland was bound to Britain by "ties of family, business and geography." See James L. Sturgis, *John Bright and the Empire* (London: Athlone Press, 1969), p. 186. During the vote on Gladstone's 1886 Home Rule Bill some ninety-three Liberal MPs voted against the government, subsequently forming the basis of a dissident Liberal Unionist faction in the July 1886 election. For Stoker's feelings about Gladstone and Parnell, see *Personal Reminiscences*, pp. 260–63.

48. Not that Stoker's friendships were ever determined purely along political lines, however. The cross-cutting ties among members of the metropolitan elite meant that it was perfectly acceptable for Stoker to have friends among the Conservatives, like Lord Randolph Churchill who sided with the Ulster Loyalists, as well as friends like the managing proprietor of the *Daily Telegraph*, the Hon. Harry Lawson, who had defected to the Liberal Unionists.

49. On Stoker's Irishness, see Farson, p. 232, and Horace Wyndham, *The Nineteen Hundreds* (1922; New York: Thomas Seltzer, 1923), pp. 117–21.

50. However, he sometimes debunks the pseudotraditional aspects of Scottish national life. In his 1894 short story "Crooken Sands," a London merchant buys what he thinks is an authentic dress tartan from an East End Scottish clothing store, to the embarrassment of his family and the ridicule of the local Scots when he wears it on holiday in Aberdeenshire. In a nasty little twist to the tale, "The Scotch All-Wool Tartan Clothing Mart" turns out to be run by two Jewish tailors, one of whom dies in the Scottish quicksands wearing an identical costume. The story was included in Stoker's posthumous collection *Dracula's Guest* (1914).

51. Bram Stoker, "The Great White Fair in Dublin," *The World's Work* (London) 9, Special Irish Number (May 1907): 570–76. A similar spirit animates his companion piece in the same issue, "The World's Greatest Shipbuilding Yard: Impressions of a Visit to Messrs. Harland and Wolff's Shipbuilding Yards at Belfast" (pp. 647–50).

52. See G. R. Searle, *The Quest for National Efficiency: A Study in British Politics and Political Thought, 1899–1914* (Berkeley: University of California Press, 1971).

53. Karl Pearson writing in the *Manchester Guardian* (March 22, 1910), quoted in G. R. Searle, *Eugenics and Politics in Britain, 1900–1914* (Leyden: Noordhoff International Publishing, 1976), p. 69.

54. Bram Stoker, "In the Valley of the Shadow," originally published in *The Grand Magazine* (July 1907) and reprinted in Peter Haining, ed., *Shades of Dracula: Bram Stoker's Uncollected Stories* (London: William Kimber, 1982), pp. 198–204.

55. Jean Laplanche and J.-B. Pontalis, "Fantasy and the Origins of Sexuality," *International Journal of Psycho-Analysis* 49, pt. 1 (1968): 13.

56. Sigmund Freud, "Creative Writers and Day-dreaming" (1908), in Albert Dickson, ed., *The Pelican Freud Library Vol. 14: Art and Literature* (Harmondsworth: Penguin, 1985), pp. 130–41.

57. Steve Neale, "Sexual Difference in Cinema: Issues of Fantasy, Narrative, and the Look," *Oxford Literary Review* 8, nos. 1–2 (1986): 124.

58. Laplanche and Pontalis (1968), p. 13.

59. Sigmund Freud, "Formulations on the Two Principles of Mental Functioning" (1911), Angela Richards, ed., *The Pelican Freud Library Vol. 11: On Metapsychology: The Theory of Psychoanalysis* (Harmondsworth: Penguin, 1984), pp. 31–44.

60. Freud, "Creative Writers and Day-dreaming" (1908), p. 141.

61. Fredric Jameson, *The Seeds of Time* (New York: Columbia University Press, 1994), pp. 74–75.

62. Gilles Deleuze, *Masochism: Coldness and Cruelty*, trans. Jean McNeil (1967; New York: Zone Books, 1991), pp. 71–72.

63. Slavoj Žižek, *Tarrying with the Negative: Kant, Hegel, and the Critique of Ideology* (Durham: Duke University Press, 1993), pp. 89–90.

64. The term "dominant fiction" (adapted from Jacques Rancière) is applied to questions of sexual identity in Kaja Silverman's *Male Subjectivity at the Margins* (New York: Routledge, 1992).

65. Ibid., p. 42.

66. Ibid.

67. Pierre Manent, *An Intellectual History of Liberalism*, trans. Rebecca Balinski (Princeton: Princeton University Press, 1994), p. 116.

68. Stoker sent *Dracula* to Gladstone on May 24, 1897, together with a letter in which he asserted that the novel was designed to "cleanse the mind by pity

& terror" (quoted by Schaffer, p. 424). Gladstone acknowledged receipt of the book three days later, saying that he had begun reading it and felt that Stoker had been "very successful in maintaining the readers [*sic*] interest in the story." W. E. Gladstone to Bram Stoker, May 27, 1897 (Hawarden), Brotherton Collection, Leeds University Library.

69. Early in December 1890, forty-five members of the Irish Party broke with Parnell, leaving their leader with only twenty-seven supporters. Parnell's opponents were led by Justin McCarthy and included William O'Brien, both of them friends of Stoker's. See Paul Bew, *C. S. Parnell* (Dublin: Gill & Macmillan, 1980), pp. 117–18.

70. John Sutherland, *The Stanford Companion to Victorian Fiction* (Stanford: Stanford University Press, 1989), p. 605.

71. Bram Stoker, *Famous Impostors* (New York: Sturgis & Walton, 1910), p. 228.


## 1 *Sexual Ethnology and Irish Nationalism*

1. Dipesh Chakrabarty, "Postcoloniality and the Artifice of History: Who Speaks for 'Indian' Pasts?" *Representations* 37 (Winter 1992): 23.

2. William E. H. Lecky, *Democracy and Liberty*, vol. 1 (1896; Indianapolis: Liberty Classics, 1981), pp. 397 and 404.

3. See *The Compact Edition of the Oxford English Dictionary*, Vol. 1 (Oxford: Oxford University Press, 1971), p. 901.

4. David Lloyd, *Nationalism and Minor Literature: James Clarence Mangan and the Emergence of Irish Cultural Nationalism* (Berkeley: University of California Press, 1987), p. ix.

5. Cf. Charles Taylor's recent claim that "on the human level, one could argue that it is reasonable to suppose that cultures that have provided the horizon of meaning for large numbers of human beings, of diverse characters and temperaments, over a long period of time . . . are almost certain to have something that deserves our admiration and respect." Charles Taylor, *Multiculturalism and "The Politics of Recognition"* (Princeton: Princeton University Press, 1992), pp. 66–67.

6. See E. J. Hobsbawm, *Nations and Nationalism since 1780: Programme, Myth, Reality* (Cambridge: Cambridge University Press, 1990), for an overview of the history of nationalism. However, Hobsbawm argues for a linear two-stage model of this history, which seriously underestimates the early development of cultural nationalism and the importance of "scientific" theories of race throughout the nineteenth century.

7. In Lecky's view, considerations of "imperial strength and unity" or "the stability of European peace" could override claims to national self-

determination. He also stressed that "scarcely any one would apply it to the dealings of civilised nations with savages, or with semi-civilised portions of the globe." *Democracy and Liberty*, vol. 1, pp. 404 and 424.

8.  Thomas Flanagan, "Literature in English, 1801–91," in W. E. Vaughan, ed., *A New History of Ireland*, vol. 5, *Ireland under the Union, I: 1801–70* (Oxford: Clarendon, 1989), p. 495. For a careful statement of some of the problems of interpretation here, see Julian Moynahan, "The Politics of Anglo-Irish Gothic: Maturin, Le Fanu, and 'The Return of the Repressed,'" in Heinz Kosok, ed., *Studies in Anglo-Irish Literature* (Bonn: Bouvier Verlag Herbert Grundmann, 1982), pp. 43–53.

9.  See W. J. McCormack's analysis of J. Sheridan Le Fanu's later novels in "J. Sheridan Le Fanu's 'Richard Marston' (1848): The History of an Anglo-Irish Text," in Francis Barker et al., eds., *1848: The Sociology of Literature* (Colchester: University of Essex, 1978), pp. 107–25.

10.  "Impressions of America," *Daily Telegraph*, December 29, 1885.

11.  "Mr. Bram Stoker: A Chat with the Author of 'Dracula,'" *The British Weekly*, July 1, 1897, p. 185. *The British Weekly* (subtitled "A Journal of Social and Christian Progress") was first published in November 1886 by Hodder and Stoughton and had as one of its chief aims the reunification of the Liberal Party which was split over Irish Home Rule.

12.  Horace Wyndham, *The Nineteen Hundreds* (New York: Thomas Seltzer, 1923), p. 118. For the contrast with Oscar Wilde, particularly Wilde's loss of his Irish accent at Oxford and his determination to be "beyond rather than behind the English," see Richard Ellmann, *Oscar Wilde* (New York: Vintage, 1988), p. 38.

13.  *With Walt Whitman in Camden*, vol. 4, ed. Horace Traubel (Carbondale: Southern Illinois University Press, 1959), pp. 181–85.

14.  As F. S. L. Lyons notes, Dowden actively resisted opening his mind to "the possibility of creating a recognizably Irish literature." He once summed up the "direction of such work as I have done in literature" as "imperial or cosmopolitan," adding "though I think a literature ought to be rooted in the soil, I don't think a conscious effort to promote a provincial spirit tends in that direction." See Lyons, *Culture and Anarchy in Ireland, 1890–1939* (Oxford: Clarendon, 1979), pp. 64–65. Dowden was strongly opposed to the 1886 Home Rule Bill, though he and Stoker seem to have remained on good terms.

15.  Edward Dowden, "The Poetry of Democracy: Walt Whitman," *Westminster Review* (American edition) 96 (July 1871): 17, 22.

16.  See Douglas Grant, *Walt Whitman and His English Admirers* (Leeds: Leeds University Press, 1962). Charles Masterman's appraisal of Whitman appears in chapter 8 ("Literature and Progress") of *The Condition of England* (1909).

17.  Bram Stoker, *Personal Reminiscences of Henry Irving* (1906; New York: Macmillan, 1907), pp. 18–21. John Bright (1811–89) was the son of a Quaker

Rochdale millowner. He first entered Parliament as MP for Durham in 1843, becoming MP for Manchester from 1847 to 1857, when he transferred to Birmingham. A tireless campaigner for electoral reform, Bright served as president of the Board of Trade under Gladstone in 1868. In the same passage Stoker also mentions the oratory of the political and legal reformer Lord Brougham, who was also the first president of the National Association for the Promotion of Social Science in 1856.

18. Patrick Joyce, *Democratic Subjects: The Self and the Social in Nineteenth-Century England* (Cambridge: Cambridge University Press, 1994), p. 169.

19. Ibid., p. 156.

20. Ibid., p. 140.

21. John Bright, *Speeches on Questions of Public Policy*, vol. 1, ed. James E. Thorold Rogers (London: Macmillan, 1868), pp. 363, 367. Bright was opposed to Home Rule, calling instead for "a real and thorough working union for freedom with the people of Great Britain" (p. 385). Nevertheless, "he became a symbol of hope, so much so that the mere mention of his name could be guaranteed to elicit long and appreciative cheering on the part of Irish audiences." See James L. Sturgis, *John Bright and the Empire* (London: Athlone Press, 1969), p. 151. Details of the audience's response to his speech at a grand banquet in the Rotunda are taken from *The Times*, October 31, 1866, p. 12.

22. In commencing his speech to the working men of Dublin, Bright stressed that he "was not in good order for speaking" since he was suffering "from much cold and hoarseness"—in fact, it was for this reason that the meeting was held indoors with, as Stoker reports, many people standing outside in the street. *The Times* correspondent noted that there were "frequent" interruptions "from a very limited portion of the meeting" and that the chairman's "allusion to the Reform Bill of last session was received with considerable laughter, and among the cries from the gallery were 'Fenianism for ever.'" But this putative polarization between a dissident minority and a responsive majority clearly oversimplifies the complex feelings that Bright's visit evoked. For example, although Mr. M'Corry, the mechanic whose remarks prefaced Bright's speech, affirmed that "we cannot fail to discern kindred impulses which demand our sympathy" in "the upheavings of the mighty multitudes pressing onward in England to the goal of their emancipation," he also cautioned that Irish "aspirations inevitably tend to a different destiny, and [aim] at the attainment of a native Legislature, being helpless of any substantial remedy from the London Parliament for the numerous evils springing from misrule under which the land and the artisan alike labour." See "Mr. Bright in Ireland," *The Times*, November 3, 1866, p. 5.

23. See Daniel Farson, *The Man Who Wrote "Dracula": A Biography of Bram Stoker* (London: Michael Joseph, 1975), p. 36.

24. Edward Dowden to Bram Stoker, 3 January 1879 (Rathmines), Brotherton Collection, Leeds University Library.

25. On Stoker's support for Irish Home Rule, see his *Personal Reminiscences*, pp. 218–19, 260–63. Details of his friendship with the Wilde family can be found in Harry Ludlam, *A Biography of Bram Stoker: Creator of Dracula* (1962; London: New English Library, 1977), pp. 35–36.

26. William O'Brien to Bram Stoker, 30 July 1890 (House of Commons, London), Brotherton Collection, Leeds University Library.

27. William O'Brien (1852–1928) had edited *United Ireland* at Parnell's invitation in 1881 but had been imprisoned that same year when the Land League was outlawed. In the wake of the O'Shea divorce scandal in 1890, Parnell tried to persuade O'Brien to take over chairmanship of the Irish party, but the latter refused. O'Brien went on to dissociate himself from Parnell and to found the United Irish League in 1898. For further details of O'Brien's political career, see Joseph V. O'Brien, *William O'Brien and the Course of Irish Politics, 1881–1918* (Berkeley: University of California Press, 1976). A useful short discussion of the novel can be found in Robert Lee Wolff's introduction to the 1979 reprint; see William O'Brien, *When We Were Boys* (1890; New York: Garland Publishing, 1979).

28. See the letters to Stoker from L. F. Austin, 24 March 1891 (London), and Tighe Hopkins, 1 April 1891 (London), Brotherton Collection, Leeds University Library.

29. George Egerton to Bram Stoker, 4 May 1898 (London), Brotherton Collection, Leeds University Library.

30. Information regarding Stoker's library is taken from the Sotheby auction catalog for 7 July 1913. On Florence Stoker's collection, see David J. Skal, *Hollywood Gothic: The Tangled Web of Dracula from Novel to Stage to Screen* (New York: W. W. Norton, 1990), p. 180.

31. *The Labour World*, 29 November 1890, p. 15. Like William O'Brien, Michael Davitt (1846–1906) was an early associate of Parnell who later took a critical anti-Parnellite position. Davitt was the moving force behind the formation of the National Land League in 1879, subsequently pushing for a policy of national ownership of the land. By 1890 he was urging readers of his paper that cooperation with Gladstone's Liberal Party was essential if Home Rule was to be won. He was elected MP for North Meath in 1892, and South Mayo in 1895.

32. *Personal Reminiscences*, ch. 45. See also *The Gladstone Diaries, Vol. XII: 1887–1891*, ed. H. C. G. Matthew (Oxford: Clarendon Press, 1994), pp. 336–37. Unfortunately, *The Snake's Pass* has become one of the least discussed of all Stoker's books; for an important exception to this critical neglect, see Nicholas Daly's excellent "Irish Roots: The Romance of History in Bram Stoker's *The Snake's Pass*," *Literature and Society*, 3d series, 4 (Autumn 1995): 42–70.

33. Described as "a burly, hale, stalwart man, with keen eyes and a flowing brown beard" (*SP*, 52), Dick Sutherland is one of Stoker's early fictional self-portraits. Other playful identifications were possible too: *Punch* columnist

Sir Henry Lucy closed a letter to Stoker regarding a review of *The Snake's Pass* with "kind regards to Norah." Sir Henry Lucy to Bram Stoker, 2 December 1890 (London), Brotherton Collection, Leeds University Library.

34. See the review of *The Snake's Pass* in *Punch*, December 6, 1890, p. 269.

35. Daly, "Irish Roots." On the historiography of the Irish gombeenman, see Peter Gibbon and M. D. Higgins, "Patronage, Tradition, and Modernisation: The case of the Irish 'Gombeenman,'" *Economic and Social Review* 6, no. 1 (1974): 27–44; Liam Kennedy, "A Sceptical View on the Reincarnation of the Irish 'Gombeenman,'" *Economic and Social Review* 8, no. 3 (1977): 213–22; and Peter Gibbon and M. D. Higgins, "The Irish 'Gombeenman': Reincarnation or Rehabilitation?" *Economic and Social Review* 8, no. 4 (1977): 313–20.

36. Lady Morgan, *The Wild Irish Girl*, intro. Brigid Brophy (London: Pandora, 1986), pp. 6–7.

37. Ibid., p. 7.

38. See Christopher Morash's introduction to W. M. Thackeray, *The Irish Sketchbook* (Gloucester: Alan Sutton, 1990), pp. xiii–xix.

39. *Charles Kingsley: His Letters and Memories of His Life*, vol. 2, edited by his wife (London: Henry S. King, 1877), p. 107.

40. George Stoker, *With "The Unspeakables"; Or, Two Years' Campaigning in European and Asiatic Turkey* (London: Chapman & Hall, 1878), pp. 10 and 13. According to one of Stoker's biographers, Bram helped his brother in the preparation of this book; see Harry Ludlam, *A Biography of Bram Stoker: Creator of Dracula*, pp. 53–54.

41. The relevant portions of Major Johnson's book are reprinted in Clive Leatherdale, *The Origins of Dracula: The Background to Bram Stoker's Gothic Masterpiece* (London: William Kimber, 1987), pp. 99–107.

42. *The Snake's Pass* occupies an ill-defined position midway between two points: Galway, which acts as the center for banking and legal services, and Westport in County Mayo, which is the site of the landed estate ("me Lard's demesne") where Arthur's driver, Andy Sullivan, lives and works (*SP*, 94). Westport was an important site in the organization of the National Land League of Mayo in 1879. It was there in June of that year that Parnell urged tenants to curtail their payments of rent. As Foster points out, "Mayo had a history of tenant organization" and "a strong local tradition of Fenian influence." In this same period Michael Davitt became "the patron saint of Mayo radicalism." See R. F. Foster, *Modern Ireland, 1600–1972* (Harmondsworth: Penguin, 1989), pp. 403–4.

43. William Carleton, *The Black Prophet: A Tale of Irish Famine*, in *The Works of William Carleton*, vol. 3 (New York: Collier, 1881), p. 777.

44. Ibid., p. 781.

45. Terry Eagleton, *Heathcliff and the Great Hunger: Studies in Irish Culture* (London: Verso, 1995), p. 212.

46. On Yeats, see Margaret Chesnutt, *Studies in the Short Stories of William Carleton* (Göteborg: Acta Universitatis Gothoburgensis, 1976), p. 7.

47. *With Walt Whitman in Camden*, vol. 4, pp. 183–84.

48. Bram Stoker, "Mr. Winston Churchill Talks of His Hopes, His Work, and His Ideals to Bram Stoker," *The Daily Chronicle*, January 15, 1908, p. 8. For further discussion of Stoker's use of physiognomy, see my essay "Bram Stoker and the Crisis of the Liberal Subject," *New Literary History* 23 (Autumn 1992): 983–1002. Churchill (1874–1965) had been born into a Conservative family, but his support for Free Trade had led him to join the Liberal Party in 1904. During this period he was also an advocate of Irish Home Rule.

49. John Beddoe, *The Races of Britain: A Contribution to the Anthropology of Western Europe* (1885; London: Hutchinson, 1971), pp. 12 and 295. One of Beddoe's conclusions was "the undoubted fact that the Gaelic and Iberian races of the west, mostly dark-haired, are tending to swamp the blond Teutons of England by a reflux migration" (p. 298). Beddoe was elected president of the Anthropology Society of London in 1869 and he subsequently became president of the Royal Anthropological Institute.

50. See L. Perry Curtis, *Apes and Angels: The Irishman in Victorian Caricature* (Washington: Smithsonian Institution Press, 1971). One of the major figures in the stereotyping of the Irish was the famous cartoonist Sir John Tenniel, who was a friend of Stoker's employer Sir Henry Irving. In fairness, it should be added that similar imagery was also employed against indigenous English workers. Thus at the time of the second Reform crusade, *Punch* published a cartoon entitled "The Brummagen Frankenstein" which depicted John Bright quaking in his shoes while overshadowed by a grim-faced working-class giant and nervously affirming "I have no fe-fe-fear of ma-manhood suffrage!" Reproduced in Keith Robbins, *John Bright* (London: Routledge & Kegan Paul, 1979), p. 185.

51. R. F. Foster, *Modern Ireland*, p. 375.

52. William O'Brien, *Irish Ideas* (London: Longmans, Green & Co., 1893), p. 10 (O'Brien had given Stoker a presentation copy of his book of speeches in July 1894); Lecky, *Democracy and Liberty*, pp. 23–24. Lecky's stress upon Irish "decadence" was a standard way of indicating the country's unfitness for self-government. Cf. Trevelyan's references to a "degenerate Ireland" in the debate on the first Home Rule Bill, cited in Grenfell Morton, *Home Rule and the Irish Question* (Harlow: Longman, 1980), p. 37.

53. William O'Brien, *Irish Ideas*, pp. 10–12 and 115–16. Although O'Brien's later lecture "Toleration in the Fight for Ireland" was delivered in Belfast in November 1892, the reference to Hottentots probably derives from a rabidly anti–Home Rule speech by the Conservative Marquis of Salisbury in May 1886, in which the Irish were compared to the Hottentots in their unfitness for self-government. On the place of the Hottentot woman in nineteenth-

century sexual discourse, see Sander L. Gilman, "Black Bodies, White Bodies: Toward an Iconography of Female Sexuality in Late Nineteenth-Century Art, Medicine, and Literature," in Henry Louis Gates Jr., ed., *"Race," Writing, and Difference* (Chicago: University of Chicago Press, 1986).

54. John Beddoe, *The Races of Britain*, p. 11. Though it has ancient antecedents, "in the eighteenth century, you begin to get the idea that the farther north or up the mountain you go, the better people are—not merely in the virtues of simplicity, but also in the virtues of high and pure thought." Walter Cohen, "An Interview with Martin Bernal," *Social Text* 35 (Summer 1993): 2. See also Martin Bernal, *Black Athena: The Afroasiatic Roots of Classical Civilization, Vol. 1: The Fabrication of Ancient Greece, 1785–1985* (New Brunswick, N.J.: Rutgers University sity Press, 1987), ch. 4.

55. Judith Butler, *Bodies That Matter: On the Discursive Limits of "Sex"* (London: Routledge, 1993), p. 111.

56. Francis Galton, *Hereditary Genius: An Inquiry into Its Laws and Consequences* (1869; London: Macmillan, 1914), pp. 334–43.

57. For a brief but suggestive allegorical reading of *Dracula*, see Terry Eagleton, "Form and Ideology in the Anglo-Irish Novel," *Bullán: An Irish Studies Journal* 1 (Spring 1994): 22.

58. See Slavoj Žižek, "Formal Democracy and Its Discontents," *American Imago* 48 (Summer 1991): 181–98.

59. Lauren Berlant, *The Anatomy of National Fantasy: Hawthorne, Utopia, and Everyday Life* (Chicago: University of Chicago Press, 1991), p. 14.

60. John A. Hall, *Liberalism: Politics, Ideology, and the Market* (London: Paladin, 1988), p. 69. Hobson was particularly horrified by the upsurge of popular sentiment during the Boer War and he wrote *The Psychology of Jingoism* (1901) "to explain how the mass mind could have been so manipulated into supporting rabid nationalism and war."

61. David Kazanjian, "Notarizing Knowledge: Paranoia and Civility in Freud and Lacan," *Qui Parle* 7 (Fall 1993): 132.

62. Slavoj Žižek, "Eastern European Liberalism and Its Discontents," *New German Critique* 57 (Fall 1992): 39. For Žižek "the liberal gaze . . . is founded upon the exclusion of the Other to whom one attributes fundamentalist nationalism, and so on" (p. 40).

63. "Mr. Winston Churchill Talks of His Hopes, His Work, and His Ideals to Bram Stoker," *The Daily Chronicle*, January 15, 1908, p. 8. For a fuller account of Churchill's analysis, see Winston S. Churchill, *Liberalism and the Social Problem: Speeches 1906–1909* (London: Hodder & Stoughton, 1909), in which he argues that "the main aspirations of the British people are at the present time social rather than political. They see around them on every side, and almost every day, spectacles of confusion and misery which they cannot reconcile with any conception of humanity or justice" (p. 237).

64. Churchill, *Liberalism and the Social Problem*, p. 237.

65. Daniel Pick, *Faces of Degeneration: A European Disorder, c.1848–c.1918* (Cambridge: Cambridge University Press, 1989), p. 199.

66. On the diminution of the vampire as a feature of *Dracula*'s narrative strategy, see David Seed, "The Narrative Method of *Dracula*," *Nineteenth-Century Fiction* 40, no. 1 (1985): 61–75. For an early analysis of Stoker's use of positivist criminology, see Ernest Fontana, "Lombroso's Criminal Man and Stoker's *Dracula*," *Victorian Newsletter* 66 (Fall 1984): 25–27.

67. The quote is from Massimo d'Azeglio as cited in Hobsbawm, *Nations and Nationalism*, p. 44. On Lombrosian criminology in its Italian context, see Pick, *Faces of Degeneration*, ch. 5.

68. Pick, *Faces of Degeneration*, p. 141. Lombroso's conventional hierarchy of races was central to his national criminological enterprise. In *The White Man and the Coloured Man* (1871), Lombroso claimed that "only we White people have reached the most perfect symmetry of bodily form . . . Only we have created true nationalism . . . [and] freedom of thought" (quoted in Pick, p. 126).

69. For some suggestive remarks about the role of nationalism in *Dracula*, see Franco Moretti's 1978 essay "The Dialectic of Fear," reprinted in *Signs Taken For Wonders: Essays in the Sociology of Literary Forms* (London: Verso, 1983), pp. 92–98.

70. Matthew Arnold, *The Study of Celtic Literature* (London: Smith, Elder & Co., 1912 edition), pp. 84–88. From a different political perspective, compare Michael Davitt's claim that Irishmen are "warm-hearted, impulsive, and generous," these being the "distinguishing qualities of their race." Editorial, *The Labour World*, November 29, 1890, p. 8.

71. Raymond Williams, *The English Novel from Dickens to Lawrence* (1970; London: Hogarth Press, 1984), p. 62.

72. Walt Whitman, *Democratic Vistas* (1871; New York: Liberal Arts Press, 1949), p. 37. In the subsequent paragraph Whitman gestures toward what would soon be called eugenics to underwrite his "basic model or portrait of personality for general use for the manliness of the States": "Will the time hasten when fatherhood and motherhood shall become a science—and the noblest science?" For a useful discussion of this aspect of Whitman's work, see Dana Phillips, "Nineteenth-Century Racial Thought and Whitman's 'Democratic Ethnology of the Future,'" *Nineteenth-Century Literature* 49 (December 1994): 289–320.

73. Of course, Arthur has also made good his father's bad marriage, magically changing his parent's poverty into a second-generation success.

74. Seamus Deane, *A Short History of Irish Literature* (1986; Notre Dame: University of Notre Dame Press, 1994), p. 98. As Deane notes, one reason for Lady Morgan's success was that she seemed to offer "reparation on the part of the Irish Protestant Whigs for the oppressions of the Irish Protestant Tories." The earlier quote is from Lady Morgan, *The Wild Irish Girl*, p. 253.

75. Like the Irish countryside, the buried French gold also has a history that the novel is at pains to repress: the abortive 1798 French expedition occurred in the wake of a bloody Irish insurrection. According to Roy Foster, "the 1798 rising was probably the most concentrated episode of violence in Irish history." R. F. Foster, *Modern Ireland: 1600–1972*, p. 280.

76. Grenfell Morton, *Home Rule and the Irish Question*, p. 49. Morton cites the impact of Kane's ideas on one of the architects of the Irish Free State, Arthur Griffith, whose famous newspaper, *United Irishman*, was started in 1899 and who also founded the Gaelic Society the following year and Sinn Fein in 1905. In his 1907 essay "The Great White Fair in Dublin," Stoker draws attention to Ireland's unexploited "natural advantages," especially her "as yet but little known" mineral resources and the "vast areas of fuel-bog, sufficient alone for national wealth." See *The World's Work* (London) 9 (May 1907): 573. This article anticipates many of the themes of national development in *The Lady of the Shroud*.

77. Reprinted in Bram Stoker, *Midnight Tales*, ed. with an intro. by Peter Haining (London: Peter Owen, 1990), pp. 107–19.

78. The subtitle of one of the very few analyses of this text is entirely symptomatic: Carol A. Senf's "*The Lady of the Shroud*: Stoker's Successor to *Dracula*," *Essays in Arts and Sciences* 19 (May 1990): 82–96. Similarly, Phyllis A. Roth in her book on Stoker discusses the novel in her chapter on "The Horror Tales." See Phyllis A. Roth, *Bram Stoker* (Boston: Twayne Publishers, 1982), pp. 74–80. One reason for this analytic blindness seems to be the reliance on later editions which are heavily edited: the widely available 1966 Jarrolds "reprint" effectively omits books 7 to 9, except for a few pages.

79. See Katie Trumpener, "National Character, Nationalist Plots: National Tale and Historical Novel in the Age of *Waverley*, 1806–1830," *ELH* 60 (Fall 1993): 685–731.

80. Krishan Kumar, *Utopia and Anti-Utopia in Modern Times* (Oxford: Basil Blackwell, 1987), p. 65.

81. H. G. Wells, *A Modern Utopia* (1905; Lincoln: University of Nebraska Press, 1967), pp. 11–12.

82. Though its complexities transcend any simple generic reduction, *Dracula* too can illuminatingly be read in the light of the vogue for invasion narratives. See Stephen D. Arata, "The Occidental Tourist: *Dracula* and the Anxiety of Reverse Colonization," *Victorian Studies* 33 (Summer 1990): 621–45, and R. J. Dingley, "Count Dracula and the Martians," in Kath Filmer, ed., *The Victorian Fantasists: Essays on Culture, Society, and Belief in the Mythopoeic Fiction of the Victorian Age* (New York: St. Martin's Press, 1991).

83. Fredric Jameson, "Of Islands and Trenches: Neutralization and the Production of Utopian Discourse," in *The Ideologies of Theory, Essays 1971– 1986—Volume 2: Syntax of History* (Minneapolis: University of Minnesota Press, 1988), p. 101.

1. Gaston Bachelard, *The Poetics of Space*, trans. Maria Jolas (1958; Boston: Beacon Press, 1969), p. 39.

2. Thomas De Quincey, "On Murder Considered as One of the Fine Arts," in D. Masson, ed., *The Collected Writings of Thomas De Quincey*, 14 vols. (Edinburgh: Adam and Charles Black, 1890), 13:124.

3. Hall Caine, "The New Watchwords of Fiction," *Contemporary Review*, 57 (1890): 479–88.

4. See John Stuart Mill, *The Logic of the Moral Sciences*, intro. A. J. Ayer (London: Duckworth, 1987), ch. 5. This text reprints the sixth book of Mill's *A System of Logic* (1843).

5. See Andrew Vincent, "Classical Liberalism and Its Crisis of Identity," *History of Political Thought* 11 (Spring 1990): 143–61, and Stefan Collini, *Liberalism and Sociology: L. T. Hobhouse and the Political Argument in England 1880–1914* (Cambridge: Cambridge University Press, 1979).

6. *Spectator*, July 31, 1897, pp. 150–51.

7. Thomas De Quincey, quoted in J. Hillis Miller, *The Disappearance of God: Five Nineteenth-Century Writers* (Cambridge, Mass.: Harvard University Press, 1963), p. 64.

8. In *The Snake's Pass* Protestantism and skepticism are explicitly linked in the character of the "hard-faced" McGlown, who "much prefer[s] the facs" and who prefers a story told by someone "old enough till remember the theng itself" to any legend (*SP*, 23).

9. Bram Stoker, *The Duties of Clerks of Petty Sessions in Ireland* (Dublin: John Falconer, 1879), pp. v–vi and 27.

10. The Law List is a directory of English professional lawyers, whose ranks Jonathan Harker is about to join. The other volumes in the Count's collection include reference books containing the names or biographies of the aristocracy, the well-to-do, London businessmen, and members of the officer corps in the army and navy, as well as a plethora of government publications and a compendium of British railway timetables.

11. Auguste Comte, *La Philosophie Positive*, quoted in Jerry Palmer, "The Damp Stones of Positivism: Erich von Däniken and Paranormality," *Philosophy of Social Science* 9 (1979): 145.

12. See Terence Brown, "Edward Dowden: Irish Victorian," in *Ireland's Literature: Selected Essays* (Mullingar: Lilliput Press, 1988), p. 37.

13. See Edward Dowden, *Fragments from Old Letters: E. D. to E. D. W., 1869–1892, First Series* (London: J. M. Dent, 1914), p. 129. This letter dates from 1877. Among the other relevant texts that Dowden mentions and which are likely to have been passed on by him to Stoker are Charles Darwin's *Expression of the Emotions*, Max Müller's *Science of Religion*, and Henry Maudsley's *Body and Mind: An Inquiry into Their Connection and Mutual Influence*. See Dowden's letter of

September 7, 1873, in *Fragments from Old Letters: E. D. to E. D. W., 1869–1892, Second Series* (London: J. M. Dent, 1914), pp. 33–34.

14. Roy Foster suggests a less conventional outcome of Dowden's transcendentalism: his interest in Shelley and his circle. According to Foster, "it was Dowden's account of Shelley's experiments with demonic invocation at Eton that inspired Yeats and AE to attempt spirit-raising in the mid-1880s." R. F. Foster, "Protestant Magic: W. B. Yeats and the Spell of Irish History," in *Paddy and Mr. Punch: Connections in Irish and English History* (London: Penguin, 1993), p. 226.

15. On Stoker's continuing interest in mathematics, see Sir Gilbert Parker's letter to him, May 31, 1893 (Harpenden, Herts.), Brotherton Collection, Leeds University Library.

16. Bram Stoker, *Famous Impostors* (New York: Sturgis & Walton, 1910), p. 100.

17. Josep R. Llobera, "The Dark Side of Modernity," *Critique of Anthropology* 8, no. 2 (1988): 71–76.

18. Daniel Pick, *Faces of Degeneration: A European Disorder, c.1848–c.1918* (Cambridge: Cambridge University Press, 1989), p. 180.

19. Michael Freeden, *The New Liberalism: An Ideology of Social Reform* (Oxford: Clarendon Press, 1986), p. 178. See also his essay "Eugenics and Progressive Thought: A Study in Ideological Affinity," *Historical Journal* 22, no. 3 (1979): 645–71.

20. C. F. G. Masterman, *In Peril of Change: Essays Written in Time of Tranquility* (New York: B. W. Huebsch, 1905), pp. 175, 177.

21. Cesare Lombroso (1835–1909) was the Italian founder of positivistic criminology who originally claimed that crime could largely be explained in terms of evolutionary atavism. Lombroso greatly influenced the German physician and journalist Max Nordau (1849–1923), who helped popularize the concept of degeneration by using it as a critical tool to stigmatize developments in the arts. An English translation of Nordau's magnum opus *Entartung* (1893) was published by William Heinemann (later to become Stoker's publisher) under the title *Degeneration* in 1895. This aspect of Stoker's work has attracted increasing attention in recent years, though few studies go much beyond cataloging textual affinities. The best analysis to date remains Daniel Pick, " 'Terrors of the night': *Dracula* and 'Degeneration' in the Late Nineteenth Century," *Critical Quarterly* 30, no. 4 (1988): 71–87; but as Troy Boone notes, Pick "does not focus on how these fears are represented in narrative." See Boone's essay " 'He is English and therefore adventurous': Politics, Decadence, and *Dracula*," *Studies in the Novel* 25 (Spring 1993): 90. For a useful overview of degeneration theory's relationship to Anglo-American literary culture, see R. B. Kershner Jr., "Degeneration: The Explanatory Nightmare," *Georgia Review* 40 (Summer 1986): 416–44.

22. Colin Martindale, "Degeneration, Disinhibition, and Genius," *Journal of the History of Behavioral Science* 7 (1971): 177–82.

23. Albert Wilson (1910), quoted in Richard D. Walter, "What Became of the Degenerate? A Brief History of a Concept," *Journal of the History of Medicine* 11 (1956): 422–29.

24. Francis Galton, *Hereditary Genius: An Inquiry into Its Laws and Consequences* (1869; London: Macmillan, 1914), p. 338.

25. See Ian Hacking, "How Should We Do the History of Statistics?" *I&C* 8 (1981): 15–26. See also D. W. Forrest, *Francis Galton: The Life and Work of a Victorian Genius* (New York: Taplinger, 1974), ch. 14.

26. Greta Jones, *Social Darwinism and English Thought: The Interaction between Biological and Social Theory* (Brighton: Harvester Press, 1980), p. 35.

27. W. R. Greg, "On the Failure of Natural Selection in the Case of Man," *Fraser's Magazine* 78 (1868): 360.

28. Francis Galton, *Hereditary Genius*, pp. 328–29.

29. See Daniel Pick, *Faces of Degeneration*, pp. 176–79.

30. Reprinted in the posthumous collection *Dracula's Guest* (1914), "The Secret of the Growing Gold" was originally published in *Black & White*, January 23, 1892. The original manuscript in the Brotherton Collection in Leeds University Library indicates that the story was written between May 28 and June 12, 1891.

31. Michel Foucault, *The History of Sexuality, Volume 1: An Introduction*, trans. Robert Hurley (1976; Harmondsworth: Penguin, 1981), p. 118.

32. Interestingly, part of the challenge the madman R. M. Renfield poses to Dr. Seward's knowledge of the human mind lies in the fact that he is "so unlike the normal lunatic" (*D*, 78). For an exploration of the replacement of the idea of human nature by "a model of normal people with laws of dispersion," see Ian Hacking, *The Taming of Chance* (Cambridge: Cambridge University Press, 1990).

33. Foucault, *History of Sexuality*, pp. 118–21.

34. See Melville Macnaghten's highly enthusiastic letter to Stoker, June 30, 1897 (Metropolitan Police Office, London), Brotherton Collection, Leeds University Library. Macnaghten exclaims that he has "revelled" in *Dracula* and singles out this episode, noting that Mina's blood is "not unwillingly" taken from her by the Count. At the time of writing Macnaghten was Chief Constable in the Criminal Investigation Department, Scotland Yard. He was knighted in 1907.

35. "London Letter" (syndicated column written by Henry Lucy), *Keighley News*, July 10, 1897.

36. Franco Moretti, *Signs Taken For Wonders: Essays in the Sociology of Literary Forms* (London: Verso, 1983), p. 103.

37. See Galton's suggestion that "there is a most unusual unanimity in respect to the causes of incapacity of savages for civilization, among writers on those hunting and migratory nations who are brought into contact with advancing colonization, and perish, as they invariably do, by the contact.

They tell us that the labour of such men is neither constant nor steady; that the love of a wandering, independent life prevents their settling anywhere to work, except for a short time, when urged by want and encouraged by kind treatment." Galton, *Hereditary Genius*, p. 334.

38. On the popularity of phrenology as a naturalistic science of social life, revealing "progress in action in the world," see Patrick Joyce, *Democratic Subjects: The Self and the Social in Nineteenth-Century England* (Cambridge: Cambridge University Press, 1994), pp. 171–73. Joyce stresses its links with popular Liberalism. On the general importance of popular physiology in the early nineteenth century, see Roger Cooter, "The Power of the Body: The Early Nineteenth Century," in Barry Barnes and Steven Shapin, eds., *Natural Order: Historical Studies of Scientific Culture* (Beverly Hills: Sage, 1979), pp. 73–92.

39. On the historical uses of physiognomy, see Jeanne Fahnestock, "The Heroine of Irregular Features: Physiognomy and Conventions in Heroine Descriptions," *Victorian Studies* 24 (Spring 1981): 325–50, and Mary Cowling, *The Artist as Anthropologist: The Representation of Type and Character in Victorian Art* (Cambridge: Cambridge University Press, 1989).

40. Johann Caspar Lavater, *Essays on Physiognomy, Designed to Promote the Knowledge and the Love of Mankind*, trans. Henry Hunter (London: John Murray, 1789), vol. 1, Author's Preface.

41. Ibid., pp. 14–15, 30–31.

42. Ibid., pp. 137, 236–37; vol. 2, p. 423.

43. For example, in *The Man* (1905) the "rough voyages" undertaken by Harold An Wolf's "forebears amongst northern seas, though they had been a thousand years back, had left traces on his imagination, his blood, his nerves!" And a mid-Atlantic storm is enough to reawaken "the old Berserker spirit" (*M*, 279–80). Similarly, in *The Lady of the Shroud* (1909), Rupert Sent Leger refers to "the fighting instinct of my Viking forbears" (*LS*, 195). Note also that in *Dracula*, when Arthur Holmwood drives a stake into the heart of his fiancée Lucy, "he looked like a figure of Thor" (*D*, 259).

44. For a discussion of the Viking as a contested figure in English literary culture in a slightly earlier period, see the account of the reception of Charles Kingsley's novel *Hereward the Wake* (1866) in Bruce Haley, *The Healthy Body and Victorian Culture* (Cambridge, Mass.: Harvard University Press, 1978), pp. 216–20. Other examples would include Carlyle's enthusiasm for "the Pagan Norseman" in his book *On Heroes* (1841) and the account of Sir Henry Curtis's "Bersekir" pugnacity in H. Rider Haggard's *King Solomon's Mines* (1885).

45. See Piers Beirne, "Heredity versus Environment: A Reconsideration of Charles Goring's *The English Convict* (1913)," *British Journal of Criminology* 28 (Summer 1988): 315–39. Beirne's careful analysis gives an excellent account of the intricacies of Lombroso's English reception during the late Victorian and Edwardian periods, stressing the ways in which challenges to Lombro-

sianism moved "in the same operative direction as that initiated by Lombroso himself" (p. 336).

46. Horace Traubel, ed., *With Walt Whitman in Camden, Vol. 4* (Carbondale: Southern Illinois University Press, 1959), p. 183.

47. Stoker, *Famous Impostors*, pp. 227–29.

48. Lavater, *Essays*, 1: 30–33.

49. William B. Carpenter, *Principles of Mental Physiology, with Their Applications to the Training and Discipline of the Mind and the Study of Its Morbid Conditions*, 4th ed. (New York: D. Appleton, 1884), p. 517; hereafter cited in text. For a useful historical account of Carpenter's career, see Adrian Desmond, *The Politics of Evolution: Morphology, Medicine, and Reform in Radical London* (Chicago: University of Chicago Press, 1989), pp. 210–22.

50. Jonathan Miller has contrasted Freud's "distinctively custodial interpretation" of the unconscious with the "altogether productive" model developed by Carpenter and others, whose "contents are inaccessible not, as in psychoanalytic theory, because they are held as in strenuously preventive detention but, more interestingly, because the effective implementation of cognition and conduct does not actually *require* comprehensive awareness." Jonathan Miller, "Going Unconscious," *New York Review of Books*, April 20, 1995, p. 64.

51. See F. W. H. Myers, "Multiplex Personality," *Proceedings of the Society for Psychical Research* 4 (1886): 496–514.

52. Alan Ryan has argued that John Stuart Mill was oblivious to similar problems: "If the external world was to be constructed out of experience of a self which tried out inductive hypotheses about the course of its experience, then this presupposed a unitary self to do the experiencing, and to make the inferences. Yet the atomistic theory to which Mill was attached seemed to rule out any such self." See Alan Ryan, *J. S. Mill* (London: Routledge & Kegan Paul, 1974), p. 226.

53. See Robert M. Young, *Mind, Brain, and Adaptation in the Nineteenth Century: Cerebral Localization and Its Biological Context from Gall to Ferrier* (Oxford: Clarendon Press, 1970), esp. pp. 210–20. For a general survey of Victorian approaches to the will from a literary perspective, see John R. Reed, *Victorian Will* (Athens: Ohio University Press, 1989).

54. When David Ferrier's experimental results were first published in 1873, Carpenter erroneously interpreted them as providing support for his own position, a misreading that continued to command assent for at least another decade. Ferrier's work was not incorporated into standard textbooks until 1890. See Young, *Mind, Brain, and Adaptation*, pp. 215–20. Ironically, as Young shows, Ferrier's thoroughly modern localization of sensory-motor psychophysiology can be placed in a line of descent that goes back to the discredited late-eighteenth-century phrenology of Franz Joseph Gall. For a different view of *Dracula's* relationship to contemporary medical knowledge,

see John L. Greenway, "Seward's Folly: *Dracula* as a Critique of 'Normal Science,'" *Stanford Literature Review* 3 (Fall 1986): 213–30.

55. See Janet Oppenheim, "Manly Nerves," in her *Shattered Nerves: Doctors, Patients, and Depression in Victorian England* (New York: Oxford University Press, 1991), pp. 141–80.

56. Given the atmosphere of intense inwardness that pervades the opening chapters, it is hardly surprising that "one of the most consistent interpretations of *Dracula* has been to see it as the projection of Jonathan Harker's unconscious," in which the Count serves as his lascivious double, acting out the clerk's "repressed desires." See Elaine Showalter, "Blood Sells: Vampire Fever and Anxieties for the *fin de siècle*," *Times Literary Supplement*, January 8, 1993, p. 14.

57. Brodie-Innes to Bram Stoker, November 29, 1903 (Forres, Scotland), Brotherton Collection, Leeds University Library. J. W. Brodie-Innes (1848–1923), an Edinburgh lawyer, was one of the leading members of the Amen-Ra Temple of the Hermetic Order of the Golden Dawn. He was at the center of the internal disputes that plagued the Golden Dawn throughout the Edwardian era and became a senior figure in the breakaway Alpha and Omega Temple in 1912. Though he rightly cautions us against overinterpreting such connections, Stoker's biographer Daniel Farson tentatively suggests that the author may have been a secret member of Innes's group, noting that Innes dedicated his 1915 occult novel *The Devil's Mistress* to Stoker's memory. However, since Brodie-Innes only became praemonstrator of the dissident temple in the year of Stoker's death, Farson's hypothesis seems extremely unlikely. It is important to remember that Stoker was also the author of *Famous Impostors* as well as *Dracula*. His interests seem to have run more toward spiritualism than ritual magic. See Daniel Farson, *The Man Who Wrote "Dracula": A Biography of Bram Stoker* (London: Michael Joseph, 1975), p. 207. For further biographical details regarding Brodie-Innes, see Ellic Howe, *The Magicians of the Golden Dawn: A Documentary History of a Magical Order, 1887–1923* (London: Routledge & Kegan Paul, 1972).

58. When *The Jewel of Seven Stars* was republished in 1912, one of its more speculative chapters (16) was deleted and a "happy ending" substituted in which all the characters survive with the sole exception of Queen Tera, who through a kind of metempsychosis merges with the personality of Margaret Trelawny. In the final scene, wearing the queen's robe and jewels, Margaret at last becomes Ross's wife. As if to confirm the queen's reincarnation, Margaret urges her husband not to grieve for Tera, hinting that "she may have found the joy she sought." See Bram Stoker, *The Jewel of Seven Stars* (1912; New York: Carroll & Graf, 1989), p. 254. The 1912 edition is almost invariably used in modern reprints of the novel. There is some dispute as to whether Stoker himself actually made these changes.

59. Madame Blavatsky, quoted in Richard Ellmann, *Yeats: The Man and the Masks* (Oxford: Oxford University Press, 1979), p. 56.

60. See Philippa Levine, *The Amateur and the Professional: Antiquarians, Historians, and Archaeologists in Victorian England, 1838–1886* (Cambridge: Cambridge University Press, 1986). Levine notes that archaeology only attains full university respectability in the 1880s, partly as a result of Petrie's successful Egyptian excavations.

61. See Norman Etherington's "Rider Haggard, Imperialism, and the Layered Personality," *Victorian Studies* 22 (Autumn 1978): 71–87, which of course notes Freud's interest in this aspect of Haggard's work. For a useful account of the revamped ideology of romance, see N. N. Feltes, *Literary Capital and the Late Victorian Novel* (Madison: University of Wisconsin Press, 1993), esp. pp. 104–8.

62. See Phyllis A. Roth, *Bram Stoker* (Boston: Twayne Publishers, 1982), p. 144. Unfortunately, Roth's reading depends solely upon the later (1912) edition of the novel with its very different ending to that of the earlier book. For a brief comparison of *She*, *Dracula*, and *The Lair of the White Worm*, see Sandra M. Gilbert and Susan Gubar, *No Man's Land, Vol. 2: Sexchanges* (New Haven: Yale University Press, 1989), pp. 10–25. Gilbert and Gubar need to be read with caution, however; for an excellent corrective, see Laura Chrisman, "The Imperial Unconscious? Representations of Imperial Discourse," *Critical Quarterly* 32 (Autumn 1990): 38–58.

63. The idea of civilization as a "veneer" comes from the introduction to H. Rider Haggard's *Allan Quatermain* (1887), quoted by Etherington, "Rider Haggard," p. 78; but for a more recent resort to the same metaphor, see C. P. Snow's final novel *A Coat of Varnish* (1979). The view of man as "a fighting animal" derives from Haggard's autobiography *The Days of My Life* (1926) and is quoted by Dennis Butts in his introduction to H. Rider Haggard, *King Solomon's Mines* (1885; Oxford: Oxford University Press, 1989), p. xvii.

64. The phrase "muscular liberalism" is taken from Stefan Collini's important essay "The Idea of 'Character' in Victorian Political Thought," *Transactions of the Royal Historical Society*, 5th ser., 35 (1985): 29–50, where it is used to describe the "political aesthetic" of "manliness" promoted by "the professional and preaching classes."

65. "Intrusion, imagination, misfit" are, according to Maria Torok, the three defining "characteristics of fantasy." See her 1959 essay "Fantasy: An Attempt to Define Its Structure and Operation," in Nicolas Abraham and Maria Torok, *The Shell and the Kernel: Renewals of Psychoanalysis, Volume 1*, ed. and trans. Nicholas T. Rand (Chicago: University of Chicago Press, 1994), pp. 27–36.

66. Undated letter to Florence Farr (c. December 1895), in Clifford Bax, ed., *Florence Farr, Bernard Shaw, W. B. Yeats: Letters* (New York: Dodd, Mead, 1942), p. 51.

67. R. F. Foster, "Protestant Magic: W. B. Yeats and the Spell of Irish History," p. 212.

68. Thus, though it is certainly plausible to see "Yeats's continuing preoc-

cupation with the occult" as enabling him "to lay claim upon Irishness, while retaining a hold upon his own marginalized tradition," Stoker's Irishness appears to require a large admixture of cosmopolitan rationalism; Foster, "Protestant Magic," p. 230. Similarly, to describe Stoker as someone "living in England but regretting Ireland" (p. 220) seems to me to fail to recognize the author's own peculiar love affair with England. It is unlikely, to say the least, that Yeats could ever have described the 1897 Diamond Jubilee as (in Stoker's words) "a magnificent survey of the Empire" which "brought home, as nothing else could have done, the sense of the immense variety of the Queen's dominions." "Mr. Bram Stoker: A Chat with the Author of 'Dracula,'" *British Weekly*, July 1, 1897, p. 185.

69. The inclusion of Sir William Crookes (1832–1919) in this list is of particular interest since he was famous as a chemist and physicist, as a president of the Royal Society, *and* as a sympathizer with spiritualism. Crookes received a knighthood in 1897 (coinciding with the publication of *Dracula*), the same year that he was also made president of the Society for Psychical Research. W. B. Carpenter, together with E. Ray Lankester, was among those who criticized Crookes for lending scientific respectability to spiritualism. See Edmund E. Fournier D'Albe, *The Life of Sir William Crookes* (London: T. Fisher Unwin, 1923), and, for a more general analysis, Jon Palfreman, "Between Scepticism and Credulity: A Study of Victorian Scientific Attitudes to Modern Spiritualism," in Roy Wallis, ed., *On the Margins of Science: The Social Construction of Rejected Knowledge, Sociological Review Monograph* No. 27 (Keele, Staffordshire: University of Keele, 1979), pp. 201–36.

70. W. M. Flinders Petrie, ed., *Egyptian Tales* (London: Methuen, 1895), p. 49. Although earlier anthropologists like Bachofen and Morgan had suggested that at the beginning of history power and descent were the prerogative of mothers rather than fathers, by the 1870s this idea was being vigorously challenged and this critique led to a distinction between power or sovereignty and descent or inheritance (matrilinearity); see Rosalind Coward, *Patriarchal Precedents: Sexuality and Social Relations* (London: Routledge & Kegan Paul, 1983), chs. 1 and 2. For a recent overview of the position of women in ancient Egypt, see Eric Carlton, *Ideology and Social Order* (London: Routledge & Kegan Paul, 1977), pp. 80–84, 107–9.

71. See Billie Melman, *Women's Orients: English Women and the Middle East, 1718–1918* (Ann Arbor: University of Michigan Press, 1992), p. 268. Edwards's lecture was subsequently incorporated into her book *Pharaohs, Fellahs, and Explorers* (New York: Harper, 1891), but, as Melman makes clear, this later version abandons the polemic of her spoken text.

72. Significantly, Stoker's account of "The Bisley Boy" in *Famous Impostors* is devoted to demonstrating the strong probability that Queen Elizabeth was a man. This is the longest section of the book.

73. Edwards, *Pharaohs, Fellahs, and Explorers*, p. 281.

74. Jean Laplanche and J.-B. Pontalis, "Fantasy and the Origins of Sexuality," *International Journal of Psycho-Analysis* 49, pt. 1 (1968): 17.

75. Judith Butler, "The Force of Fantasy: Feminism, Mapplethorpe, and Discursive Excess," *differences* 2 (Summer 1990): 110.

76. Sigmund Freud, "Medusa's Head" (1922), in *Standard Edition*, Vol. 18 (London: Hogarth Press, 1955), pp. 273–74.

77. There is considerable dispute as to whether Stoker himself really edited and rewrote the ending to the novel. Harry Ludlam's biography simply claims that Stoker made the changes at the publisher's insistence (see *A Biography of Bram Stoker: Creator of Dracula*, pp. 143–44), while recent critics like Nicholas Daly have questioned whether there is any evidence to support this (see his essay "That Obscure Object of Desire: Victorian Commodity Culture and Fictions of the Mummy," *Novel* 28 [Fall 1994]: 42). This debate has little bearing on my own position since I argue that the conclusion of the 1912 edition merely inverts the terms of its predecessor, even referring back to the language of dreams with which the novel begins and especially to Margaret Trelawny's statement about Tera's dreams in chapter 15. For further discussion of the question of authorship, see my introduction to the reprint of the 1903 edition of *The Jewel of Seven Stars* (Oxford: Oxford University Press, 1996).

78. Jacqueline Rose, *The Haunting of Sylvia Plath* (London: Virago, 1991), p. 151. Rose is arguing that the images of female purity and terror both presuppose "the imago of the phallic woman who, because she contains all things, threatens the man at the very core."

79. See Alasdair MacIntyre, *Whose Justice? Which Rationality?* (London: Duckworth, 1988), p. 347.

80. C. F. G. Masterman, *The Condition of England*, ed. J. T. Boulton (1909; London: Methuen, 1960), pp. 95–96.

81. John Stuart Mill, *On Liberty*, ed. Gertrude Himmelfarb (1859; Harmondsworth: Penguin, 1974), p. 69.

82. For a discussion of Britain's world position at this time and contemporary perceptions of it, see A. L. Friedberg, *The Weary Titan: Britain and the Experience of Relative Decline, 1895–1905* (Princeton: Princeton University Press, 1988).

83. Janet Oppenheim, *Shattered Nerves: Doctors, Patients, and Depression in Victorian England* (Oxford: Oxford University Press, 1991), p. 150.

84. See Pick, *Faces of Degeneration*, p. 126.

85. Indeed, this point can be extended to argue that the novel represents the victory of an emergent information society over its premodern competitors, though there are dangers of overgeneralization here. See Regenia Gagnier, "Evolution and Information, or Eroticism and Everyday Life, in *Dracula* and Late Victorian Literature," in Regina Barreca, ed., *Sex and Death in Victorian Literature* (London: Macmillan, 1990), pp. 140–57, and Thomas Richards,

*The Imperial Archive: Knowledge and the Fantasy of Empire* (London: Verso, 1993), esp. ch. 2.

86. See Carol A. Senf, "*Dracula:* Stoker's Response to the New Woman," *Victorian Studies* 26 (Autumn 1982): 33–49. For the perceived links between the New Woman and literary decadence, see Linda Dowling, "The Decadent and the New Woman in the 1890's," *Nineteenth-Century Fiction* 33 (March 1979): 434–53.

87. On the growing numbers of women in public services and commerce considered in a literary context, see Peter Keating, *The Haunted Study: A Social History of the English Novel 1875–1914* (London: Secker & Warburg, 1989), p. 181.

88. Flora Shaw (1852–1929) was a key figure in British imperialist politics. A friend of Rhodes and Chamberlain, she was privy to the planning of the Jameson Raid in 1895, keeping in touch with Rhodes by secret code and publishing premature reports in *The Times.* As described by her husband's biographer Margery Perham, Flora Shaw "always wore black" and "never played the woman as a short cut to her professional objectives." Nevertheless, "public men, however cautious, found it surprisingly easy to give away official information to such an interviewer." See Margery Perham, *Lugard: The Years of Authority 1898–1945* (London: Collins, 1960), pp. 54–66.

89. See Leonore Davidoff, "Class and Gender in Victorian England," in J. L. Newton, M. P. Ryan, and J. R. Walkowitz, eds., *Sex and Class in Women's History* (London: Routledge & Kegan Paul, 1983), pp. 17–21.

90. John Buchan, *Memory Hold-the-Door* (London: Hodder & Stoughton, 1940), p. 286. Strictly speaking this passage deals with external threats to "the European tradition," but in Buchan's imaginary (as in De Quincey's and Stoker's) the two are inextricably linked. In his 1924 novel *The Three Hostages,* the character Dr. Greenslade "theorizes" that "the barriers between the conscious and the subconscious . . . are growing shaky and the two worlds are getting mixed," corroding "the clear psychology of most civilized human beings." See John Buchan, *The Three Hostages* (1924; Harmondsworth: Penguin, 1953), p. 14.

91. The early chapters of Stoker's *Lady Athlyne* (1908) see its aristomilitary hero languishing in a Boer prisoner-of-war camp, for example. Elsewhere, as in *The Lady of the Shroud* (1909), Stoker preferred to choose his heroes from the disreputable branches of titled families.

92. See Bram Stoker, *Original Foundation Notes and Data for Dracula,* Rosenbach Museum and Library, Philadelphia. On the basis of this material, Joseph S. Bierman in his article "The Genesis and Dating of *Dracula* from Bram Stoker's Working Notes," *Notes and Queries* 24, no. 1 (1977): 39–41, argues that the author had begun work on the novel as early as 1890.

93. In *A Glimpse of America,* Stoker's brief remarks on "negroes" occur in a discussion of "tramps, and other execrations of civilization." Stoker notes coolly that in cases where "some outrage has been committed, particularly

when a woman has been the victim" and "a negro has been the delinquent, he is almost invariably lynched." Stoker's implied judgment seems to be that such "dangerous element[s]" bring this kind of "ruthless severity" upon themselves; see *A Glimpse of America: A Lecture Given at the London Institution, 28 December 1885* (London: Sampson Low, Marston & Co., 1886), pp. 14–15. Though the racist passages in *The Lair of the White Worm* are among the crudest ever written, I would suggest that they add little to the language of race that Stoker develops more insidiously elsewhere. But it is perhaps worth noting that even where the greater part of Stoker's original 1911 text has been reprinted the violence of the author's racist excesses has led publishers to edit out his more gratuitously offensive statements; see, for example, the 1966 paperback edition retitled *The Garden of Evil* (New York: Paperback Library, 1966).

94. Bram Stoker, *Personal Reminiscences of Henry Irving* (1906; rev. ed., New York: Macmillan, 1907), pp. 164 and 215–16.

95. Beatrice Webb's diary, quoted in J. Morris, *Pax Britannica: The Climax of an Empire* (New York: Harcourt, Brace & World, 1968), p. 26.


## 3 *Sexualitas Aeternitatis*

1. Jeffrey Moussaieff Masson, trans. and ed., *The Complete Letters of Sigmund Freud to Wilhelm Fliess, 1887–1904* (Cambridge, Mass.: Harvard University Press, 1985), p. 465. This letter, dated July 26, 1904, concerns the origins of Otto Weininger's ideas on bisexuality, ideas which Fliess regarded as his own and which he believed had passed into Weininger's hands via Freud.

2. Ford Madox Ford, *Women and Men* (Paris: Three Mountains Press, 1923), pp. 30–33. I owe this reference to Denise Riley. Arthur Mizener's biography of Ford dates this essay, originally conceived as the first part of a longer but uncompleted project, from early 1911. It was first published in *The Little Review* in 1918. See Arthur Mizener, *The Saddest Story: A Biography of Ford Madox Ford* (New York: World Publishing Company, 1971), pp. 210, 297.

3. Mrs. Emmeline Pankhurst, quoted in Asa Briggs, "The Political Scene," in Simon Nowell-Smith, ed., *Edwardian England, 1901–1914* (London: Oxford University Press, 1964), p. 98. For a discussion of conflicts within the Liberal Party on the question of women's suffrage, see Claire Hirshfield, "Fractured Faith: Liberal Party Women and the Suffrage Issue in Britain, 1892–1914," *Gender and History* 2 (Summer 1990): 173–97.

4. The quotation is from a letter by Harold Hodge, editor of the *Saturday Review*, cited in Roy Porter and Lesley Hall, *The Facts of Life: The Creation of Sexual Knowledge in Britain, 1650–1950* (New Haven: Yale University Press, 1995), p. 164. The publication details are taken from William Heinemann's 1910 reissue of *Sex and Character.*

5. Quoted in Emile Delavenay, "Lawrence, Otto Weininger, and 'Rather Raw Philosophy,'" in Christopher Heywood, ed., *D. H. Lawrence: New Studies* (New York: St. Martin's, 1987), p. 137.

6. Greta Jones, *Social Hygiene in Twentieth-Century Britain* (London: Croom Helm, 1986), p. 15.

7. Arnold I. Davidson, "Sex and the Emergence of Sexuality," *Critical Inquiry* 4 (Autumn 1987): pp. 21–22. In an important revision of Foucault's *Histoire de la sexualité* (1976), Davidson argues that this nonanatomical understanding of sexual identity creates the possibility of our modern concept of sexuality and distinguishes it from a purely biological notion of sex. He locates the conditions for this radical shift in what, following Ian Hacking, he dubs "the psychiatric style of reasoning" (p. 23).

8. Publisher's Note to William Heinemann's 1910 edition of Weininger's *Sex and Character*, p. vii.

9. Georges Canguilhem, "What Is a Scientific Ideology?" in *Ideology and Rationality in the History of the Life Sciences*, trans. Arthur Goldhammer (Cambridge, Mass.: MIT Press, 1988), p. 38.

10. Publisher's Note to William Heinemann's 1910 edition of *Sex and Character*, pp. v–vi.

11. Dugald Williamson, "The Novel and Its Neighbors," *Southern Review* 22 (November 1989): 224–43. For a more general application of this Foucauldian perspective, see Ian Hunter, David Saunders, and Dugald Williamson, *On Pornography: Literature, Sexuality, and Obscenity Law* (New York: St. Martin's, 1993).

12. Bram Stoker, "The Censorship of Fiction," *Nineteenth Century* 54 (July–December 1908): 479–87. For a useful general discussion of Victorian fiction's status as a means of moral edification, see Kenneth Graham, *English Criticism of the Novel, 1865–1900* (Oxford: Clarendon Press, 1965).

13. One thinks too of Mina Harker's "man's brain" (*D*, 404) and Queen Tera's "kingship and masculinity" (*JSS*, 176), though, as I go on to show, the case of Stephen Norman in *The Man* is undoubtedly the most complex example.

14. My focus here is upon the dialogic relationship between Stoker's renormativization of heterosexuality and a variety of sexualizing texts ranging from the technical to the literary. But I would certainly anticipate that the future development of queer readings of Stoker's work as a whole (going beyond *Dracula*) would change the configuration of my arguments.

15. In Sarah Grand's *The Heavenly Twins*, the character Angelica Hamilton-Wells also dresses up as a man. She wishes to know "the benefit of free intercourse" with a "masculine mind," unencumbered by the usual "masculine prejudices" against the opposite sex. See *The Heavenly Twins*, intro. Carol A. Senf (1893; Ann Arbor: University of Michigan Press, 1992), p. 458.

16. This short story originally appeared in *Collier's Magazine* in November

1888; it is reprinted in its original form as "Death in the Wings" in Bram Stoker, *Midnight Tales*, ed. Peter Haining (London: Peter Owen, 1990), 59–70. Stoker subsequently included a revised version in his collection *Snowbound: The Record of a Theatrical Touring Party* (London: Collier, 1908); this later variant is reprinted as "A Star Trap" in *The Bram Stoker Bedside Companion*, ed. Charles Osborne (New York: Taplinger, 1973), from which the above quotations are taken (pp. 102, 113).

17. Bram Stoker, "The Censorship of Stage Plays," *Nineteenth Century* 46 (July–December 1909): 987. Stoker took a keen personal interest in the report: he had given evidence before its authors, the Joint Committee of both Houses of Parliament, appointed to inquire into the censorship of plays, on August 13, 1909.

18. See, for example, James Ashcroft Noble, "The Fiction of Sexuality," *Contemporary Review* 67 (1895): 490–98.

19. See George Egerton's letter to Stoker, September 27, 1898 (London), Brotherton Collection, Leeds University Library.

20. Ferrero's thesis was skeptically reviewed by Stoker's Irish friend Stephen Gwynn in his essay "Bachelor Women," *Contemporary Review* 73 (June 1898): 866–75. Karl Pearson's 1885 lecture "The Woman's Question," in which he depicts the decadence of female consumption as the mirror image of the decadence of prostitution, is reprinted in *The Ethic of Freethought and Other Addresses and Essays* (1887; London: Adam and Charles Black, 1901), pp. 354–78.

21. Sigmund Freud, "Lecture 33: Femininity," in *The Pelican Freud Library*, Vol. 2, *New Introductory Lectures on Psychoanalysis* [1933], ed. James Strachey and Angela Richards (Harmondsworth: Penguin, 1973), p. 149.

22. Esmé Wingfield-Stratford, *The Victorian Sunset* (New York: William Morrow, 1932), p. 376. As the author notes succinctly: "The army corps was beaten, not at one point only, but at all."

23. J. A. Spender, "The Liberal Party—Past and Future," *Contemporary Review* 82 (August 1902): 156.

24. J. A. Hobson, extract from *The Psychology of Jingoism* (1901), in Michael Freeden, ed., *J. A. Hobson: A Reader* (London: Unwin Hyman, 1988), p. 192.

25. Kaja Silverman, *Male Subjectivity at the Margins* (New York: Routledge, 1992), ch. 2. Her working definition refers to "any historical event, whether socially engineered or of natural occurrence, which brings a large group of male subjects into such an intimate relation with lack that they are at least for the moment unable to sustain an imaginary relation with the phallus, and so withdraw their belief from the dominant fiction. Suddenly the latter is radically de-realized, and the social formation finds itself without a mechanism for achieving consensus" (p. 55).

26. A number of commentators looking back on the South African conflict have seen it as a dress rehearsal for the First World War. See, for example,

Compton Mackenzie's view that "everything which has been attributed to the effect of the European War 1914–18 had been already brought about in this country by the Boer War." Compton Mackenzie, *Literature in My Time* (London: Rich & Cowan, 1933), p. 100. But the scale of destruction should be kept in perspective. Just under one million British troops died in World War I, compared to the 29,000 fatalities suffered during the Boer War, which, together with an additional 16,000 deaths from disease, amounted to the loss of one-tenth of the British armed forces in South Africa. Still, as Eric Hobsbawm notes, "such costs were far from negligible." E. J. Hobsbawm, *The Age of Empire, 1875–1914* (New York: Vintage Books, 1989), p. 306.

27. Harry Ludlam, *A Biography of Bram Stoker, Creator of Dracula* (1962; London: New English Library, 1977), p. 152.

28. Review of *The Man*, *Punch*, September 27, 1905, p. 234.

29. Sarah Grand, *The Heavenly Twins* (1992), p. 321. Of course, Angelica's proposal to Mr. Kilroy is a far more petulantly expressive act, accompanied as it is by her "stamping her foot at him." The history of the woman's offer of her own hand in marriage in the late-nineteenth-century and early-twentieth-century British novel remains to be written.

30. See the review of *The Gates of Life* (the abridged version of *The Man* which Stoker produced for the American market) in the *Nation*, August 20, 1908, p. 63. Cf. *Punch*, September 27, 1905, p. 234.

31. For an interesting discussion of Iota's *A Yellow Aster*, see Ann L. Ardis, *New Women, New Novels: Feminism and Early Modernism* (New Brunswick: Rutgers University Press, 1990), pp. 91–95.

32. When Freud says of women that "their super-ego is never so inexorable, so impersonal, so independent of its emotional origins as we require it to be in men," he is providing a theoretical substantiation of the charges "which critics of every epoch have brought up against women." See his essay "Some Psychical Consequences of the Anatomical Distinction between the Sexes" (1925), in Sigmund Freud, *On Sexuality: Three Essays on the Theory of Sexuality and Other Works* (Harmondsworth: Penguin, 1977), p. 342.

33. Uncle Gilbert Rowly is the late Margaret Norman's older brother and a member of the local squirearchy. Aunt Laetitia, who becomes Stephen's guardian after Squire Norman's death, is Gilbert Rowly's father's younger sister. She was also Margaret's guardian following the death of the elder Squire Rowly.

34. Radclyffe Hall, *The Well of Loneliness* (1928; New York: Covici Friede Publishers, 1929), p. 8. Stephen Gordon's mother sees in her daughter "a blemished, unworthy, maimed reproduction" of her husband (ibid.). For an incisive review of critical approaches to this text, see Teresa de Lauretis, "Sexual Indifference and Lesbian Representation," in Henry Abelove, Michèle Aina Barale and David M. Halperin, eds., *The Lesbian and Gay Studies Reader* (New York: Routledge, 1993), pp. 141–58.

35. Somerville Hall was founded in Oxford in 1879 as a women's college, but it was not considered part of the university, and no degrees were awarded to women until 1920. On the early history of this institution, see Susan J. Leonardi, *Dangerous by Degrees: Women at Oxford and the Somerville College Novelists* (New Brunswick: Rutgers University Press, 1989), ch. 1. The university settlement movement dates from the 1880s and aimed at the moral improvement of the poor. One of the best recent accounts of the movement (focusing on the questions of masculinity it raises) is Seth Koven's essay "From Rough Lads to Hooligans: Boy Life, National Culture, and Social Reform," in Andrew Parker, Mary Russo, Doris Sommer, and Patricia Yaeger, eds., *Nationalisms and Sexualities* (New York: Routledge, 1992), pp. 365–91.

36. As Esmé Wingfield-Stratford explains: "What had happened was simply that the power of the modern rifle had asserted itself in a way that had been predicted by a Polish civilian, Ivan Bloch, two years before, but which up to the time of the Great War, the soldiers had steadily refused to take into their calculations." See *The Victorian Sunset*, p. 376. The "booming cannon and shrieking shell" on the opening page of *The Man* clearly refer to the impact of the Boers' howitzers and field guns.

37. See Joseph Allen Boone, *Tradition Counter Tradition: Love and the Form of Fiction* (Chicago: University of Chicago Press, 1987), p. 97.

38. As Stefan Collini notes, duty and character are so intimately linked in Smiles's writing that his two books *Character* (1871) and *Duty* (1880) are practically impossible to tell apart "without looking at the title-page." See Stefan Collini, *Public Moralists: Political Thought and Intellectual Life in Britain, 1850–1930* (Oxford: Oxford University Press, 1991) p. 100. It is perhaps worth adding that, as late as 1902, the Irish historian W. E. H. Lecky revived these ideas in a Smilesian tract entitled *The Map of Life: Conduct and Character.*

39. George Gissing, *The Odd Women* (1893; New York: W. W. Norton, 1977), p. 77.

40. D. W. Forrest, *Francis Galton: The Life and Work of a Victorian Genius* (New York: Taplinger, 1974), p. 206.

41. Superficially at least, Leonard remains a banker's son: while he shows little skill in handling money, the only way in which he can get beyond "animal passion" in a relationship with a woman is to think of her as an "asset" or [stock] "option" (*M*, 264, 269).

42. The same combination of grace and languor define Everard Barfoot's sensuality in *The Odd Women*: "The lower half of his forehead was wrinkled, and when he did not fix his look on anything in particular, his eyelids drooped, giving him for the moment an air of languor. On sitting down, he at once abandoned himself to a posture of the completest ease, which his admirable proportions made graceful" (p. 77).

43. Significantly, her Aunt Laetitia suggests that it is literally Stephen's good breeding which saves her from real wrongdoing: "Your race, your father and

mother, your upbringing, yourself and the truth and purity which are yours" (*M*, 249). Note, however, that this defense, like that of Mr. Stonehouse, also rests upon a minimization of gender differences.

44. Not all Liberals would have regarded Weininger's socialist affiliation as a problem. In this period, "New Liberal" intellectuals like L. T. Hobhouse and J. A. Hobson were arguing for a convergence between liberalism and socialism. Characteristic of New Liberal thinking was a "new trust . . . in social action via the state—not as a necessary evil but as the just and right way of attaining human ends. Personality was considered in varying degrees to be social and had to be expressed as such both in individual conduct and in social institutions." Michael Freeden, *The New Liberalism: An Ideology of Social Reform* (Oxford: Clarendon Press, 1986), p. 257. Weininger's formulation relies more closely on philosophical idealism than this, but his view of the state as a higher, moral agency, "a union of all the separate individual aims, as the higher unit combining the purposes of the lower units" and bolstered by the "ethical notion of free combination," is quite consonant with some strands of New Liberal thought. See Otto Weininger, *Sex and Character* (New York: Putnam's, 1908), p. 307; hereafter cited in parentheses in the text.

45. Weininger's *Geschlect und Charakter* was originally published in Vienna in 1903, the same year in which the author committed suicide at the age of twenty-three. For an overview of Weininger's life, work, and influence, see Jacques Le Rider, *Le cas Otto Weininger: Racines de l'antiféminisme et de l'antisémitisme* (Paris: Presses Universitaires de France, 1982). My account of Weininger's work is not in any way intended to be exhaustive; my primary aim is to tease out the sexual politics that governed the way in which *Sex and Character* was received in Britain.

46. For an account of the relationship between Freud, Fliess, and Weininger and the dispute between them over the question of bisexuality, see Peter Heller, "A Quarrel over Bisexuality," in Gerald Chapple and Hans H. Schulte, eds., *The Turn of the Century: German Literature and Art, 1890–1915* (Bonn: Bouvier Verlag Herbert Grundmann, 1981).

47. In Weininger's additive law of sexual attraction, "an identical relation can be made out in each case of maximum sexual attraction" consisting of "the constant sum formed by the total masculinity and the total femininity" of the individuals involved (p. 31). Note that Weininger makes many qualifications to this "empirical law," emphasizing that it is by no means "the only law of sexual affinity" and that, due to the multitude of other variables present, "cases of undisturbed action of sexual affinity are rare" (p. 36).

48. Compare this statement with Weininger's own summary: "This law shows that, whilst innumerable gradations of sexuality exist, there always may be found pairs of beings the members of which are almost perfectly adapted to one another" (p. 43). Where Weininger does speak of degeneracy, he locates it in those marriages or liaisons where the laws of sexual

attraction are violated. Thus, in a notable example of his own Jewish self-hatred, he argues that "the degeneration of modern Jews may be traced in part to the fact that amongst them marriages for other reasons than love are specially common" (p. 44). Little of this comes through in a more recent selective reading of Weininger, Slavoj Žižek's Lacanian analysis, which is content to argue for *Sex and Character*'s tacit "inversion of the anti-feminist ideological apparatus" overtly proclaimed by Weininger himself, a species of unconscious knowledge alleged to have resulted in the author's suicide. See "Otto Weininger, or, 'Woman doesn't exist,'" in Slavoj Žižek, *The Metastases of Enjoyment: Six Essays on Woman and Causality* (London: Verso, 1994), pp. 137–64.

49. In his study of Edwardian England, Esmé Wingfield-Stratford notes that in the early years of the twentieth century popular interest in science shifted from biology to physics, with radium coming to be regarded as "the symbol of a veritable revolution." Similarly, new research which depicted the atom as made up of "tiny centres of electrical energy" created a growing sense of the ethereality of the material world, a loss of substance that Wingfield-Stratford melodramatically compares to the narrative development of Poe's story "The Masque of the Red Death." See Esmé Wingfield-Stratford, *The Victorian Aftermath, 1901–1914* (London: Routledge, 1933), pp. 130–31.

50. In a letter replying to Stoker's queries regarding the marriage laws in Scotland, the Bishop of Edinburgh informed the author that "perfectly *valid* marriages" can be contracted by a couple's simply declaring themselves to be man and wife in front of witnesses and then ratifying the agreement before a magistrate. The Rt. Rev. John Dowden to Bram Stoker, January 20, 1901 (Edinburgh), Brotherton Collection, Leeds University Library. Part of the importance of this letter is that it shows that Stoker was thinking about key episodes in *Lady Athlyne* at least seven and a half years before the novel was published.

51. This brief summary simplifies the couple's situation considerably. Athlyne wishes to create the most respectable impression he possibly can, so that Joy will be free to take "her husband's" car back to Ambleside in order to meet her father, even though he himself has to stay at the police station. Their "marriage" is also made technically possible by the fact that Athlyne owns an estate in Scotland and therefore has "undoubted domicile in Scotland for certain legal purposes" in accordance with an 1856 act of Parliament (*LA*, 298).

52. D. H. Lawrence, *The Trespasser* (1912; Harmondsworth: Penguin, 1960), pp. 13 and 30. Lawrence's self-criticisms can be found in his letter of February 11, 1911, to Heinemann's general editor Frederick Atkinson. A month before the novel was accepted for publication Lawrence was still complaining that the hated book was "too florid, too 'chargé.'" See James T. Boulton, ed., *The Letters of D. H. Lawrence: Volume 1, September 1901–May 1913* (Cambridge:

Cambridge University Press, 1979), pp. 229–30 and 358. Interestingly, Ford Madox Ford remembers early drafts of the novel as "much . . . more phallic than is the book as it stands and much more moral in the inverted-puritanic sense" (p. 178, n. 2).

53. D. H. Lawrence, *Apropos of Lady Chatterley's Lover* (London: Martin Secker, 1931), p. 77. On the sexual politics of Lawrence's first novel, see Margaret Storch, "The Lacerated Male: Ambivalent Images of Women in *The White Peacock*," *D. H. Lawrence Review* 21 (Summer 1989): 117–36.

54. *The Trespasser*, p. 30. An episode in which the two lovers wander along the seashore, lingering by "the lovely little rock-pools," expands upon this contrast: "She loved the trifles and the toys, the mystery and the magic of things. She would not own life to be relentless. It was either beautiful, fantastic, or weird, or inscrutable, or else mean and vulgar, below consideration. He had to get a sense of the anemone and a sympathetic knowledge of its experience, into his blood, before he was satisfied. To Helena an anemone was one more fantastic pretty figure in her kaleidoscope" (pp. 64–65). For a pioneering analysis of the philosophical convergences and contrasts between Lawrence and Weininger, see Janko Lavrin, "Sex and Eros (On Rozanov, Weininger, and D. H. Lawrence)," *European Quarterly* 1 (August 1934): 88–96. The case for Weininger's direct influence upon Lawrence is argued by Emile Delavenay in "Lawrence, Otto Weininger, and 'Rather Raw Philosophy.'"

55. The *Nottinghamshire Guardian Literary Supplement*, July 2, 1912, quoted in *The Letters of D. H. Lawrence*, 1:425, n. 3. In *The White Peacock*, the gamekeeper Annable's paternal exhortation to "be a good animal, true to your animal instinct" and Leslie Tempest's "animal vigour" seem to indicate attractive traits in characters who are by no means unproblematically attractive. See D. H. Lawrence, *The White Peacock* (1911; Harmondsworth: Penguin, 1982), pp. 89 and 208.

56. D. H. Lawrence, *Women in Love* (1920; New York: Viking, 1975), p. 289.

57. David Trotter, *The English Novel in History, 1895–1920* (London: Routledge, 1993), p. 192. Significantly, Trotter places *Women in Love* in a genealogy which he traces back to the "mystical-eugenic union[s]" found in Sarah Grand and George Egerton, and later developed by George Gissing and E. M. Forster. However, while *Women in Love* should be seen as a "formal and ideological" solution to a problem originating in the 1890s, it by no means follows that it represents an altogether successful solution (p. 193). For a reading which brings into focus the self-defeating quality of Lawrence's narrative strategy, see Tony Pinkney, *D. H. Lawrence and Modernism* (Iowa City: University of Iowa Press, 1990), pp. 79–99.

58. See Ed Cohen, *Talk on the Wilde Side: Toward a Genealogy of a Discourse on Male Sexualities* (New York: Routledge, 1993), esp. ch. 2.

59. See Bentley B. Gilbert, "Health and Politics: The British Physical Deterioration Report of 1904," *Bulletin of the History of Medicine* 39 (1965): 143–53.

Gilbert argues that the report led directly to the social reform legislation brought in by the Liberals after 1906.

60. David Cannadine estimates that between 1870 and 1914 approximately 10 percent of aristocratic marriages were to American brides. See Cannadine, *The Decline and Fall of the British Aristocracy* (New York: Anchor, 1992), p. 347. The marriage in 1874 of Winston Churchill's father, Lord Randolph Churchill, to the New York heiress Jennie Jerome was a famous and early example of this trend.

61. The phrase "questions of fact" is used euphemistically by L. T. Hobhouse in his classic 1911 text *Liberalism* to refer to those difficult situations where "the concrete teaching of history and the practical insight of statesmanship" dictate limitations on the "elementary rights" of other races and nations. See Hobhouse, *Liberalism and Other Writings*, ed. James Meadowcroft (Cambridge University Press, 1994), p. 20.


## Coda: Travels in Romania

1. Branka Magas, *The Destruction of Yugoslavia: Tracking the Break-Up, 1980–92* (London: Verso, 1993), p. 320.

2. Edgar Reichmann, "Le retour des vampires," *Le Monde*, May 27, 1994, p. viii. My translation.

3. For a different political spin, consider the opening lines of Martin Walker's article "Spectre of Cold War Returns," *Manchester Guardian Weekly*, August 25, 1991, p. 7: "If the corpse of the Cold War is clambering from its grave, the West's timorous and complacent leaders must agonise whether they failed to drive a stake through its heart when they had the chance." Of course, such examples are legion.

4. See John Gray, "Agonistic Liberalism," *Social Philosophy and Policy* 12 (Winter 1995): 111.

5. Jean Baudrillard, *Symbolic Exchange and Death*, trans. Iain Hamilton Grant (London: Sage, 1993), 125–26.

6. Unless otherwise indicated, all quotations are taken directly from the film of *Bram Stoker's Dracula* (Columbia Pictures, 1992), which differs in detail from the published screenplay.

7. See Bram Stoker, *Original Foundation Notes and Data for Dracula*, Rosenbach Museum and Library, Philadelphia.

8. Stuart Hall, "What Is This 'Black' in Black Popular Culture?" in *Black Popular Culture*, a Project by Michele Wallace, ed. Gina Dent (Seattle: Bay Press, 1992), p. 32.

9. Since it is both a myth of uncanny return and a myth which is itself forever returning, one might almost see *Dracula* as the most quintessential of myths, the myth of myths. I owe this point to Rachel Bowlby.

10. Claude Lévi-Strauss, *Mythologiques: Le Cru et le Cuit* (Paris: Plon, 1964), p. 26, and Roland Barthes, *Mythologies*, trans. Annette Lavers (St. Albans: Paladin, 1973), p. 142.

11. Claude Lévi-Strauss, "A Confrontation," *New Left Review* 62 (July–August 1970): 63.

12. Lecercle sees a convergence in this formula between Hegelian-Marxist analyses of myth and Lévi-Strauss's early view that myth provides "a logical model capable of overcoming a contradiction (an impossible achievement if, as it happens, the contradiction is real)." See Claude Lévi-Strauss, *Structural Anthropology*, trans. Claire Jacobson and Brooke Schoepf (Harmondsworth: Penguin, 1977), p. 229. But it is clear that there is a debt to Althusserian Marxism here too: ideology as the imaginary relation of subjects to their real conditions of existence.

13. Jean-Jacques Lecercle, *Frankenstein: Mythe et Philosophie* (Paris: PUF, 1988), pp. 75–77 (my translation). Lecercle's brief remarks on *Dracula* are introduced by way of illustrative contrast to his analysis of *Frankenstein*. *Dracula* is precisely "l'autre grand mythe fantastique." Reichmann makes a similar point about the sexualization of the vampire when he notes that writers and artists gave the history of Vlad the Impaler "une connotation érotique." Edgar Reichmann, "Le retour des vampires," p. viii.

14. Lecercle, p. 122. At this point it becomes necessary to separate out two somewhat different aspects of Lecercle's argument. For if his analysis of myth remains theoretically indebted to earlier models that have increasingly been viewed as resting upon highly questionable foundations—reflectionism, structuralism, and the like—in practice, Lecercle's reading of myth as a process of articulation suggests an unstable mix of structurally heterogeneous elements that ultimately evades any fixed order of causality. See Jacques Derrida, "Structure, Sign, and Play in the Discourse of the Human Sciences," in *Writing and Difference*, trans. Alan Bass (London: Routledge & Kegan Paul, 1978).

15. When *Children of the Night* recently appeared as a mass market paperback from Warner Books it was hyped as "the brilliant vampire novel by America's new prince of horror," and featured an encomium by Stephen King on its cover.

16. "His Bloody Valentine," Francis Ford Coppola in interview with Manohla Dargis, *Village Voice*, November 24, 1992, p. 66.

17. According to Coppola: "I made a big point that when Dracula dies he just becomes a man, I found that very Christ-like somehow. There are those figures in our lives, and maybe that's what Christ really means, who are the ones that must die or the ones who must court evil, they do it for us. In the end, it's the sacrificial role Christ plays—he who must die" (quoted in Dargis, p. 66).

18. For analyses of the homosexual subtext in *Dracula*, see Christopher

Craft's classic essay " 'Kiss Me with those Red Lips': Gender and Inversion in Bram Stoker's *Dracula*," *Representations* 8 (1984): 107–33, and also Marjorie Howes, "The Mediation of the Feminine: Bisexuality, Homoerotic Desire, and Self-Expression in Bram Stoker's *Dracula*," *Texas Studies in Language and Literature* 30, no. 1 (1988): 104–19.

19. Ishioka Eiko quoted in Francis Ford Coppola, Ishioka Eiko, and David Seidner, *Coppola and Eiko on "Bram Stoker's Dracula*," ed. Susan Dworkin (San Francisco: Collins San Francisco, 1992), p. 41.

20. Ibid.

21. Francis Ford Coppola, quoted in Francis Ford Coppola and James V. Hart, *Bram Stoker's Dracula: The Film and the Legend* (New York: Newmarket Press, 1992), p. 64.

22. Coppola and Hart, *Bram Stoker's Dracula: The Film and the Legend*, pp. 30 and 47.

23. Ryszard Kapuscinski, foreword to Edward Behr, *Kiss the Hand You Cannot Bite: The Rise and Fall of the Ceauşescus* (New York: Villard Books, 1991), p. xi.

24. Peter Millar, "The Family a Nation Learned to Loathe," *Sunday Times*, December 24, 1989, p. A13.

25. John Sweeney, *The Life and Evil Times of Nicolae Ceauşescu* (London: Hutchinson, 1991), p. 20.

26. Ibid., p. 24. Readers curious as to how Sweeney's political sociology of Romania can find space for the 1989 revolution will be reassured to learn that the least orientalized parts of the country were the first to rebel. For an alternative view, see Sam Beck, "What Brought Romanians to Revolt," *Critique of Anthropology* 11, no. 1 (1991): 7–31.

27. David Edgar, "Whirlpools on the Danube," *Manchester Guardian Weekly*, March 13, 1991, p. 26. For a recent survey of East European ethnic politics, see Stephen R. Bowers, "Ethnic Politics in Eastern Europe," *Conflict Studies* 248 (London: Research Institute for the Study of Conflict and Terrorism, 1992), pp. 1–25.

28. Laszlo Kurti, "Transylvania, Land Beyond Reason: Toward an Anthropological Analysis of a Contested Terrain," *Dialectical Anthropology* 14, no. 1 (1989): 21–23. Note that Count Dracula tells Jonathan Harker that he belongs to the Szekely, thereby proudly asserting what are entirely uncertain origins (*D*, 40).

29. George Galloway and Bob Wylie, *Downfall: The Ceauşescus and the Romanian Revolution* (London: Futura, 1991), p. 54.

30. Jill Neimark, "Romanian Roulette," *Village Voice*, October 1, 1991, p. 28.

31. Dan Simmons, *Children of the Night* (New York: Putnam's, 1992), p. 221. Subsequent references are given in parentheses.

32. Vampires are at their most human in Anne Rice's trend-setting *Interview with the Vampire* (1976). But note the opposed tendency for humans (at least *female* humans) to turn into monsters in contemporary thrillers like *Fatal*

*Attraction* and *Single White Female.* See Judith Williamson, "Nightmare on Madison Avenue," *New Statesman,* January 15, 1988, pp. 28–29.

33. While both texts gingerly flirt with the theme of AIDS, neither lets it dominate the narrative. Of the two, the relation of Coppola's film to AIDS is the most vague, the most puzzling, and possibly the most cynical. Despite an assortment of references to the disease in the movie's publicity and in published extracts from the director's production diary, Coppola is on record as saying that "the only direct connection between *Bram Stoker's Dracula* and AIDS is that if his film succeeds, he'll go on to make 'a real film about AIDS,' tentatively titled *The Cure.*" Laurie Winer, "Death Becomes Him," *Harper's Bazaar* 3370 (October 1992): 172.

34. In Stoker's novel, though Dracula dies with "a look of peace" on his face, it is his extinction at the hands of the book's male heroes (not Mina's) that is important, for he does not die as a man as he does in the film, but immediately crumbles to dust (*D*, 447).

35. Etienne Balibar, "Racism and Nationalism," in Etienne Balibar and Immanuel Wallerstein, *Race, Nation, Class: Ambiguous Identities* (London: Verso, 1991), p. 61. As Balibar's examples suggest, transnational racisms are typically reinscribed in nationalist ideologies, part of what he terms "the cycle of historical reciprocity of nationalism and racism" in which each can emerge out of the other. See Balibar, p. 53.

36. Balibar, p. 57. Importantly, Balibar's argument is not antihumanist per se; rather, he distinguishes between different *humanisms* in terms of their compatibility/incompatibility with racism. In practical terms, humanism can serve as "a politics and an ethics of the defense of civil rights without limitations or exceptions." However, when humanism is conceived theoretically as "a doctrine which makes man as a species the origin and end of declared and established rights," then the way is open for any number of racist exclusions. See Balibar, pp. 62–64.

37. Tzvetan Todorov, *The Fantastic: A Structural Approach to a Literary Genre,* trans. Richard Howard (Ithaca: Cornell University Press, 1975), p. 168.

38. Homi K. Bhabha, "Culture's In Between," *Artforum* 32 (September 1993): 211.

# Bibliography

## Primary Sources

"An Irish American Comedy." Review of Bram Stoker's *Lady Athlyne*. *The World's Work* (London) 12 (July 1908): 174.

Arnold, Matthew. *The Study of Celtic Literature*. 1867. London: Smith, Elder & Co., 1912.

Beddoe, John. *The Races of Britain: A Contribution to the Anthropology of Western Europe*. 1885. London: Hutchinson, 1971.

Bright, John. *Speeches on Questions of Public Policy*. 2 vols. Edited by James E. Thorold Rogers. London: Macmillan, 1868.

Buchan, John. *The Three Hostages*. 1924. Harmondsworth: Penguin, 1953.

———. *Memory Hold-the-Door*. London: Hodder & Stoughton, 1940.

Caine, Hall. "The New Watchwords of Fiction." *Contemporary Review* 57 (1890): 479–88.

Carleton, William. *The Black Prophet: A Tale of Irish Famine*. 1847. Reprinted in vol. 3 of *The Works of William Carleton*, 777–935. New York: Collier, 1881.

Carlyle, Thomas. *On Heroes, Hero-Worship, and the Heroic in History*. 1841. Edited by Carl Niemeyer. Lincoln: University of Nebraska Press, 1966.

Carpenter, William B. *Principles of Mental Physiology, with Their Applications to the Training and Discipline of the Mind and the Study of Its Morbid Conditions*. 4th ed. New York: D. Appleton, 1884.

Churchill, Winston S. *Liberalism and the Social Problem: Speeches 1906–1909*. London: Hodder & Stoughton, 1909.

D'Albe, Edmund E. Fournier. *The Life of Sir William Crookes*. London: Fisher Unwin, 1923.

De Quincey, Thomas. "On Murder Considered as One of the Fine Arts." 1854. Rpt. in vol. 13 of *The Collected Writings of Thomas De Quincey*, edited by David Masson, 9–124. Edinburgh: Adam and Charles Black, 1890.

Dowden, Edward. "The Poetry of Democracy: Walt Whitman." *Westminster Review* (U.S. ed.) 96 (July 1871): 16–32.

———. *Fragments from Old Letters: E. D. to E. D. W., 1869–1892*. First Series. London: Dent, 1914.

———. *Fragments from Old Letters: E. D. to E. D. W., 1869–1892*. Second Series. London: Dent, 1914.

"Editorial." *The Labour World*, November 29, 1890, p. 8.

Edwards, Amelia B. *Pharaohs, Fellahs, and Explorers*. New York: Harper, 1891.

*Egyptian Tales*. Edited by W. M. Flinders Petrie. London: Methuen, 1895.

*Florence Farr, Bernard Shaw, W. B. Yeats: Letters*. Edited by Clifford Bax. New York: Dodd, Mead, 1942.

Ford, Ford Madox. *Women and Men*. Paris: Three Mountains Press, 1923.

Galton, Francis. *Hereditary Genius: An Inquiry into Its Laws and Consequences*. 1869. London: Macmillan, 1914.

Gissing, George. *The Odd Women*. 1893. New York: Norton, 1977.

Gladstone, William E. *The Gladstone Diaries*. Vol. 14: 1887–1891. Edited by H. C. G. Matthew. Oxford: Clarendon, 1994.

Grand, Sarah. *The Heavenly Twins*. 1893. Introduced by Carol A. Senf. Ann Arbor: University of Michigan Press, 1992.

Greg, William R. "On the Failure of Natural Selection in the Case of Man." *Fraser's Magazine* 78 (September 1868): 353–62.

Gwynn, Stephen. "Bachelor Women." *Contemporary Review* 73 (June 1898): 866–75.

Haggard, H. Rider. *King Solomon's Mines*. 1885. Edited by Dennis Butts. Oxford: Oxford University Press, 1989.

———. *She: A History of Adventure*. 1887. Edited by Daniel Karlin. Oxford: Oxford University Press, 1991.

Hall, Radclyffe. *The Well of Loneliness*. 1928. New York: Covici Friede, 1929.

Hobhouse, L. T. *Liberalism and Other Writings*. 1911. Edited by James Meadowcroft. Cambridge: Cambridge University Press, 1994.

"Impressions of America." *Daily Telegraph*, December 29, 1885, n.p.

James, Henry. "Mr. Henry Irving's *MacBeth*." 1875. Reprinted in *The Scenic Art: Notes on Acting and the Drama, 1872–1901*, edited by Allan Wade. New York: Hill & Wang, 1957.

Johnson, Major E. C. *On the Track of the Crescent*. 1885. Excerpted in *The Origins of Dracula: The Background to Bram Stoker's Gothic Masterpiece*, edited by Clive Leatherdale, 97–107. London: William Kimber, 1987.

Kingsley, Charles. *Charles Kingsley: His Letters and Memories of His Life*. Edited by his wife. 2 vols. London: Henry S. King, 1877.

Lavater, Johann Caspar. *Essays on Physiognomy, Designed to Promote Knowledge and the Love of Mankind*. 5 vols. Translated by Henry Hunter. London: John Murray, 1789.

Lawrence, D. H. *The Letters of D. H. Lawrence*. Vol. 1: September 1901–May 1903. Edited by James T. Boulton. Cambridge: Cambridge University Press, 1979.

———. *The White Peacock*. 1911. Harmondsworth: Penguin, 1982.

———. *The Trespasser*. 1912. Harmondsworth: Penguin, 1960.

———. *Women in Love*. 1920. New York: Viking, 1975.

———. *Apropos of Lady Chatterley's Lover*. London: Martin Secker, 1931.

Lecky, William E. H. *Democracy and Liberty*. 2 vols. 1896. Indianapolis: Liberty Classics, 1981.

Lucy, Henry. "London Letter." *Keighley News* July 10, 1897, n.p.

MacArthur, James. "Books and Bookmen." *Harper's Weekly*, February 20, 1904, p. 276.

Mackenzie, Compton. *Literature in My Time.* London: Rich & Cowan, 1933.

Masterman, Charles F. G. *In Peril of Change: Essays Written in Time of Tranquility.* New York: Huebsch, 1905.

———. *The Condition of England.* 1909. Edited by J. T. Boulton. London: Methuen, 1960.

Mill, John Stuart. *The Logic of the Moral Sciences.* 1843. Introduced by A. J. Ayer. London: Duckworth, 1987.

———. *On Liberty.* 1859. Edited by Gertrude Himmelfarb. Harmondsworth: Penguin, 1974.

Morgan, Lady. *The Wild Irish Girl.* 1806. Introduced by Brigid Brophy. London: Pandora, 1986.

"Mr. Bright in Ireland." *The Times,* October 31, 1866, p. 12.

"Mr. Bright in Ireland." *The Times,* November 3, 1866, p. 5.

Myers, Frederic W. H. "Multiplex Personality." *Proceedings of the Society for Psychical Research* 4 (1886): 496–514.

"New Books and Magazines." Review of Stoker's *The Snake's Pass. The Labour World,* November 29, 1890, p. 15.

Noble, James Ashcroft. "The Fiction of Sexuality." *Contemporary Review* 67 (1895): 490–98.

O'Brien, William. *When We Were Boys.* 1890. Introduced by Robert Lee Wolff. New York: Garland, 1979.

———. *Irish Ideas.* London: Longmans, Green & Co., 1893.

Pearson, Karl. "The Woman's Question." 1885. In *The Ethic of Freethought and Other Addresses and Essays,* 354–78. 1887. London: Adam and Charles Black, 1901.

"Publisher's Note." Otto Weininger's *Sex and Character.* 1904. London: Heinemann, 1910.

Review of Stoker's *The Snake's Pass. Punch,* December 6, 1890, p. 269.

Review of Stoker's *Dracula. Spectator,* July 31, 1897, pp. 150–51.

Review of Stoker's *The Man. Punch,* September 27, 1905, p. 234.

Review of Stoker's *The Gates of Life. Nation,* August 20, 1908, p. 63.

Spender, J. A. "The Liberal Party—Past and Future." *Contemporary Review* 82 (August 1902): 153–65.

Stoddart, Jane. ["Lorna"]. "Mr. Bram Stoker. A Chat with the Author of *Dracula.*" The British Weekly, July 1, 1897, p. 185.

Stoker, Bram. *The Duties of Clerks of Petty Sessions in Ireland.* Dublin: John Falconer, 1879.

———. *A Glimpse of America: A Lecture Given at the London Institution, 28 December 1885.* London: Sampson Low, Marston, 1886.

———. *The Snake's Pass.* 1890. Dingle Co. Kerry: Brandon, 1990.

———. *Original Foundation Notes and Data for "Dracula."* Philadelphia: Rosenbach Museum and Library, c.1890–c.1897.

———. *Dracula.* 1897. Harmondsworth: Penguin, 1979.

------. *The Mystery of the Sea.* London: Heinemann, 1902.

------. *The Jewel of Seven Stars.* London: Heinemann, 1903.

------. *The Man.* London: Heinemann, 1905.

------. *Personal Reminiscences of Henry Irving.* 1906. Rev. ed. London: Heinemann, 1907.

------. "The Great White Fair in Dublin." *The World's Work* (London) 9 (May 1907), Special Irish Number: 570–76.

------. "The World's Greatest Shipbuilding Yard: Impressions of a Visit to Messrs. Harland and Wolff's Shipbuilding Yards at Belfast." *The World's Work* (London) 9 (May 1907), Special Irish Number: 647–50.

------. "Mr. Winston Churchill Talks of His Hopes, His Work, and His Ideals to Bram Stoker." *Daily Chronicle,* January 15, 1908, p. 8.

------. *Lady Athlyne.* New York: Paul R. Reynolds, 1908.

------. "The Work of William De Morgan: An Artist, Manufacturer, and Inventor Who Began Writing Novels at the Age of Sixty-Four." *The World's Work* (London) 12 (July 1908): 160–64.

------. "The Censorship of Fiction." *The Nineteenth Century and After* 64 (July–December 1908): 479–87.

------. *Snowbound: The Record of a Theatrical Touring Party.* London: Collier, 1908.

------. "A Star Trap." 1908. In *The Bram Stoker Bedside Companion,* edited by Charles Osborne, 102–14. New York: Taplinger, 1973.

------. *The Lady of the Shroud.* 1909. London: William Rider, 1925.

------. "The Censorship of Stage Plays." *The Nineteenth Century and After* 66 (July–December 1909): 974–89.

------. *Famous Impostors.* New York: Sturgis & Walton, 1910.

------. *The Lair of the White Worm.* London: William Rider, 1911.

------. *The Jewel of Seven Stars.* 1912. New York: Carroll & Graf, 1989.

------. *Dracula's Guest.* 1914. Dingle Co. Kerry: Brandon, 1990.

------. *The Garden of Evil.* Reprint of *The Lair of the White Worm.* New York: Paperback Library, 1966.

------. *Shades of Dracula: Bram Stoker's Uncollected Stories.* Edited by Peter Haining. London: William Kimber, 1982.

------. *Midnight Tales.* Edited by Peter Haining. London: Peter Owen, 1990.

Stoker, George. *With "The Unspeakables"; Or, Two Years' Campaigning in European and Asiatic Turkey.* London: Chapman & Hall, 1878.

Thackeray, William M. *The Irish Sketchbook.* 1843. Introduced by Christopher Morash. Gloucester: Alan Sutton, 1990.

Traubel, Horace. *With Walt Whitman in Camden: Vol. 4, 21 January–7 April 1889.* Edited by Sculley Bradley. Carbondale: Southern Illinois University Press, 1959.

Weininger, Otto. *Sex and Character.* 1904. New York: Putnam's, 1908.

Wells, H. G. *A Modern Utopia.* 1905. Lincoln: University of Nebraska Press, 1967.

Whitman, Walt. *Democratic Vistas.* 1871. New York: The Liberal Arts Press, 1949.

Wyndham, Horace. *The Nineteen Hundreds.* 1922. New York: Thomas Seltzer, 1923.


## Secondary Sources

Aldiss, Brian W. *Dracula Unbound.* New York: HarperCollins, 1991.

Arata, Stephen D. "The Occidental Tourist: *Dracula* and the Anxiety of Reverse Colonization." *Victorian Studies* 33 (Summer 1990): 621–45.

Ardis, Ann L. *New Women, New Novels: Feminism and Early Modernism.* New Brunswick: Rutgers University Press, 1990.

Auerbach, Nina. *Romantic Imprisonment: Women and Other Glorified Outcasts.* New York: Columbia University Press, 1985.

Bachelard, Gaston. *The Poetics of Space.* 1958. Translated by Maria Jolas. Boston: Beacon, 1969.

Balibar, Etienne. "Racism and Nationalism." In *Race, Nation, Class: Ambiguous Identities,* by Etienne Balibar and Immanuel Wallerstein, 37–67. London: Verso, 1991.

Baudrillard, Jean. *Symbolic Exchange and Death.* 1976. Translated by Iain Hamilton Grant. London: Sage, 1993.

Beck, Sam. "What Brought Romanians to Revolt." *Critique of Anthropology* 11, no. 1 (1991): 7–31.

Berlant, Lauren. *The Anatomy of National Fantasy: Hawthorne, Utopia, and Everyday Life.* Chicago: University of Chicago Press, 1991.

Bernal, Martin. *Black Athena: The Afroasiatic Roots of Classical Civilization.* Vol. 1, *The Fabrication of Ancient Greece, 1785–1985.* New Brunswick: Rutgers University Press, 1987.

Bew, Paul. *C. S. Parnell.* Dublin: Gill & Macmillan, 1980.

Bhabha, Homi K. "Culture's In Between." *Artforum* 32 (September 1993): 167–68, 211–14.

Bierman, Joseph S. "The Genesis and Dating of *Dracula* from Bram Stoker's Working Notes." *Notes and Queries* 24, no. 1 (1977): 39–41.

———. "*Dracula:* Prolonged Childhood Illness and the Oral Triad." *American Imago* 29 (Summer 1972): 186–98.

Bierne, Piers. "Heredity versus Environment: A Reconsideration of Charles Goring's *The English Convict* (1913)." *British Journal of Criminology* 28 (Summer 1988): 315–39.

Boone, Joseph Allen. *Tradition Counter-Tradition: Love and the Form of Fiction.* Chicago: University of Chicago Press, 1987.

Boone, Troy. " 'He is English and therefore adventurous': Politics, Decadence, and *Dracula.*" *Studies in the Novel* 25 (Spring 1993): 76–91.

Bowers, Stephen R. "Ethnic Politics in Eastern Europe." *Conflict Studies* 248. London: The Research Institute for the Study of Conflict and Terrorism, 1992.

Briggs, Asa. "The Political Scene." In *Edwardian England, 1901–1914,* edited by Simon Nowell-Smith, 43–101. London: Oxford University Press, 1964.

Bristow, Joseph. "Post-sexuality? The Wilde Centenary." *Radical Philosophy* 71 (May/June 1995): 2–4.

Brown, Terence. "Edward Dowden: Irish Victorian." In *Ireland's Literature: Selected Essays,* 29–48. Mullingar: Lilliput, 1988.

Burn, W. L. *The Age of Equipoise: A Study of the Mid-Victorian Generation.* London: Allen & Unwin, 1964.

Butler, Judith. "The Force of Fantasy: Feminism, Mapplethorpe, and Discursive Excess." *differences* 2 (Summer 1990): 105–25.

———. *Bodies That Matter: On the Discursive Limits of "Sex."* New York: Routledge, 1993.

Canguilhem, Georges. *Ideology and Rationality in the History of the Life Sciences.* 1977. Translated by Arthur Goldhammer. Cambridge, Mass.: MIT Press, 1988.

Cannadine, David. *The Decline and Fall of the British Aristocracy.* 1990. New York: Anchor Books, 1992.

Carlton, Eric. *Ideology and Social Order.* London: Routledge, 1977.

Chakrabarty, Dipesh. "Postcoloniality and the Artifice of History: Who Speaks for 'Indian' Pasts?" *Representations* 37 (Winter 1992): 1–26.

Chesnutt, Margaret. *Studies in the Short Stories of William Carleton.* Göteburg: Acta Universitatis Gothoburgensis, 1976.

Chrisman, Laura. "The Imperial Unconscious? Representations of Imperial Discourse." *Critical Quarterly* 32 (Autumn 1990): 38–58.

Cohen, Ed. *Talk on the Wilde Side: Toward a Genealogy of a Discourse on Male Sexualities.* New York: Routledge, 1993.

Cohen, Walter. "An Interview with Martin Bernal." *Social Text* 35 (Summer 1993): 1–24.

Collini, Stefan. *Liberalism and Sociology: L. T. Hobhouse and the Political Argument in England, 1880–1914.* Cambridge: Cambridge University Press, 1979.

———. "The Idea of 'Character' in Victorian Political Thought." *Transactions of the Royal Historical Society* (5th ser.) 35 (1985): 29–50.

———. *Public Moralists: Political Thought and Intellectual Life in Britain, 1850–1930.* Oxford: Oxford University Press, 1991.

Comerford, R. V. "Ireland 1850–70: Post-famine and Mid-Victorian." In *Ireland under the Union I: 1801–70,* edited by W. E. Vaughan, 372–95. Vol. 5 of *A New History of Ireland.* Oxford: Clarendon, 1989.

Cooter, Roger. "The Power of the Body: The Early Nineteenth Century." In *Natural Order: Historical Studies of Scientific Culture,* edited by Barry Barnes and Steven Shapin, 73–92. Beverly Hills: Sage, 1979.

Coppola, Francis Ford, et al. *Coppola and Eiko on "Bram Stoker's Dracula."* Edited by Susan Dworkin. San Francisco: Collins San Francisco, 1992.

——, and James V. Hart. *Bram Stoker's Dracula: The Film and the Legend.* New York: Newmarket Press, 1992.

Coward, Rosalind. *Patriarchal Precedents: Sexuality and Social Relations.* London: Routledge & Kegan Paul, 1983.

Cowling, Mary. *The Artist as Anthropologist: The Representation of Type and Character in Victorian Art.* Cambridge: Cambridge University Press, 1989.

Craft, Christopher. " 'Kiss Me with those Red Lips': Gender and Inversion in Bram Stoker's *Dracula.*" *Representations* 8 (1984): 107–33.

Curtis, L. Perry. *Apes and Angels: The Irishman in Victorian Caricature.* Washington: Smithsonian Institution Press, 1971.

Dalby, Richard. *Bram Stoker: A Bibliography of First Editions.* London: Dracula Press, 1983.

Daly, Nicholas. "That Obscure Object of Desire: Victorian Commodity Culture and Fictions of the Mummy." *Novel* 28 (Fall 1994): 24–51.

——. "Irish Roots: The Romance of History in Bram Stoker's *The Snake's Pass.*" *Literature and History.* 3d series, 4 (Autumn 1995): 42–70.

Dargis, Manohla. "His Bloody Valentine." *Village Voice,* November 24, 1992, p. 66.

Davidoff, Leonore. "Class and Gender in Victorian England." In *Sex and Class in Women's History,* edited by Judith L. Newton et al., 17–71. London: Routledge, 1983.

Davidson, Arnold I. "Sex and the Emergence of Sexuality." *Critical Inquiry* 4 (Autumn 1987): 16–48.

Deane, Seamus. *A Short History of Irish Literature.* 1986. Notre Dame: University of Notre Dame Press, 1994.

De Lauretis, Teresa. "Sexual Indifference and Lesbian Representation." In *The Lesbian and Gay Studies Reader,* edited by Henry Abelove et al, 141–58. New York: Routledge, 1993.

Delavenay, Emile. "Lawrence, Otto Weininger, and 'Rather Raw Philosophy.' " In *D. H. Lawrence: New Studies,* edited by Christopher Heywood, 137–57. New York: St. Martin's Press, 1987.

Deleuze, Gilles. *Masochism: Coldness and Cruelty.* Translated by Jean McNeil. 1967. New York: Zone Books, 1991.

Derrida, Jacques. "Structure, Sign, and Play in the Discourse of the Human Sciences." 1966. Reprinted in *Writing and Difference,* translated by Alan Bass, 278–93. London: Routledge, 1978.

Desmond, Adrian. *The Politics of Evolution: Morphology, Medicine, and Reform in Radical London.* Chicago: University of Chicago Press, 1989.

Diawara, Manthia. "Canonizing Soundiata in Mande Literature: Toward a Sociology of Narrative Elements." *Social Text* 31/32 (1992): 154–68.

Dingley, R. J. "Count Dracula and the Martians." In *The Victorian Fantasists: Essays on Culture, Society, and Belief in the Mythopoeic Fiction of the Victorian Age*, edited by Kath Filmer, 13–24. New York: St. Martin's Press, 1991.

Dowling, Linda. "The Decadent and the New Woman in the 1890's." *Nineteenth-Century Fiction* 33 (March 1979): 434–53.

Eagleton, Terry. "Form and Ideology in the Anglo-Irish Novel." *Bullán: An Irish Studies Journal* 1 (Spring 1994): 17–26.

——. *Heathcliff and the Great Hunger: Studies in Irish Culture*. London: Verso, 1995.

Edgar, David. "Whirlpools on the Danube." *Manchester Guardian Weekly*, March 13, 1991, p. 26.

Ellmann, Richard. *Yeats: The Man and the Masks*. 1948. Rev. ed. Oxford: Oxford University Press, 1979.

——. *Oscar Wilde*. New York: Vintage, 1988.

Etherington, Norman. "Rider Haggard, Imperialism, and the Layered Personality." *Victorian Studies* 22 (Autumn 1978): 71–87.

Fahnestock, Jeanne. "The Heroine of Irregular Features: Physiognomy and Conventions in Heroine Descriptions." *Victorian Studies* 24 (Spring 1981): 325–50.

Farson, Daniel. *The Man Who Wrote "Dracula": A Biography of Bram Stoker*. London: Michael Joseph, 1975.

Feltes, N. N. *Literary Capital and the Late Victorian Novel*. Madison: University of Wisconsin Press, 1993.

Flanagan, Thomas. "Literature in English, 1801–91." In *Ireland Under the Union, I: 1801–70*, edited by W. E. Vaughan, 482–522. Vol. 5 of *A New History of Ireland*. Oxford: Clarendon, 1989.

Fontana, Ernest. "Lombroso's Criminal Man and Stoker's *Dracula*." *Victorian Newsletter* 66 (Fall 1984): 25–27.

Forrest, D. W. *Francis Galton: The Life and Work of a Victorian Genius*. New York: Taplinger, 1974.

Foster, R. F. *Modern Ireland, 1600–1972*. Harmondsworth: Penguin, 1989.

——. "Protestant Magic: W. B. Yeats and the Spell of Irish History." In *Paddy and Mr. Punch: Connections in Irish and English History*. London: Allen Lane, 1993.

Foucault, Michel. *The History of Sexuality, Vol. 1: An Introduction*. 1976. Translated by Robert Hurley. Harmondsworth: Penguin, 1981.

——. "Truth and Power." In *Power/Knowledge: Selected Interviews and Other Writings, 1972–1977*, edited and translated by Colin Gordon, 109–33. Brighton: Harvester, 1980.

Freeden, Michael. *The New Liberalism: An Ideology of Social Reform*. 1978. Rev. ed. Oxford: Clarendon, 1986.

——. "Eugenics and Progressive Thought: A Study in Ideological Affinity." *Historical Journal* 22, no. 3 (1979): 645–71.

——, ed. *J. A. Hobson: A Reader*. London: Unwin Hyman, 1988.

Freud, Sigmund. "Creative Writers and Day-dreaming." 1908. Reprinted in
*Art and Literature*, translated by James Strachey and edited by Albert Dickson, 129–41. Vol. 14 of *The Pelican Freud Library*. Harmondsworth: Penguin, 1985.

———. "Formulations on the Two Principles of Mental Functioning." 1911. Reprinted in *On Metapsychology: The Theory of Psychoanalysis*, translated by James Strachey and edited by Angela Richards, 29–44. Vol. 11 of *The Pelican Freud Library*. Harmondsworth: Penguin, 1984.

———. "Medusa's Head." 1922. In *The Standard Edition of the Complete Psychological Works*, edited by James Strachey. Vol. 18. London: Hogarth Press, 1955.

———. "Some Psychical Consequences of the Anatomical Distinction between the Sexes." 1925. Reprinted in *On Sexuality: Three Essays on the Theory of Sexuality and Other Works*, translated by James Strachey and edited by Angela Richards. Vol. 7 of *The Pelican Freud Library*. Harmondsworth: Penguin, 1977.

———. "Lecture 33: Femininity." 1933. Reprinted in *New Introductory Lectures on Psychoanalysis*, translated by James Strachey and edited by James Strachey and Angela Richards. Vol. 2 of *The Pelican Freud Library*. Harmondsworth: Penguin, 1973.

———. *The Complete Letters of Sigmund Freud to Wilhelm Fliess, 1887–1904*. Translated and edited by Jeffrey Moussaieff Masson. Cambridge, Mass.: Harvard University Press, 1985.

Friedberg, Aaron L. *The Weary Titan: Britain and the Experience of Relative Decline, 1895–1905*. Princeton: Princeton University Press, 1988.

Gagnier, Reginia. "Evolution and Information, or Eroticism and Everyday Life, in *Dracula* and Late Victorian Literature." In *Sex and Death in Victorian Literature*, edited by Regina Barreca, 140–57. London: Macmillan, 1990.

Galloway, George, and Bob Wylie. *Downfall: The Ceauşescus and the Romanian Revolution*. London: Futura, 1991.

Gelder, Ken. *Reading the Vampire*. London: Routledge, 1994.

Gibbon, Peter, and M. D. Higgins. "Patronage, Tradition, and Modernisation: The Case of the Irish 'Gombeenman.'" *Economic and Social Review* 6, no. 1 (1974): 27–44.

———. "The Irish 'Gombeenman': Re-incarnation or Rehabilitation?" *Economic and Social Review* 8, no. 4 (1977): 313–20.

Gilbert, Bentley B. "Health and Politics: The British Physical Deterioration Report of 1904." *Bulletin of the History of Medicine* 39 (1965): 143–53.

Gilbert, Sandra M., and Susan Gubar. *No Man's Land*. Vol. 2 of *Sexchanges*. New Haven: Yale University Press, 1989.

Gilman, Sander L. "Black Bodies, White Bodies: Toward an Iconography of Female Sexuality in Late Nineteenth-Century Art, Medicine, and Literature." In *"Race," Writing, and Difference*, edited by Henry Louis Gates Jr., 223–61. Chicago: University of Chicago Press, 1986.

Glover, David. "Bram Stoker and the Crisis of the Liberal Subject." *New Literary History* 23 (Autumn 1992): 983–1002.

———. Introduction. *The Jewel of Seven Stars,* by Bram Stoker. Oxford: Oxford University Press, 1996.

Graham, Kenneth. *English Criticism of the Novel, 1865–1900.* Oxford: Clarendon, 1965.

Grant, Douglas. *Walt Whitman and His English Admirers.* Leeds: Leeds University Press, 1962.

Gray, John. "Agonistic Liberalism." *Social Philosophy and Policy* 12 (Winter 1995): 111–35.

Greenway, John L. "Seward's Folly: *Dracula* as a Critique of 'Normal Science.'" *Stanford Literature Review* (Fall 1986): 213–30.

Hacking, Ian. "How Should We Do the History of Statistics?" *I&C* 8 (1981): 15–26.

———. *The Taming of Chance.* Cambridge: Cambridge University Press, 1990.

Haley, Bruce. *The Healthy Body and Victorian Culture.* Cambridge, Mass.: Harvard University Press, 1978.

Hall, John A. *Liberalism: Politics, Ideology, and the Market.* London: Paladin, 1987.

Hall, Stuart. "Cultural Studies and Its Theoretical Legacies." In *Cultural Studies,* edited by Lawrence Grossberg, Cary Nelson, and Paula Treichler, 277–94. New York: Routledge, 1992.

———. "What is this 'Black' in Black Popular Culture?" In *Black Popular Culture: A Project by Michele Wallace,* edited by Gina Dent, 21–33. Seattle: Bay Press, 1992.

———, and Bill Schwarz. "State and Society, 1880–1930." In *Crises in the British State, 1880–1930,* edited by Mary Langan and Bill Schwarz, 7–32. London: Hutchinson, 1985.

Heller, Peter. "A Quarrel over Bisexuality." In *The Turn of the Century: German Literature and Art, 1890–1915,* edited by Gerald Chapple and Hans H. Schulte. Bonn: Bouvier Verlag Herbert Grundmann, 1981.

Hindle, Maurice. Introduction. *Dracula,* by Bram Stoker. Harmondsworth: Penguin, 1993.

Hirshfield, Claire. "Fractured Faith: Liberal Party Women and the Suffrage Issue in Britain, 1892–1914." *Gender and History* 2 (Summer 1990): 173–97.

Hobsbawm, Eric J. *The Age of Empire, 1875–1914.* 1987. New York: Vintage, 1989.

———. *Nations and Nationalism since 1780: Programme, Myth, Reality.* Cambridge: Cambridge University Press, 1990.

Howe, Ellic. *The Magicians of the Golden Dawn: A Documentary History of a Magical Order, 1887–1923.* London: Routledge, 1972.

Howes, Marjorie. "The Mediation of the Feminine: Bisexuality, Homoerotic Desire, and Self-Expression in Bram Stoker's *Dracula.*" *Texas Studies in Language and Literature* 30, no. 1 (1988): 104–19.

Hunter, Ian, David Saunders, and Dugald Williamson. *On Pornography: Literature, Sexuality, and Obscenity Law.* London: Macmillan, 1993.

Jameson, Fredric. "Of Islands and Trenches: Neutralization and the Production of Utopian Discourse." 1977. Reprinted in *Syntax of History*, vol. 2 of *The Ideologies of Theory, Essays 1971–1986*, 75–101. Minneapolis: University of Minnesota Press, 1988.

———. *The Seeds of Time.* New York: Columbia University Press, 1994.

Jones, Greta. *Social Darwinism and English Thought: The Interaction between Biological and Social Theory.* Brighton: Harvester, 1980.

———. *Social Hygiene in Twentieth Century Britain.* London: Croom Helm, 1986.

Joyce, Patrick. *Democratic Subjects: The Self and the Social in Nineteenth-Century England.* Cambridge: Cambridge University Press, 1994.

Kapuscinski, Ryszard. Foreword to *Kiss the Hand You Cannot Bite: The Rise and Fall of the Ceauşescus*, by Edward Behr. New York: Villard Books, 1991.

Kazanjian, David. "Notarizing Knowledge: Paranoia and Civility in Freud and Lacan." *Qui Parle* 7 (Fall 1993): 102–39.

Keating, Peter. *The Haunted Study: A Social History of the English Novel, 1875–1914.* London: Secker & Warburg, 1989.

Kennedy, Liam. "A Sceptical View on the Reincarnation of the Irish 'Gombeenman.'" *Economic and Social Review* 8, no. 3 (1977): 213–22.

Kershner, R. B., Jr. "Degeneration: The Explanatory Nightmare." *Georgia Review* 40 (Summer 1986): 416–44.

Koven, Seth. "From Rough Lads to Hooligans: Boy Life, National Culture, and Social Reform." In *Nationalisms and Sexualities*, edited by Andrew Parker et al, 365–91. New York: Routledge, 1992.

Kumar, Krishan. *Utopia and Anti-Utopia in Modern Times.* Oxford: Blackwell, 1987.

Kurti, Laszlo. "Transylvania, Land beyond Reason: Toward an Anthropological Analysis of a Contested Terrain." *Dialectical Anthropology* 14, no. 1 (1989): 21–52.

Laplanche, Jean, and J.-B. Pontalis. "Fantasy and the Origins of Sexuality." *International Journal of Psycho-Analysis* 49, no. 1 (1968): 1–18.

Lavrin, Janko. "Sex and Eros (On Rozanov, Weininger, and D. H. Lawrence)." *European Quarterly* 1 (August 1934): 88–96.

Lecercle, Jean-Jacques. *Frankenstein: Mythe et Philosophie.* Paris: PUF, 1988.

Leonardi, Susan J. *Dangerous by Degrees: Women at Oxford and the Somerville College Novelists.* New Brunswick: Rutgers University Press, 1989.

Le Rider, Jacques. *Le cas Otto Weininger: Racines de l'antiféminisme et de l'antisémitisme.* Paris: Presses Universitaires de France, 1982.

Levine, Philippa. *The Amateur and the Professional: Antiquarians, Historians, and Archaeologists in Victorian England, 1838–1886.* Cambridge: Cambridge University Press, 1986.

Lévi-Strauss, Claude. "The Structural Study of Myth." 1955. Reprinted in

*Structural Anthropology*, translated by Claire Jacobson and Brooke Schoepf, 206–31. Harmondsworth: Penguin, 1977.

——. *Mythologiques: Le Cru et le Cuit.* Paris: Plon, 1964.

——. "A Confrontation." *New Left Review* 62 (July–August 1970): 57–74.

Llobera, Josep R. "The Dark Side of Modernity." *Critique of Anthropology* 8, no. 2 (1988): 71–76.

Lloyd, David. *Nationalism and Minor Literature: James Clarence Mangan and the Emergence of Irish Cultural Nationalism.* Berkeley: University of California Press, 1987.

Ludlam, Harry. *A Biography of Dracula: The Life Story of Bram Stoker.* 1962. Reprinted as *A Biography of Bram Stoker, Creator of Dracula.* London: New English Library, 1977.

Lyons, F. S. L. *Culture and Anarchy in Ireland, 1890–1939.* Oxford: Clarendon, 1979.

McCormack, William J. "J. Sheridan Le Fanu's 'Richard Marston': The History of an Anglo-Irish Text." In *1848: The Sociology of Literature*, edited by Francis Barker et al, 107–25. Colchester: University of Essex, 1978.

MacIntyre, Alasdair. *Whose Justice? Which Rationality?* London: Duckworth, 1988.

Magas, Branka. *The Destruction of Yugoslavia: Tracking the Break-Up, 1980–92.* London: Verso, 1993.

Manent, Pierre. *An Intellectual History of Liberalism.* 1987. Translated by Rebecca Balinski. Princeton: Princeton University Press, 1994.

Martindale, Colin. "Degeneration, Disinhibition, and Genius." *Journal of the History of Behavioral Science* 7 (1971): 177–82.

Melman, Billie. *Women's Orients: English Women and the Middle East, 1718–1918.* Ann Arbor: University of Michigan Press, 1992.

Millar, Peter. "The Family a Nation Learned to Loathe." *Sunday Times*, December 24, 1989, p. A13.

Miller, Jonathan. "Going Unconscious." *New York Review of Books*, April 20, 1995, pp. 59–65.

Miller, J. Hillis. *The Disappearance of God: Five Nineteenth-Century Writers.* Cambridge, Mass.: Harvard University Press, 1963.

Mishima, Yukio. *Sun and Steel.* Translated by John Bester. New York: Kodansha, 1980.

Mizener, Arthur. *The Saddest Story: A Biography of Ford Madox Ford.* New York: World Publishing, 1971.

Moore, Suzanne. "Flying the Flag of Convenience." *The Guardian*, July 20, 1995, sec. 2, p. 5.

Moretti, Franco. "The Dialectic of Fear." 1978. Reprinted in *Signs Taken for Wonders: Essays in the Sociology of Literary Forms*, translated by David Forgacs, pp. 83–108. London: Verso, 1983.

Morris, James. *Pax Britannica: The Climax of Empire.* New York: Harcourt, 1968.

Morton, Grenfell. *Home Rule and the Irish Question.* Harlow: Longman, 1980.

Moynahan, Julian. "The Politics of Anglo-Irish Gothic: Maturin, Le Fanu, and 'The Return of the Repressed.'" In *Studies in Anglo-Irish Literature,* edited by Heinz Kosok, 43–53. Bonn: Bouvier Verlag Herbert Grundmann, 1982.

Neale, Steve. "Sexual Difference in Cinema—Issues of Fantasy, Narrative, and the Look." *Oxford Literary Review* 8, nos. 1–2 (1986): 123–32.

Neimark, Jill. "Romanian Roulette." *Village Voice,* October 1, 1991, p. 28.

O'Brien, Joseph V. *William O'Brien and the Course of Irish Politics, 1881–1918.* Berkeley: University of California Press, 1976.

Oppenheim, Janet. *Shattered Nerves: Doctors, Patients, and Depression in Victorian England.* New York: Oxford University Press, 1991.

Palfreman, Jon. "Between Scepticism and Credulity: A Study of Victorian Scientific Attitudes to Modern Spiritualism." In *On the Margins of Science: The Social Construction of Rejected Knowledge. Sociological Review* Monograph no. 27, 201–36. Keele, Staffordshire: University of Keele, 1979.

Palmer, Jeremy N. J. "The Damp Stones of Positivism: Erich von Däniken and Paranormality." *Philosophy of Social Science* 9 (1979): 129–47.

Perham, Margery. *Lugard: The Years of Authority, 1898–1945.* London: Collins, 1960.

Phillips, Dana. "Nineteenth-Century Racial Thought and Whitman's 'Democratic Ethnology of the Future.'" *Nineteenth-Century Literature* 49 (December 1994): 289–320.

Pick, Daniel. "'Terrors of the night': *Dracula* and 'Degeneration' in the Late Nineteenth Century." *Critical Quarterly* 30, no. 4 (1988): 71–87.

———. *Faces of Degeneration: A European Disorder, c.1848–c.1918.* Cambridge: Cambridge University Press, 1989.

Pinkney, Tony. *D. H. Lawrence and Modernism.* Iowa City: University of Iowa Press, 1990.

Porter, Roy, and Lesley Hall. *The Facts of Life: The Creation of Sexual Knowledge in Britain, 1650–1950.* New Haven, Yale University Press, 1995.

Pozzuoli, Alain. *Bram Stoker: Prince des Ténèbres.* Paris: Librairie Séguier, 1989.

Pugh, Martin. *The Making of Modern British Politics, 1867–1939.* Oxford: Blackwell, 1982.

Reed, John R. *Victorian Will.* Athens: Ohio University Press, 1989.

Reichmann, Edgar. "Le retour des vampires." *Le Monde,* May 27, 1994, Le Monde des Livres, p. viii.

Richards, Thomas. *The Imperial Archive: Knowledge and the Fantasy of Empire.* London: Verso, 1993.

Robbins, Keith. *John Bright.* London: Routledge, 1979.

Rose, Jacqueline. *The Haunting of Sylvia Plath.* London: Virago, 1991.

Roth, Phyllis A. *Bram Stoker.* Boston: Twayne, 1982.

Ryan, Alan. *J. S. Mill.* London: Routledge, 1974.

Schaffer, Talia. "'A Wilde Desire Took Me': The Homoerotic History of *Dracula.*" *ELH* 61 (Summer 1994): 381–425.

Searle, G. R. *The Quest for National Efficiency: A Study in British Politics and Political Thought, 1899–1914.* Berkeley: University of California Press, 1971.

———. *Eugenics and Politics in Britain, 1900–1914.* Leyden: Noordhoff, 1976.

Seed, David. "The Narrative Method of *Dracula.*" *Nineteenth-Century Fiction* 40, no. 1 (1985): 61–75.

Senf, Carol A. "*Dracula:* Stoker's Response to the New Woman." *Victorian Studies* 26 (Autumn 1982): 33–49.

———. "*The Lady of the Shroud:* Stoker's Successor to *Dracula.*" *Essays in Arts and Sciences* 19 (May 1990): 82–96.

Showalter, Elaine. "Blood Sells: Vampire Fever and Anxieties for the *Fin-de-siècle.*" *Times Literary Supplement,* January 8, 1993, p. 14.

Shuster, Seymour. "*Dracula* and Surgically Induced Trauma in Children." *British Journal of Medical Psychology* 46, no. 3 (1973): 259–70.

Simmons, Dan. *Children of the Night.* New York: Putnam's, 1992.

Silverman, Kaja. *Male Subjectivity at the Margins.* New York: Routledge, 1992.

Sinfield, Alan. *Cultural Politics—Queer Reading.* Philadelphia: University of Pennsylvania Press, 1994.

Skal, David J. *Hollywood Gothic: The Tangled Web of Dracula from Novel to Stage to Screen.* New York: Norton, 1990.

Storch, Margaret. "The Lacerated Male: Ambivalent Images of Women in *The White Peacock.*" *D. H. Lawrence Review* 21 (Summer 1989): 117–36.

Sturgis, James L. *John Bright and the Empire.* London: Athlone Press, 1969.

Sutherland, John. *The Stanford Companion to Victorian Fiction.* Stanford: Stanford University Press, 1989.

Sweeney, John. *The Life and Evil Times of Nicolae Ceauşescu.* London: Hutchinson, 1991.

Taylor, Charles. *Multiculturalism and "The Politics of Recognition."* Princeton: Princeton University Press, 1992.

Todorov, Tzvetan. *The Fantastic: A Structural Approach to a Literary Genre.* 1970. Translated by Richard Howard. Ithaca: Cornell University Press, 1975.

Torok, Maria. "Fantasy: An Attempt to Define Its Structure and Operation." 1959. Reprinted in Nicolas Abraham and Maria Torok's *The Shell and the Kernel: Renewals of Psychoanalysis,* translated and edited by Nicholas T. Rand, 27–36. Chicago: University of Chicago Press, 1994.

Trotter, David. *The English Novel in History, 1895–1920.* London: Routledge, 1993.

Trumpener, Katie. "National Character, Nationalist Plots: National Tale and Historical Novel in the Age of *Waverley.*" *ELH* 60 (Fall 1993): 685–731.

Vincent, Andrew. "Classical Liberalism and Its Crisis of Identity." *History of Political Thought* 11 (Spring 1990): 143–61.

Walker, Martin. "Spectre of Cold War Returns." *Manchester Guardian Weekly*, August 25, 1991, p. 7.

Walter, Richard D. "What Became of the Degenerate? A Brief History of a Concept." *Journal of the History of Medicine* 11 (1956): 422–29.

Wicke, Jennifer. "Vampiric Typewriting: *Dracula* and Its Media." *ELH* 59 (Summer 1992): 467–93.

Williams, Raymond. *The Long Revolution.* 1961. Harmondsworth: Penguin, 1965.

———. *The English Novel from Dickens to Lawrence.* 1970. London: Hogarth Press, 1984.

Williamson, Dugald. "The Novel and Its Neighbors." *Southern Review* 22 (November 1989): 224–43.

Williamson, Judith. "Nightmare on Madison Avenue." *New Statesman* 15 (January 1988): 28–29.

Winer, Laurie. "Death Becomes Him." *Harper's Bazaar* 3370 (October 1992): 172.

Wingfield-Stratford, Esmé. *The Victorian Sunset.* New York: William Morrow, 1932.

———. *The Victorian Aftermath, 1901–1914.* London: Routledge, 1933.

Young, Robert M. *Mind, Brain, and Adaptation in the Nineteenth Century: Cerebral Localization and Its Biological Context from Gall to Ferrier.* Oxford: Clarendon, 1970.

Žižek, Slavoj. "Formal Democracy and Its Discontents." *American Imago* 48 (Summer 1991): 181–98.

———. "Eastern European Liberalism and Its Discontents." *New German Critique* 57 (Fall 1992): 25–49.

———. *Tarrying with the Negative: Kant, Hegel, and the Critique of Ideology.* Durham: Duke University Press, 1993.

———. "Otto Weininger, or, 'Woman doesn't exist.'" In *The Metastases of Enjoyment: Six Essays on Woman and Causality,* 137–64. London: Verso, 1994.

# Index

Aldiss, Brian W., 1
Allen, Grant, 106
Arnold, Matthew, 46

Balibar, Etienne, 150–151, 189 n.35, 189 n.36
Balkans, 10, 13, 19, 26, 33, 52–56, 136
Barthes, Roland, 138–139
Baudrillard, Jean, 137
Beddoe, John, 37, 39, 73
Berserker, 73–74, 117, 171 n.43, 171 n.44. *See also* Vikings
Bhabha, Homi, 152
Biography, 2–6, 15, 27
Biopolitics, 21, 69, 136–137, 145–146
Bisexuality, 4, 126, 127, 178 n.1, 183 n.46
Blood, 35, 40–41, 71, 73, 85, 117, 122, 131–132, 134, 136–150 passim. *See also* Vampires
Boer War, First (1880–81), 139
Boer War, Second (1899–1902), 20, 97, 102, 108, 116, 133, 165 n.60, 180 n.26, 182 n.36
Boucicault, Dion, 31
Boyd-Carpenter, Mrs. A. M., 4
*Bram Stoker's Dracula. See* Coppola, Francis Ford
Bright, John, 11, 27–28, 157 n.47, 160 n.17, 161 n.21, 161 n.22
British Empire, 23, 56, 62, 69, 85, 97, 99, 174–175 n.68
Brodie-Innes, J. W., 81, 173 n.57
Buchan, John, 98, 177 n.90
Bulwer-Lytton, Edward, 54
Bunyan, John, 14–15
Burton, Sir Richard, 26, 143
Butler, Judith, 39

Caine, Hall, 29, 59, 104, 155 n.32
Campbell-Bannerman, Sir Henry, 100

Canguilhem, Georges, 102
Carleton, William, 29, 32, 34–35
Carlyle, Thomas, 37
Carpenter, Edward, 121
Carpenter, W. B., 76–79, 84, 86, 93, 172 n.50, 175 n.69
Catholicism, 25, 29, 46, 49, 51; magic and, 87; nationalism and, 50
Ceauşescu, Nicolae, 136, 144–146
Celts, 38, 46, 80. *See also* Arnold, Matthew
Chadwick, Edwin, 101
Character, 8, 19–20, 46, 59–60, 74, 77–79, 82, 85–86, 117, 152; Gladstone and, 30; national, 46, 47, 53, 92; physiognomy and, 11, 19, 71–72, 75, 84; reserve and, 75; science of, 19, 60, 78; tests of, 50, 92
Charcot, Jean Martin, 79, 83
Chesney, Sir George, 54
*Children of the Night. See* Simmons, Dan
Churchill, Winston, 8, 36, 42–43, 164 n.48, 165 n.63, 186 n.60
Collins, Wilkie, 43, 62
Coppola, Francis Ford, 2, 21, 136–137, 140–144, 148–151
Cosmopolitanism, 27, 28, 53, 150, 160 n.14, 174–175 n.68
Criminal anthropology, 11, 19, 44, 47, 60, 68, 74–75, 95
Crookes, Sir William, 89, 175 n.69
Cross-dressing, 75, 90, 105, 179 n.15

Dalby, Richard, 7
Daly, Nicholas, 31
Darwinism, 65, 68, 72
Davitt, Michael, 12, 30, 37, 162 n.31
Daydreams, 15–16. *See also* Fantasy
Degeneration, 19–20, 37–42, 49, 60, 65–71, 79, 86, 93, 110, 113, 119–120, 128, 132, 134, 164 n.52, 169 n.21,

Degeneration (*cont.*)
183–184 n.48; upper class and,
67–68; urban working class and,
68–69. *See also* Lombroso, Cesare;
Nordau, Max; Pseudosciences;
Science: race and; Stoker, Bram:
*Dracula*
Deleuze, Gilles, 17
De Morgan, William, 11
De Quincey, Thomas, 58, 61
Determinism, 60, 72, 75, 77, 78, 80–
81, 92, 123. *See also* Carpenter,
W. B.; Free will; Mill, John Stuart
Dicey, A. V., 41
Dixie, Lady Florence, 105
Dowden, Edward, 6, 27, 28, 64, 160
n.14, 168 n.13
*Dracula. See* Stoker, Bram: *Dracula*
Dreams, 15–16, 78, 83, 88, 91

Eagleton, Terry, 34
Edgeworth, Maria, 29, 30
Edwards, Amelia, 90
Egerton, George, 29, 105–107
Ellis, Havelock, 74, 121
Ethnicity, etymology of, 22–23. *See
also* Race
Ethnology, 23, 35–42, 47, 99, 123. *See
also* Race; Whitman, Walt
Eugenics, 14, 20, 40, 42, 47, 66, 69,
93–94, 101, 119, 131, 133, 134, 166
n.72, 185 n.57

Fantasy, 15–18, 39, 42, 50, 55, 71, 86,
90–92, 102, 103, 105, 120, 122, 132,
138, 143; conscious, 16–18; the real
and, 16. *See also* Daydreams
Femininity, 18, 45, 47, 48, 83, 88–89,
91–92, 95, 107, 112, 114, 120, 124,
126–128, 183 n.47
Feminism, 14, 17, 20, 89, 100, 102,
105–106, 109, 115, 119, 124. *See also*
Suffrage: women's
Ferrero, Guglielmo, 107
Ferrier, David, 79, 172 n.54

Ford, Ford Madox, 100–102, 125,
184–185 n.52
Forster, E. M., 134
Foster, R. F., 87
Foucault, Michel, 69, 104, 179 n.7
*Frankenstein*, 139; the Irish and, 37;
working-class voters and, 164 n.50
Free will, 60, 77, 78, 80–81, 84, 92;
and liberalism, 92–93. *See also* Determinism; Mill, John Stuart
Freud, Sigmund, 16, 42, 79, 91–92,
107, 111, 122, 150, 172 n.50, 174 n.61,
181 n.32; on feminine superego, 111;
on Medusa, 91. *See also* Fantasy;
Psychoanalysis

Galton, Francis, 40–42, 67–68, 73,
119, 170 n.37
Garnett, David, 101
Gelder, Ken, 4
Gissing, George, 119
Gladstone, W. E., 12, 14, 18–19, 26–
27, 28–29, 30, 49, 51, 59, 157 n.47,
158 n.68, 162 n.31. *See also* Irish
Home Rule; Liberalism
Gombeenmen, 30–31, 163 n.35
Gothic, 2, 15, 19, 35, 58, 59, 134, 146,
151; Anglo-Irish, 25–26; Oriental,
81
Grand, Sarah, 106, 109–110, 179 n.15
Greg, W. R., 68
Gypsies, 40–41, 71

Haggard, H. Rider, 29, 85, 174 n.61,
174 n.63
Haining, Peter, 15
Hall, Radclyffe, 21, 103, 113, 181 n.34
Hall, Stuart, 138, 154 n.16
Heinemann, William, 9, 102–103,
169 n.21
Hermetic Order of the Golden
Dawn, 1, 81, 84, 87, 173 n.57
Heterosexuality, 3–4, 20, 103, 131,
142–143, 179 n.14
Hobbes, Thomas, 22

Hobhouse, L. T., 12, 186 n.61
Hobson, J. A., 42
Homosexuality, 69, 133, 156 n.44, 187 n.18
Humanism, 150–151, 189 n.36; science and, 63
Human nature, 54, 59
Hysteria, 27, 61, 69, 79, 93, 99, 108; male hysteria, 20, 47, 70, 80, 143

Identity: national, 13, 23, 25, 41; sexual, 98, 102, 112–113, 121, 126, 179 n.7
Iota (Kathleen Mannington Caffyn), 106, 110
Irish Great Famine, 24, 32
Irish Home Rule, 12–13, 19, 23–25, 26, 28–30, 35, 36–38, 46, 50–51, 157 n.46, 162 n.31, 164 n.52, 164 n.53. See also Nationalism; Stoker, Bram: Ireland and
Irving, Sir Henry, 7, 9, 11, 12, 26. See also Stoker, Bram: Henry Irving and

James, Henry, 9, 76
Jameson, Fredric, 16
Jane Eyre, 117
Johnson, Major E. C., 34

Kane, Sir Robert, 51
Kazanjian, David, 42
Kingsley, Charles, 32, 37
Kipling, Rudyard, 14, 29

Lankester, E. Ray, 68, 175 n.69
Laplanche, Jean, and J.-B. Pontalis, 16
Lavater, Johann Caspar, 72–76
Law, 10, 17, 18, 40, 43–44, 62, 71, 105, 114, 130–131, 152
Lawrence, D. H., 21, 103, 104, 131–132, 133, 184 n.52, 185 n.54, 185 n.55
Lecercle, Jean-Jacques, 138–140, 187 n.13, 187 n.14. See also Myth

Lecky, William E. H., 22, 24–25, 37–38, 159 n.7, 182 n.38
Le Fanu, Sheridan, 29, 87
Lévi-Strauss, Claude, 138–139
Liberalism, 5, 9, 11, 20–21, 27, 36, 41–43, 45, 55, 56, 60, 65, 90, 114, 134, 152; antifeminism and, 90, 100–101, 106, 125–126; Boer War and, 108; and citizenship, theory of, 41–42, 92, 139–140, 152; individualism and, 11–12, 41, 56, 59, 60, 92–93, 103, 137; Irish liberals, 49, 51; Liberal Party, 5, 12, 27, 51, 66, 100; "muscular liberalism," 85; nationalism and, 24; New Liberals, 12, 93, 183 n.44; progress and, 14, 24, 27, 42, 65, 137; Young Liberals, 100. See also Bright, John; Gladstone, W. E.; Irish Home Rule; Science: liberalism and; Stoker, Bram: liberalism and
Liberty, 55, 60
Llobera, Josep, 65
Lodge, Sir Oliver, 10
Lombroso, Cesare, 43–44, 66, 68, 74, 76, 95–96, 169 n.21. See also Criminal anthropology

Marriage plots, 19, 30–32, 49–57 passim, 94, 97, 109, 116–124, 128–135 passim
Masculinity, 18, 19, 45, 47–48, 79–80, 81, 85, 86, 89, 92, 94–95, 108, 114, 119, 126, 128, 174 n.65, 183 n.47; emotion and, 45–47, 80; imperial masculinity, 133; "law of masculine supremacy," 56. See also Hysteria
Masterman, C. F. G., 10, 27, 66, 93
Maudsley, Henry, 68, 168 n.13
Medicine, 5, 10–11, 18, 65, 69, 72, 73, 77, 126, 152; sexual medicine, 103, 104
Melman, Billie, 90
Mental physiology, 19, 60, 77–79. See also Carpenter, W. B.

Mesmer, Franz Anton, 64
Mill, John Stuart: on free will, 60, 78–79, 93; nationalism and, 24
Modernity, 2, 9, 15, 42, 44, 48, 52, 54, 56, 58–59, 60–61, 66, 72, 137, 152
Morgan, Lady, 30–31, 49
Mummies, Egyptian, 59, 82, 88–89, 91
Myers, Frederic W. H., 78
Myth, 21, 52, 136–151 passim, 186 n.9, 187 n.12, 187 n.13, 187 n.14

National independence, 51–53
Nationalism, 22–25, 44, 47–48, 144–145, 150, 152, 159 n.6, 166 n.68, 166 n.69, 189 n.35; Irish nationalism, 23–24, 28, 51, 152. See also Irish Home Rule
National Liberal Club, 28
New Women, 45, 89, 95, 97, 109, 177 n.86; New Women novelists, 105–107, 109–110, 134
Nordau, Max, 66, 74, 96, 169 n.21

O'Brien, William, 12, 29, 37–39, 162 n.27
Occult, 54, 81, 86–88, 173 n.57, 174–175 n.68; revival, 84

Pankhurst, Mrs. Emmeline, 100. See also Suffragettes
Parnell, Charles, 12, 19, 28
Parnell, Fanny, 37
Pearson, Karl, 14, 107, 133
Phrenology, 11, 36, 71, 119, 171 n.38; 172 n.54. See also Physiognomy
Physical Deterioration Report (1904), 133
Physiognomy, 11, 19, 36–37, 39, 43–44, 60, 67, 71–76, 78, 119, 123. See also Lavater, Johann Caspar; Phrenology
Positivism, 64–65, 69, 74, 86, 151
Protestantism, 46, 49, 61; Irish Protestantism, 9, 23, 24, 39, 49, 51, 87,

96. See also Catholicism; Stoker, Bram: religion and
Pseudosciences, 11, 36, 65, 102. See also Phrenology; Physiognomy
Psychical research, 60, 78, 175 n.69
Psychoanalysis, 16–17, 172 n.50. See also Daydreams; Fantasy; Freud, Sigmund; Unconscious
Psychology, 65, 76–78, 84–85, 103, 128. See also Carpenter, W. B.

Queer readings, 4, 105, 179 n.14

Race, 20, 22–23, 26, 38–42, 44, 46–48, 56, 65, 67–68, 70, 73, 75, 98–99, 110, 115, 117, 119, 121–123, 133–134, 143–144; Ireland and, 14, 19, 35–39 passim. See also Degeneration; Ethnology; Science
Regeneration, 14, 20, 95, 104, 134
Reichmann, Edgar, 136
Rice, Anne, 2, 188 n.32
Robins, Elizabeth, 106
Romance, 10, 15, 19, 20, 26, 30, 44, 59, 65, 85, 92, 104, 105, 134, 152
Rose, Jacqueline, 92
Russell, Ken, 6

Saberhagen, Fred, 2
Science, 5, 10–11, 13–14, 18, 43, 45, 47, 52, 60, 62–66, 71, 77, 82–87, 89, 118–119, 139, 140, 184 n.49; ancient and modern, 85, 87, 90; liberalism and, 11, 14, 92–93; "national efficiency" and, 13; race and, 14, 19, 23, 24, 36–37, 48, 72–73, 95, 101; religion and, 17, 81, 86–87, 95
Scotland, 13, 105, 128, 130, 157 n.50
Secrecy, 1–4, 75, 105
Sex and Character. See Weininger, Otto
"Sex novel," 20, 102–105, 107
Sexology, 11, 14, 20, 101–104, 131, 134, 152. See also Weininger, Otto
Sexual equality, 90, 114–115, 124
Sexuality, 14, 20, 39, 47, 93, 97, 107,

*About the Author*
David Glover is Lecturer in the Department of English
at the University of Southampton, England.

*Library of Congress Cataloging-in-Publication Data*

Glover, David.

Vampires, mummies, and liberals : Bram Stoker and the politics of popular
fiction / by David Glover.

p. cm.

Includes bibliographical references and index.

ISBN 0-8223-1803-2 (cloth : alk. paper). — ISBN 0-8223-1798-2 (paper : alk.
paper)

1. Stoker, Bram, 1847–1912—Criticism and interpretation—History. 2. Popular
literature—Great Britain—History and criticism. 3. Politics and literature—
Great Britain—History. 4. Horror tales, English—History and criticism.
5. Vampires in literature. 6. Mummies in literature. 7. Sex in literature. I. Title.

PR6037.T617Z67 1996

823'.8—dc20          95-53796   CIP